IMAGES
of America

THE CAJON PASS

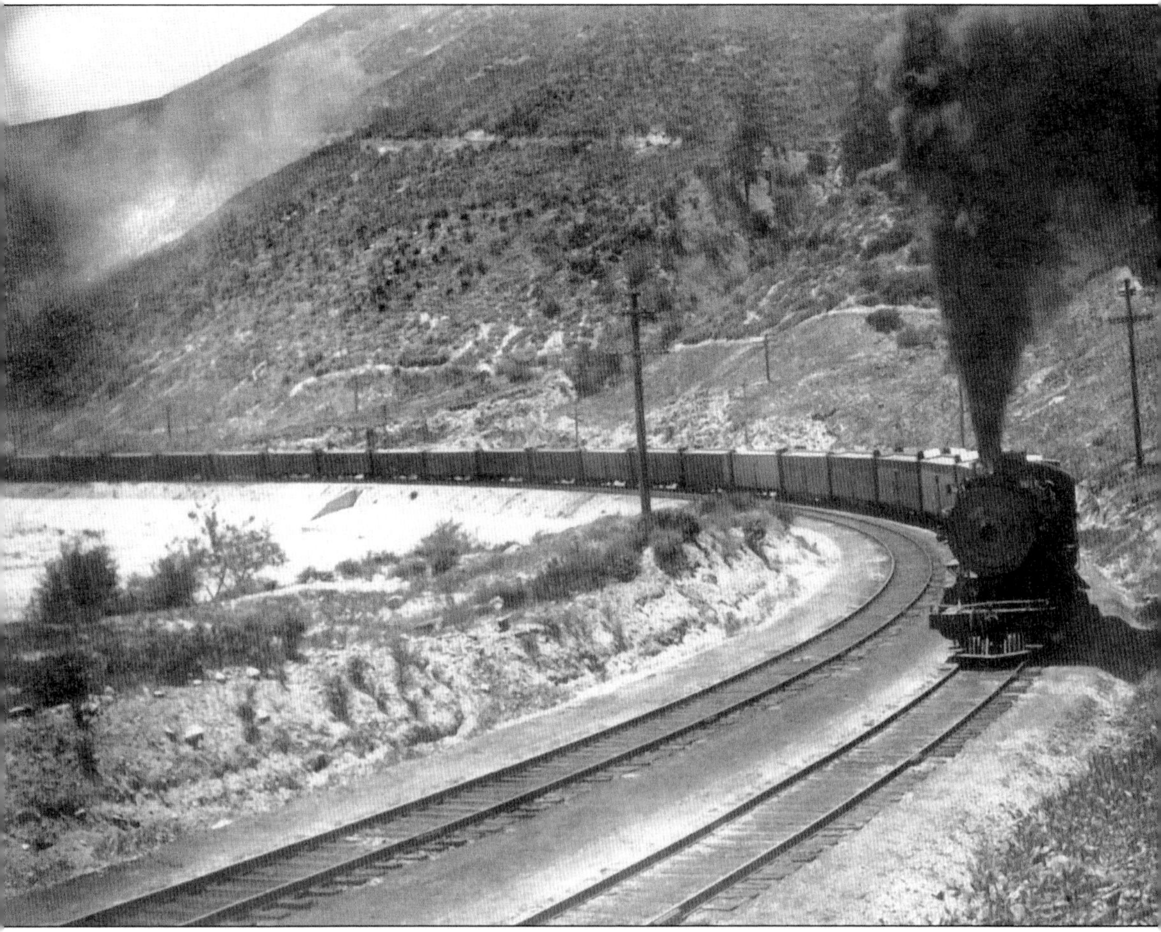

Trains Changed Cajon Pass. This photograph was probably taken by Edward Ehwegen, telegrapher at the Cajon Station between 1910 and 1937. Londa Bailey of Keenbrook and Stella Zula Ehwegen of Cajon were sisters. Hervey and Londa Bailey's grandson, Ray Bailey, generously shared his photographs of early life at Keenbrook and Cajon. (RB.)

On the Cover: The Baileys of Keenbrook and the Ehwegens (pronounced Ay-vay-gan) of Cajon Station enjoyed entertaining guests in unusual ways—like standing astride the special turtle-back tender of a 3000 class articulated Mallet steam locomotive. Nine huge Atchison, Topeka, and Santa Fe (ATSF) 3000 Series locomotives made especially for the San Bernardino/Barstow/Bakersfield slow-speed freight run pulled through Cajon Pass between 1911 and 1918, when each one was dismantled and made into two regular engines. (RB.)

IMAGES
of America

THE CAJON PASS

Alice Eby Hall

ARCADIA
PUBLISHING

ISBN 978-0-7385-7075-4

Published by Arcadia Publishing
Charleston, South Carolina

Printed in the United States of America

Library of Congress Control Number: 2009922876

For all general information contact Arcadia Publishing at:
Telephone 843-853-2070
Fax 843-853-0044
E-mail sales@arcadiapublishing.com
For customer service and orders:
Toll-Free 1-888-313-2665

Visit us on the Internet at www.arcadiapublishing.com

Lovingly dedicated to my husband, Roger,
who is enthusiastic about historical research.

Contents

ACKNOWLEDGMENTS

My husband, Roger, and I have both lived at the southern portal to Cajon Pass since the 1940s and have wanted to imprint our love for the area on others. We appreciated help.

Many people who gave me information and photographs for *Devore—A Scrapbook* continued their help with this book: Gwen Lamson Mulholland shared her mother's photographs and journals (GLM); Arturo Garcia, of Country Corners Café, allowed use of pictures on the café walls (AG); Liz King, local authority on yucca, gave photographs and information (LK); David and Nikki Malki donated their 2005 aerial photographs (DNM); Elizabeth Grogan offered photographs and memories of Glen Helen (EG); Hilda Schultz contributed pictures of Keenbrook (HS); Robert Mathews provided photographs from both sides of the Summit (RM); Linda Ruddell Harris sent old Ruddell Hill photographs (LRH); Loy Beach shared his photograph of the steamer engine at Blue Cut (LB); Katie Hade bestowed local photographs taken for her 4-H project (KH); and George Sneed (GS) offered Cajon Pass photographs and memories.

Since the Devore book was published, new people have come forward with material for this Cajon Pass book. Richard Thompson and Steven Shaw of the San Bernardino Historical and Pioneer Society (SBHPS) were invaluable with advice, pictures, and shared experiences with their own books. I became "acquainted" with rail fans online. I am particularly appreciative of the photographs sent by Dr. Gary Gray (GG) and Don Toles (DT). Also online, I met history buff John Thompson, who gave good advice, and Brad Eells and Pam Morey of the Forest Fire Lookout Association, who contributed a photograph, compliments of Cleveland National Forest (CNF). Theodore Jenkins (TJ) shared pictures of the Blue Cut of 60 years ago. Jarrel B. Glover, manager of the Historical Society and Museum for the California Department of Forestry and Fire Protection (CDFM), was helpful with forestry history. Alex Garcilazo (AlG), whose birth certificate lists Devore as his birthplace, found local photographs. Jack Brown, Stater Brothers CEO and high school classmate of the author, donated a historic photograph (JB). Paul Mowbray took great Devore flood photographs (PM), and C. A. Stevens donated the Summit Inn pictures (CS). The Arda Haenszel California Room in San Bernardino's Feldheym Library is an excellent source of pictures and information (AHCRFL).

And I am especially indebted to Ray Bailey (RB) for early photographs of Keenbrook and Cajon and Carol Carr, director of the Victor Valley Museum, which also now has the photographs collected by the Mohave Historical Society (MHS/VVM), for most of the pictures of the high desert and some of Cajon Pass.

Graphics labeled (AH) or (RH) reside in the author's files.

INTRODUCTION

The lifestyles we enjoy today are contingent upon efforts expended by those who came before us. Their dreams and goals, when met, have enabled us to pursue ours.

Cajon (Kah-hone, "box" in Spanish) Pass is still sparsely populated compared with the rest of Southern California. It presents a harsh, difficult environment to those who wish to traverse or settle in it. The Santa Ana winds tear down structures. Great diurnal temperature differences bring rocks to the surface and leave a person wondering how he should dress—for scorching days or frigid nights. The brittle, oily vegetation feeds wildfires, and when fires are also fanned by native winds, there is little that can stop them. Land that has been stripped of plants by fires lies bare and ready to move in muddy sheets when surplus rains fall. Settlers without perseverance move to other locations quickly.

The southern side of Cajon Pass originates within the Rancho Muscupiabe and the San Bernardino National Forest. This does not resemble what most people picture when they hear the word "forest." The largest plants in a chaparral forest are the oak trees—live oak, scrub oak, and holly-leaf cherry, which resembles oak. Chaparral also boasts yucca, sage (white and black), buckthorn (ceanothus or wild lilac), poison oak, Yerba Santa, buckwheat, elderberry, and the beautiful red-trunked manzanita, most of which attract bees. Chaparral biomes support animals as small as mice or kangaroo rats and as large as mountain lions, which feed on deer. Coyotes and bobcats also abound to help predatory birds like hawks, eagles, owls, and vultures clean up remains of rodents like cottontail rabbits. A favorite bird is the road runner. Reptiles—lizards (a favorite is the "horned toad") and snakes, including the rattler—are plentiful.

This vegetation is found up to Cajon Summit (4,200 feet for cars, less for trains), but once the elevation drops on the north side of the summit, the traveler quickly finds himself in the high Mojave (Moe-hah-vee) Desert. High desert supports more vegetation than low desert. Desert vegetation is sparse and dominated by the Joshua tree, juniper tree, and mesquite, surrounded by various cacti and wildflowers that appear after a rain. This biome supports many rodents like the kangaroo rat and jackrabbit. These are preyed upon by coyotes, bobcats, and birds of prey. Reptiles abound, including various kinds of rattlesnakes, the most feared being the Mojave green. The desert has attracted people interested in mining, as gold and silver have often been found, and lime is plentiful. Other people reside in the desert for health reasons, the dry warm air being easy on the lungs. Some early pioneers used thousands of acres of land to graze large herds of cattle, which were moved from desert floor to mountain highlands as necessary for ample feed.

Settlers have always been concerned about water supply. On the southern side of Cajon Pass, flowing water has been plentiful in the many canyons that feed Cajon Creek (or Wash when it is dry), and wells have not had to be particularly deep. Many settlers were able to develop springs or methods to capture free-running creek water. Since the San Andreas and Devore or Peters Faults line the San Bernardino Mountains and the Glen Helen and San Jacinto Faults run along the San Gabriel Mountains, considerable groundwater is trapped between faults, giving settlers easy access to it. Cajon Creek ran all year until it was tapped for urban water. Now it only runs after storms.

On the northern, desert side of Cajon Pass, water has been more of a problem. The Mojave River runs northward and then east from the hills for about 120 miles, but it is often underground—a location that limits loss to evaporation. When it runs on the surface, farms and settlements have grown and prospered. Early settlers who lived farther away from the river often had to haul water for domestic purposes and were unable to do anything other than dry farming. Those who drill wells have to go sometimes hundreds of feet to find enough water. Construction of the California Aqueduct continues, but it has brought enough water from the Oroville Dam on the Feather River in Northern California to encourage urban lifestyles in the Mojave Desert near Cajon Pass.

Pioneers who have conquered problems of Cajon Pass have left their marks in crumbling buildings, names of canyons, water sources, caves, or tunnels, and legends. Residents who followed have built upon remains and wondered about where place names originated. Names of early settlers like Crowder, Swarthout, Cable, Hopper, Pittman, Bailey, Wilson, and Medlin and more modern names like Ruddell are still found on railroad and forestry maps in canyons of the pass.

The only community in the pass south of the summit is Devore, located in the most northern point of the Muscupiabe Rancho. Devore is named after John A. Devore, vice president of Kenwood Corporation (Commercial Company), a manufacturer of railroad uniforms. J. A. Devore left Chicago to manage Kenwood land holdings at the southern portal of Cajon Pass. He died after only seven years in the community that bears his name, but his vision of natural beauty combined with productivity and man-made attractiveness has directed the course of the quaint rural neighborhood.

Near the top of Cajon Pass on the north side in the Baldy Mesa area is another, new bedroom community, Oak Hills, a planned rural community. Its name comes from the chaparral vegetation found there.

Desert cities like Hesperia and Victorville grew up around river crossings or railroad water stations, expanded with the completion of Highways 66, 91, and 395, and burgeoned when I-15 was completed in the late 1960s and northern water arrived via aqueduct a few years later. Today these cities rival those "down below" in convenience and goods and services available.

Hesperia, promoted in the 1880s by water developer Robert Widney, was named for Hesperus, the Greek god of the west. Victorville was named for J. N. Victor, who was superintendent of California Southern Railway and oversaw the extension of that line in 1885 through Cajon Pass and the town of Victor into Barstow. The city name of Victor was later changed to Victorville at the request of the post office as a result of confusion with Victor, Colorado.

Highway 15 has handled almost 13,000 vehicles per hour—compared with 8,200 at the Highway 5 summit. Some people might see Cajon Pass as only a corridor they speed through on their way to somewhere else, but its charm and natural beauty attract others to hike, picnic, prospect, or spend their lives there. Various hues of green, blue, and purple beckon hiker and artist into layer after stratum of hills and mountains. Rifts of slate and schist call geologist and prospector into hidden canyons and rills. Bunnies and bees and all manner of creatures between and beyond summon biologist and conservationist into secret glades and glens. This almost forgotten habitat continues to thrive in a blend of modern and natural.

One

Knowing Cajon Pass

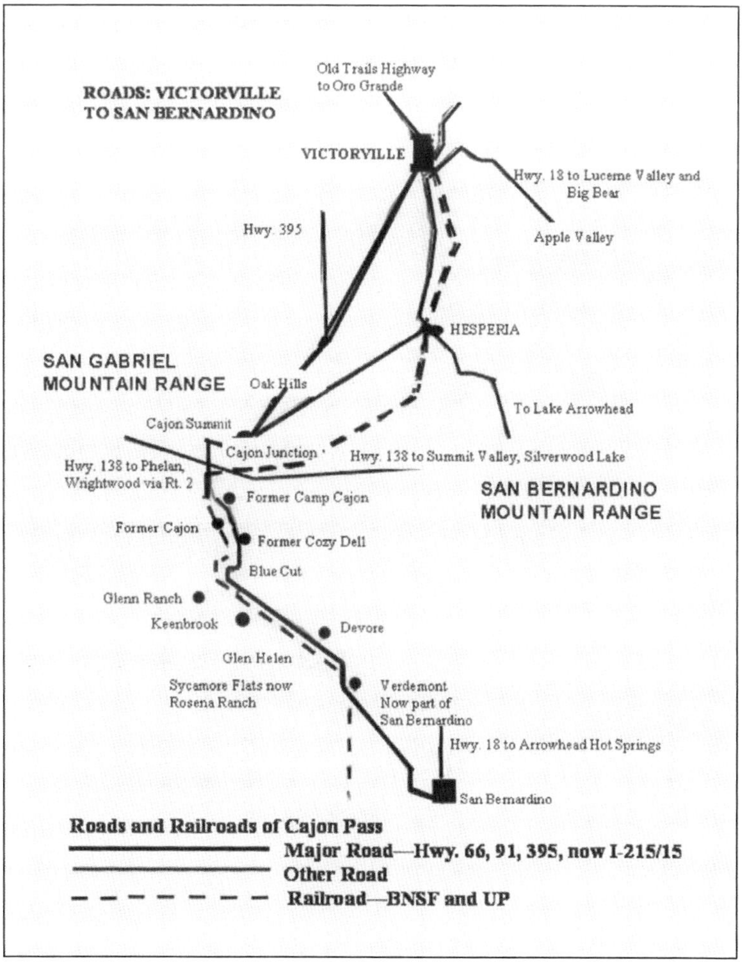

Cajon Pass, the Way. The San Gabriel and San Bernardino Mountain Ranges are the only transverse ranges in California. That is, they run east and west instead of north and south as the other mountain ranges do, effectively isolating Southern California from Northern on the east side. An easy way across those ranges was sought and finally found at Cajon Pass, elevation about 4,200 feet, which separates the two ranges. (AH.)

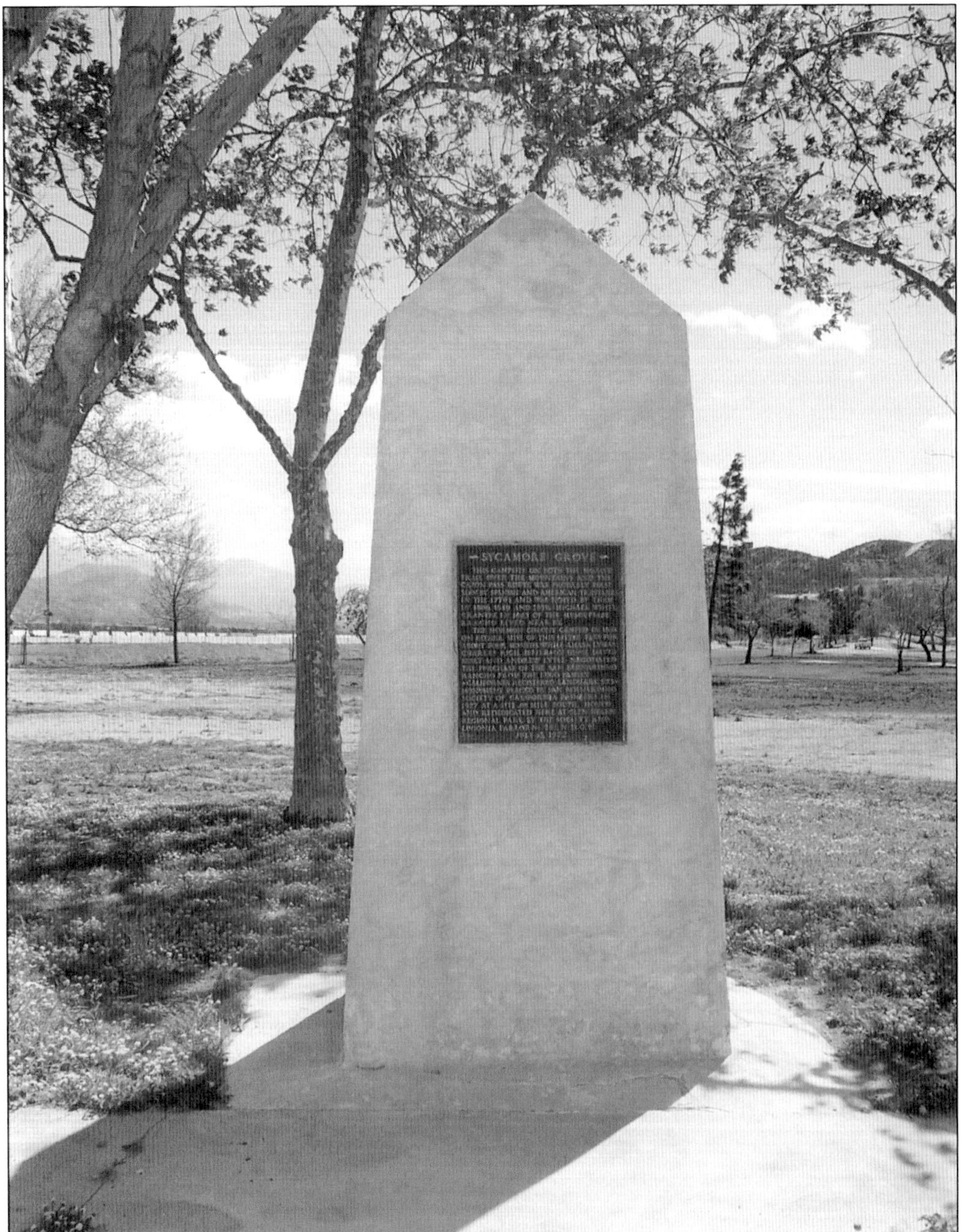

SYCAMORE GROVE MONUMENT. This monument, moved from Sycamore Flats to Glen Helen Park in 1972, marked the campsite on both the Mojave Trail over the mountains and the Cajon Pass Route. These routes were "probably first seen by Spanish and American travelers in the 1770s and were noted by them in 1806, 1849, and 1850. The Mormon colony camped in 1851 on the other side of this little Glen Helen Pass for about four months." A monument to pioneer women was erected in 1977 near Sycamore Grove to replace the one moved to Glen Helen. Cajon Pass Camp Site and Crowder Canyon Archeological Dig are both listed in the National Register of Historic Places, but the address of both is restricted. (AH.)

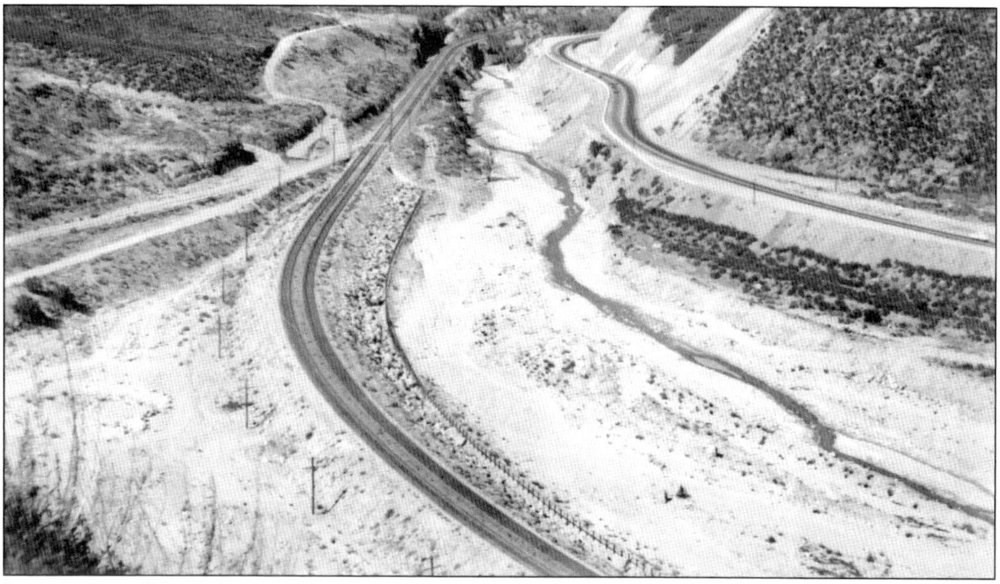

Looking up Cajon Canyon. An early postcard shows Cajon Canyon where it narrows at Blue Cut, the lower narrows, with Route 66 at the right, the railroad curving up the center with Cajon Creek barely running between. Railroad or residential roads show at the left. Today's view is not very much different. (SBHPS.)

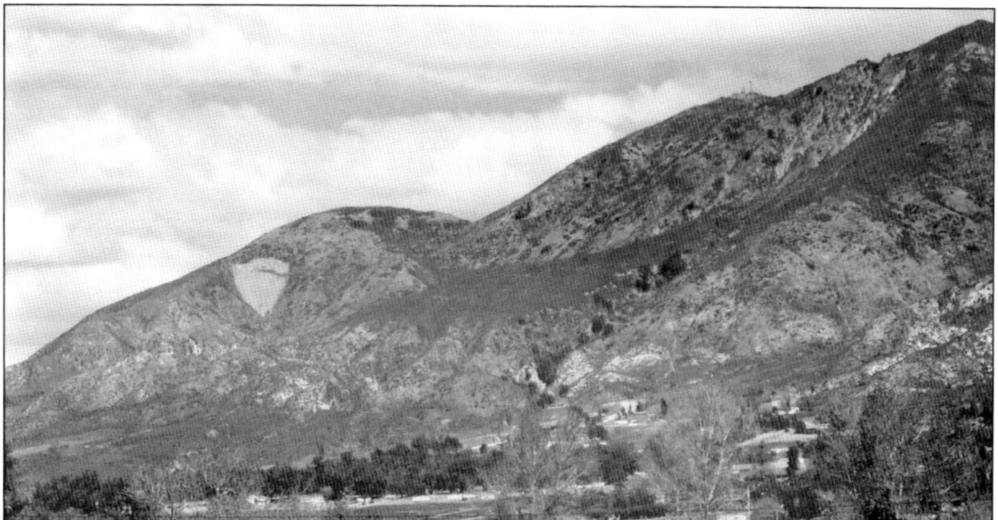

Unstable Land. Cajon Pass, laced with faults and constructed of decomposed granite, schist, and other soft, somewhat crumbly rocks, tends to slough off in wet years. High on the hill below Cajon Mountain, the 2005 slide rivals the famous San Bernardino arrowhead in shape if not in size. Local faults keep earthquakes in residents' thoughts. (RH.)

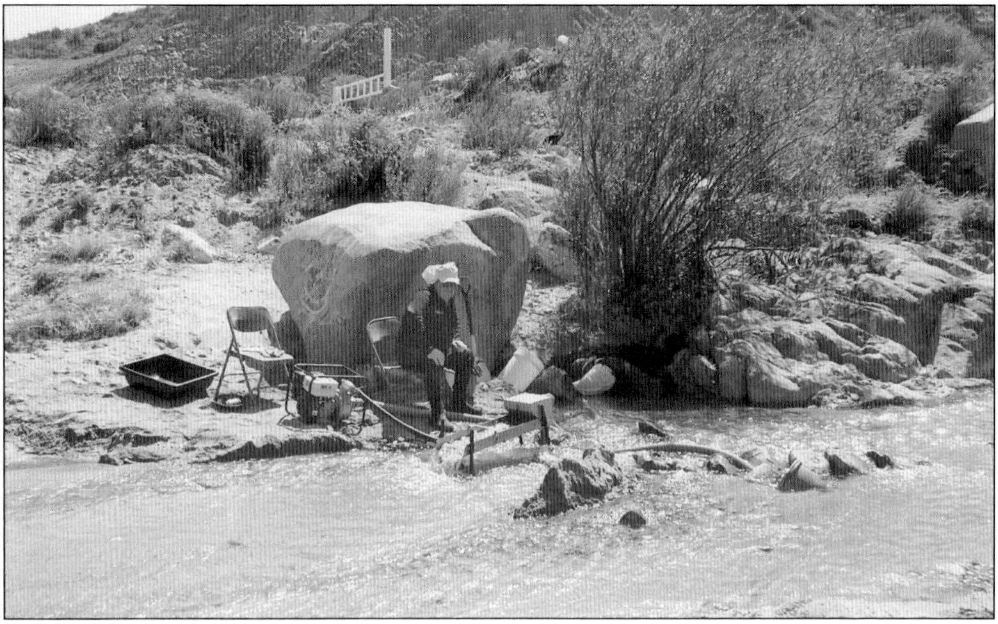

The Pass Has Many Uses. Hikers, off-roaders, artists, poets, photographers, geologists, archeologists, and prospectors ply their trades in Cajon Pass. Prospectors near water use pans, sluice boxes, and/or dredges, like the two from Oak Hills pictured, to look for "color" in the creek. One man is almost submerged as he probes for richer deposits. This popular location is where Cajon Creek crosses Swarthout Canyon Road. (RH.)

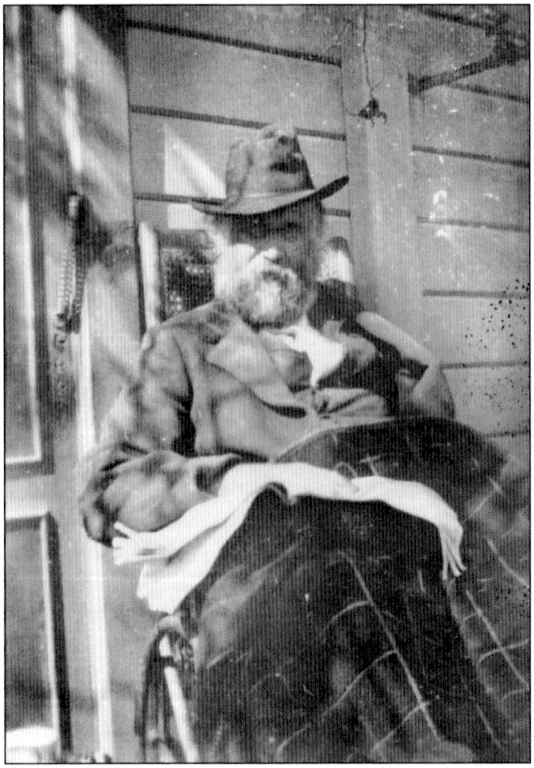

An Early Prospector. Monroe Stewart prospected in the 19th century. He cut a deal with two French prospectors to not infringe on their Kimbark Canyon claims if they would leave his alone in Cable Canyon. Stewart, the grandfather of George Sneed, longtime Devore resident, held patents on dry washers, which are important prospecting tools in dry areas. (GS.)

For Desert Prospecting. Patented in 1867, Monroe Stewart's dry washer or gold separator was manufactured in four sizes and was praised by many prospectors. Back then, a hand crank caused the bellows to blow away lighter material like sand and gravel, leaving the heavier gold behind. Nowadays, gasoline engines usually drive the bellows. (GS.)

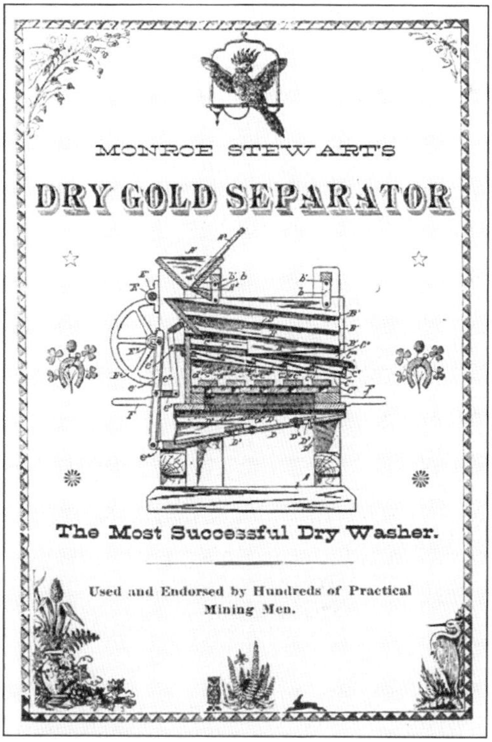

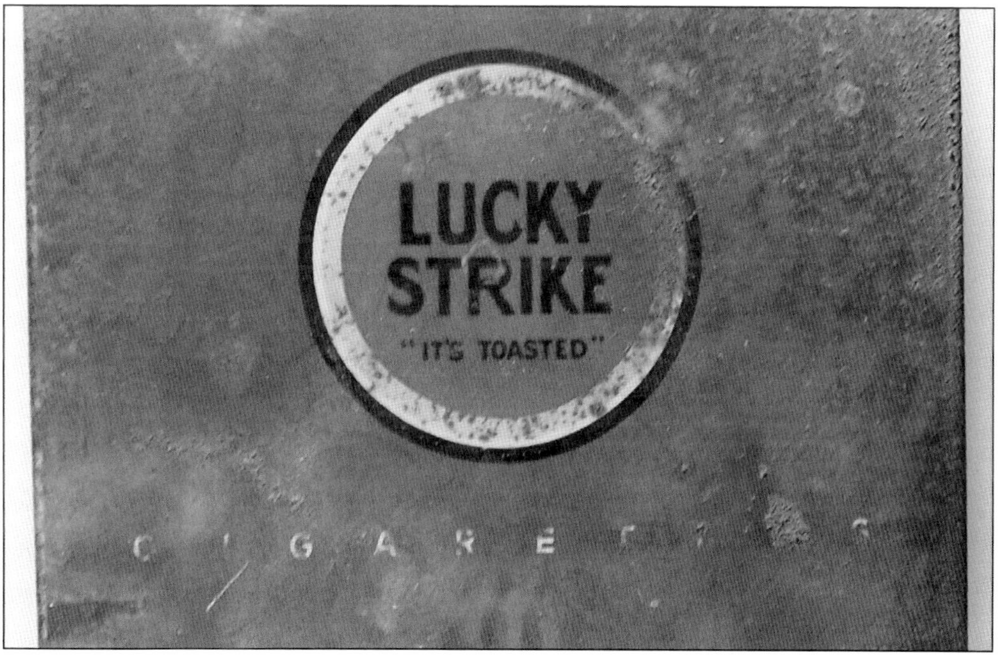

Prospector's Artifact. Found between Medlin (Middleman) Falls and Medlin (Lethan) Springs in Devore, this old cigarette case contained papers claiming the Hornet Springs lode dated March 1, 1942. Claim papers should not be removed from the site as they identify where the claim is located. A blasting cap container accompanied this find. Historians and archeologists find excitement in such items. (AH.)

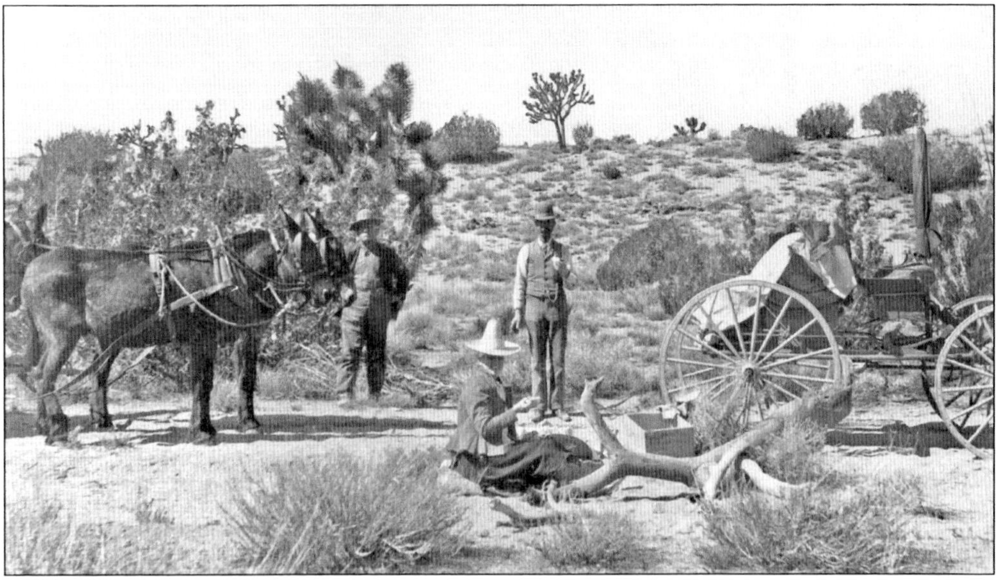

King of the High Desert. North of Cajon Pass summit, a person might see the intriguing Joshua trees (*Yucca brevifolia*) standing isolated in the desert surrounded primarily by sand and maybe mesquite or juniper trees. The Joshua tree was probably named by the Mormons during their 1851 trek from Utah to Southern California. They fancied that the plant resembled Joshua praying or pointing his sword at the town of Ai. (MHS/VVM.)

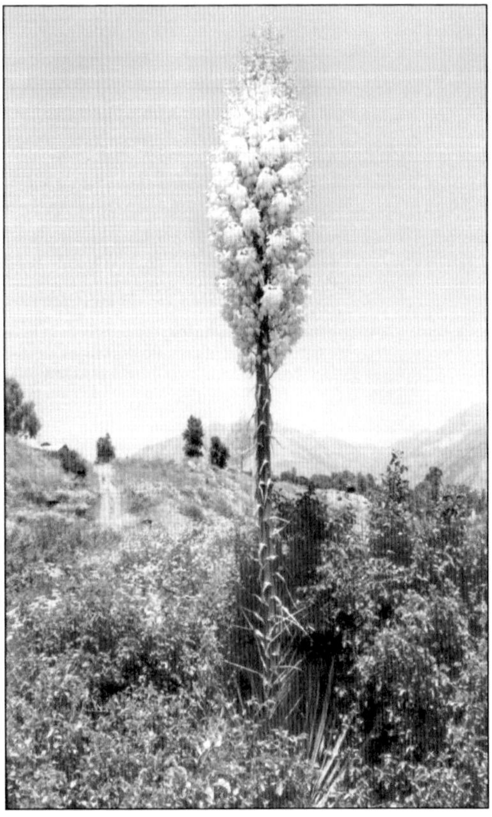

Queen of the Lower Pass. South of Cajon Pass summit, the viewer is more likely to see the stately *Hesperoyucca* dwarfing the chaparral vegetation in its vicinity. *Hesperoyucca whipplei*, found specifically at the lower end of Cajon Pass, is popular with researchers because it shows characteristics of all five subspecies. Because of that, these yuccas are called "Cajon Pass mixed swarms." (LK.)

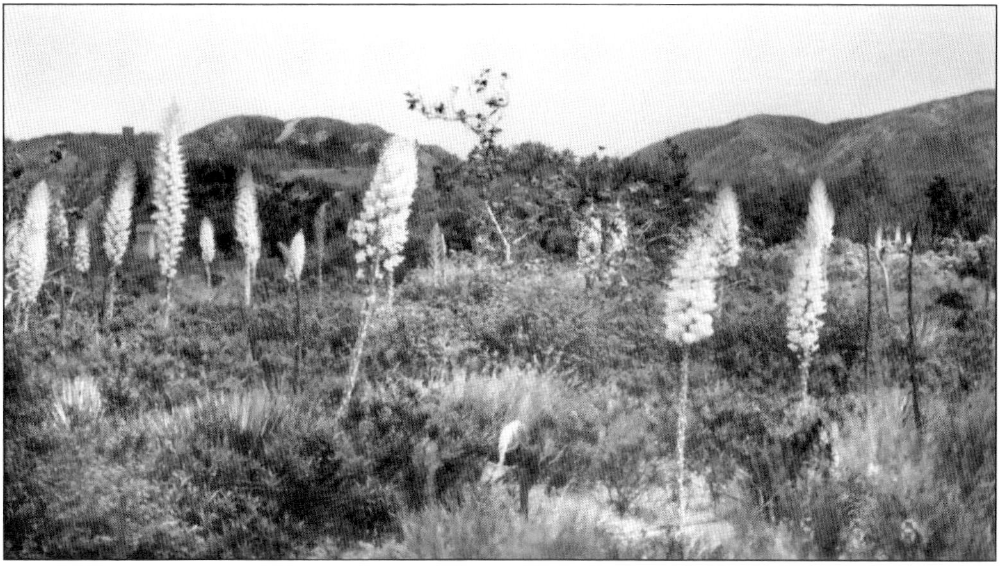

The Cajon Pass Mixed Swarm. Native Americans used yucca fruits, blossoms, and stalks for food. The roots, which contain saponin, were used as soap. Fibers from the sword-like leaves were used to make cloth for blankets and mattresses, and whole leaves were used to make sandals, mats, and baskets. This cluster, formerly Bayonet Park, has been torn out for a warehouse complex on land now within the San Bernardino city limits. (LK.)

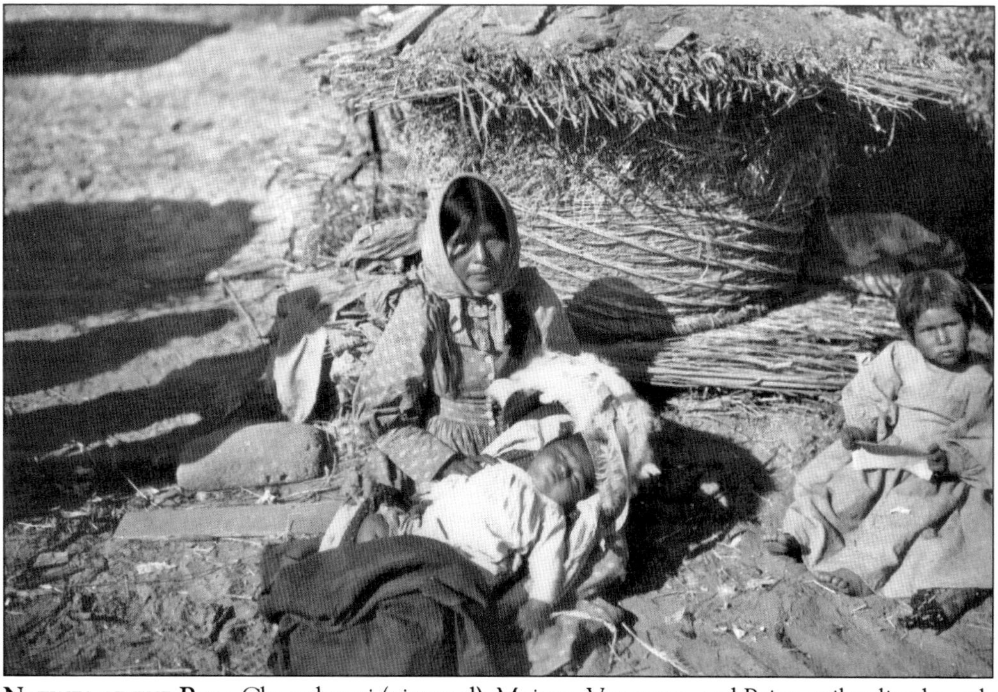

Natives of the Pass. Chemehuevi (pictured), Mojave, Vanyume, and Paiute tribes lived north of Cajon Pass. Serranos lived more on the south side of the Summit. Serrano people were the most gentle, living on what they could hunt or gather, grinding acorns using stone metates. Chemehuevi wove baskets. Vanyume used hides. Mojave and Paiute tribes were likely to steal livestock, especially horses, and settlers feared them. (MHS/VVM.)

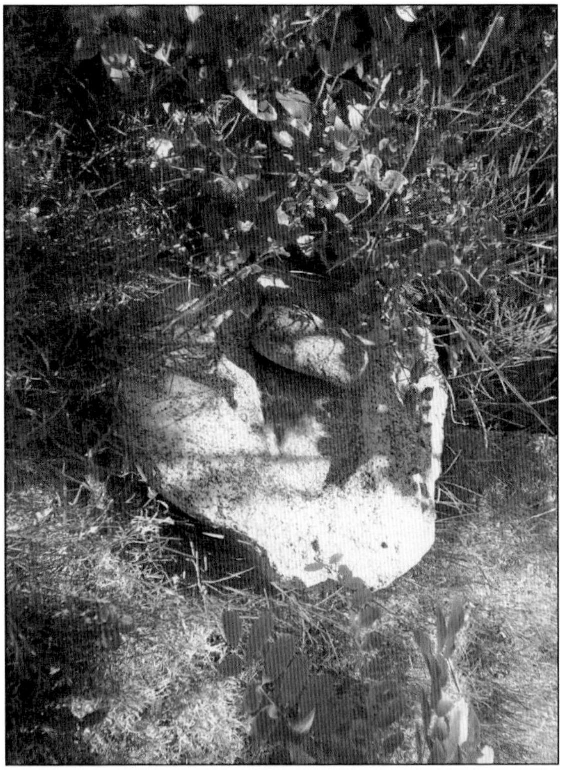

Relics of the Past. The metate, mortar stone and pestle, at left were found by lifetime resident of Devore Florence Lange Valencia, and they still reside where Kimbark and Little or East Kimbark Canyons meet in Devore. Just above this site, a huge collective or community grinding stone drew local school students on field trips. It has disappeared, probably buried by floodwaters. Petroglyphs, such as those pictured below, are found throughout the high desert. Besides things pictured, professional and amateur archeologists find interest in artifacts like bone whistles, arrowheads, and other tools. (Left, RH; below, MHS/VVM.)

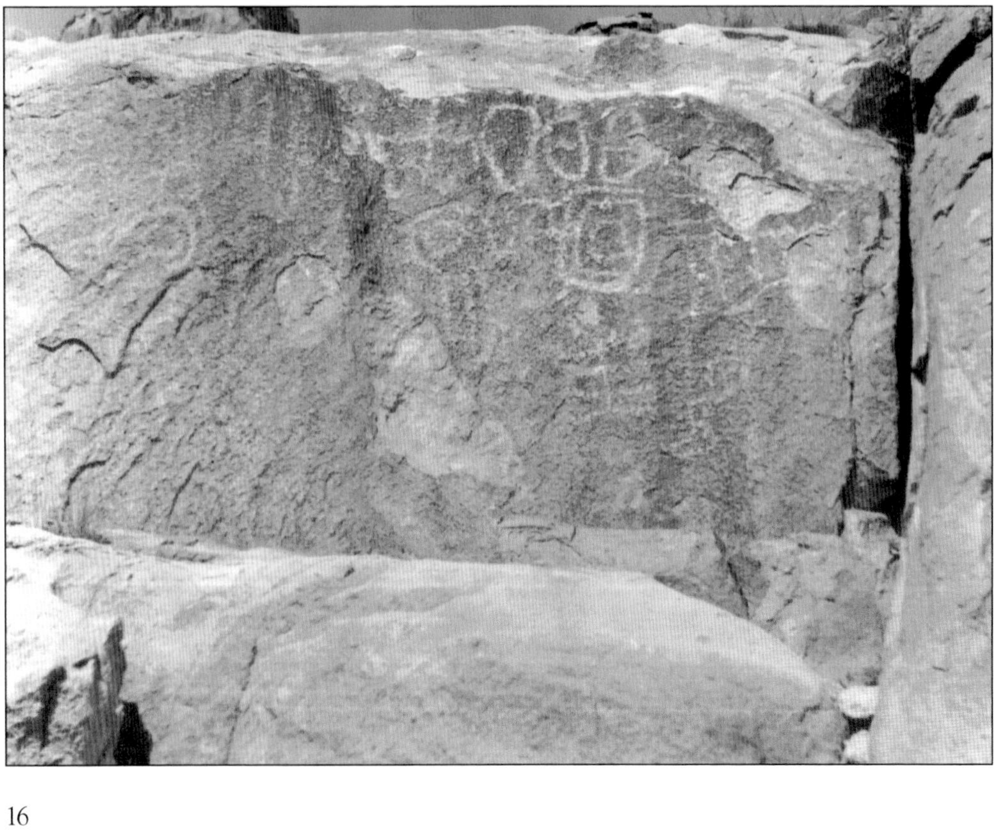

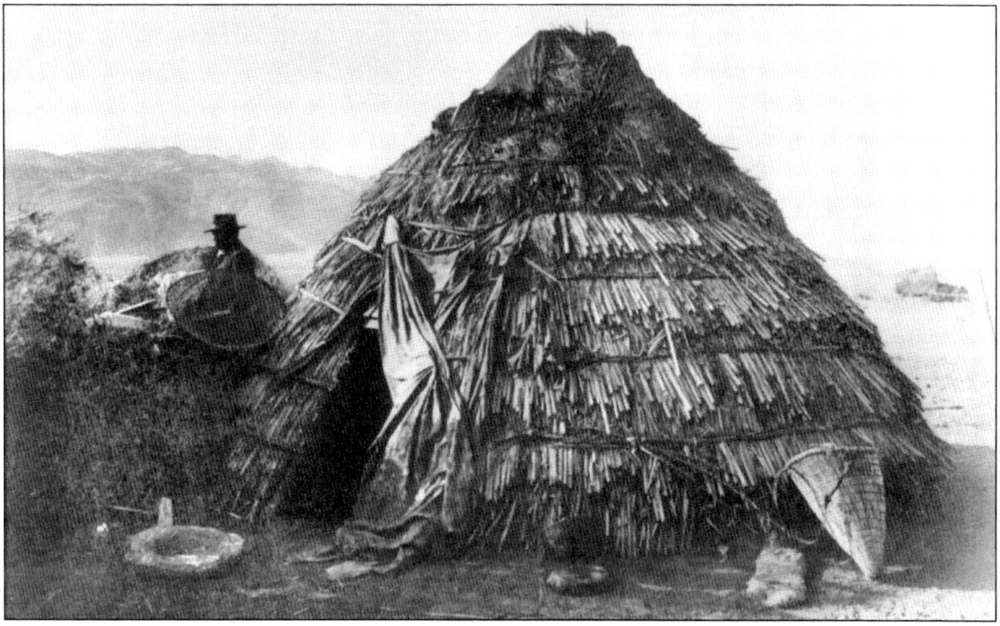

Native Impact. Early anthropologists and historians were thrilled when they came across native dwelling places like the Paiute winter house or *siwanopi* (house of straw) in the desert. A smoke hole at the top of the thatched or canvas roof draws air pollutants from the interior. Modern seekers are more likely to find tools and trinkets than abodes. (MHS/VVM.)

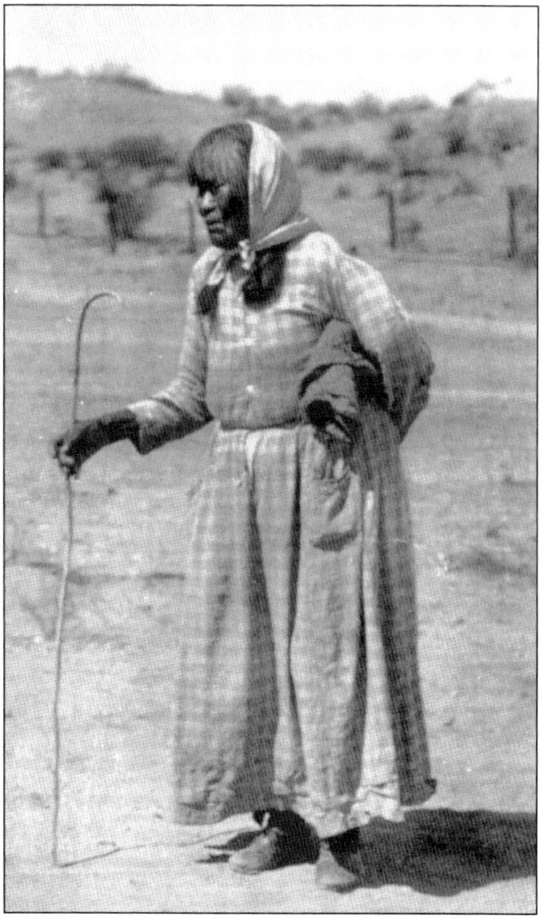

Indian Maria. Maria Chapuli, a chief's widow, was a beloved fixture around Victorville for over 100 years. Born in 1856, she lived among neighbors who appreciated her until 1960. (MHS/VVM.)

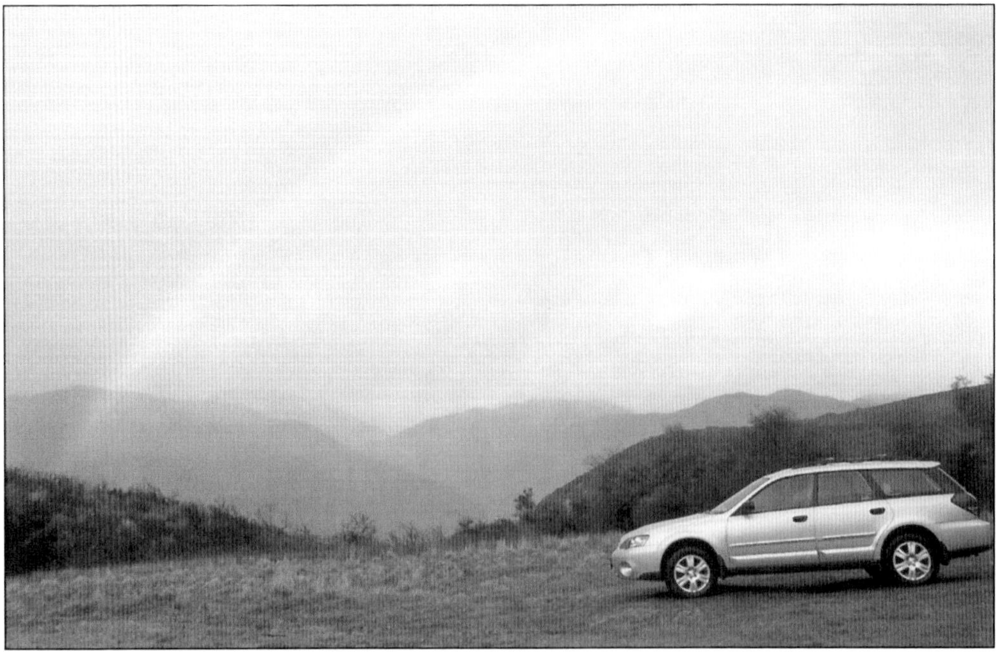

Spectacular Views. Layers of mountains and hills in various shades and hues in any type of atmosphere or weather tempt the artist, thrill the hiker, satisfy the poet, and invite every seeker of science or art to return and continue sampling what Cajon Pass has to offer. The above picture, taken from the relatively level west end of San Bernardino Range, views the more rugged San Gabriel Range. This is the view from the author's back door. The lower picture from an early postcard was taken from Applewhite Road up the San Gabriels from Keenbrook and views Cajon Pass and the San Bernardino Range to the southeast. The view is very similar today. (Above, AH; below, RB.)

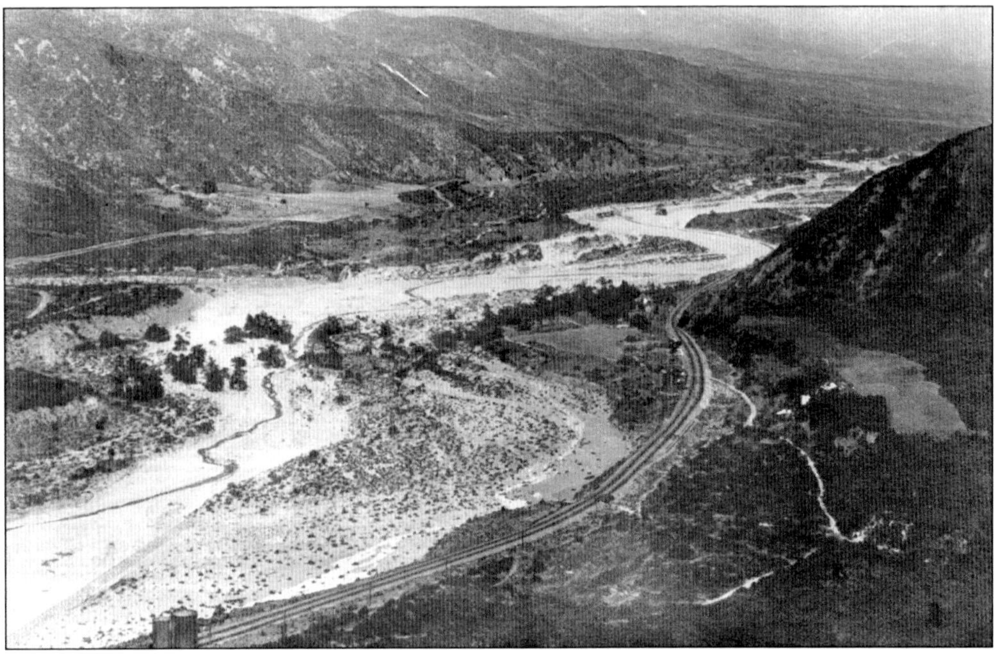

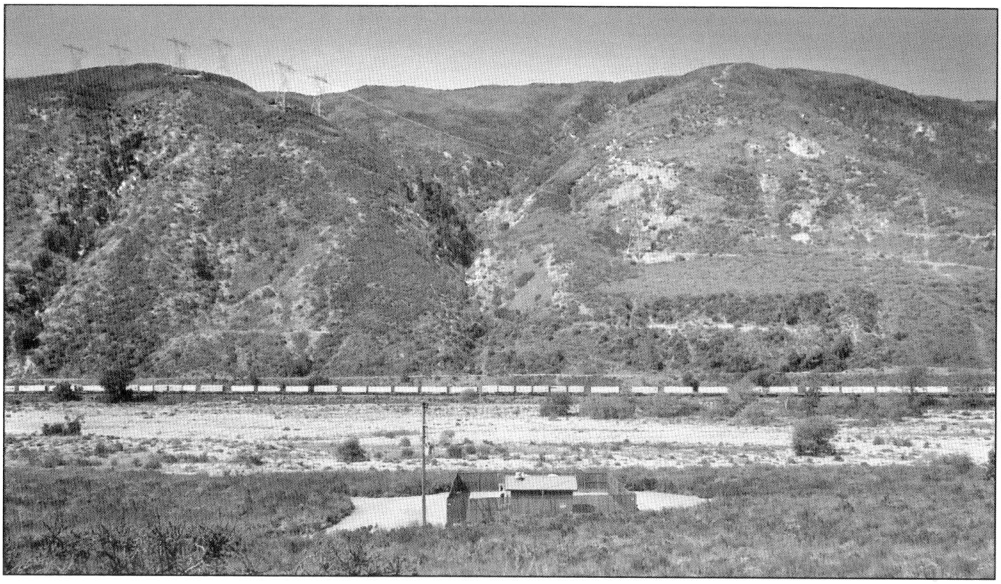

Water in Cajon Pass. Feeder canyons make Cajon Canyon dependable enough so that Robert N. C. Wilson spent decades in the 19th century finding, diverting, and developing water for the Muscoy Water Company, Glen Helen Farms, and Sycamore Flats. The deteriorated Muscoy Water ditch is visible on the hills right of the feeder canyon, above and parallel with the train. San Bernardino water facilities in the foreground are on the old Vincent homestead. (RH.)

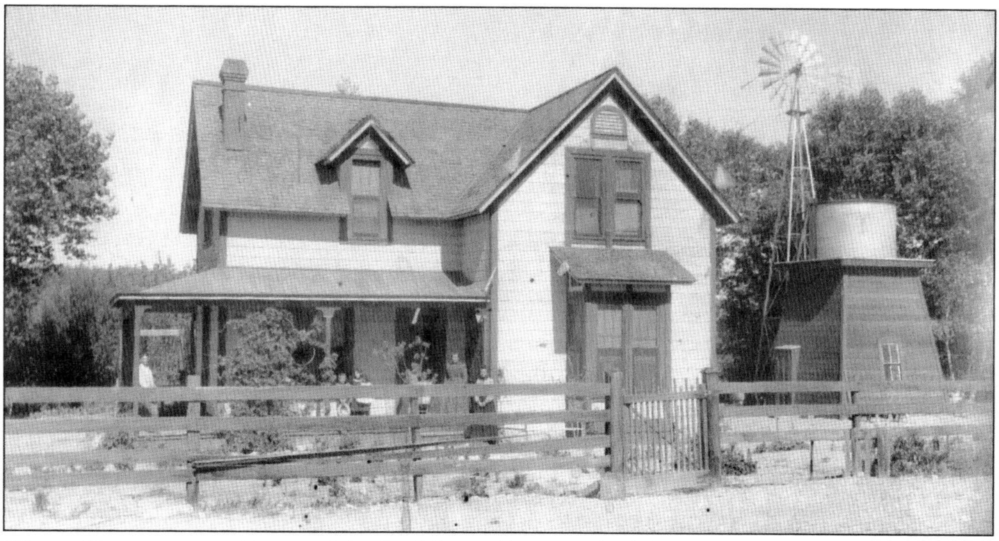

Water North of the Summit. North of Cajon Summit, the Mojave River is often subterranean. The farther a settler goes from the river, the deeper his wells must be drilled. When the river reaches the surface, the area becomes settled rapidly. Water from wells, rivers, or from long hauls is stored in water tanks, like the one shown. This 1900 Varney house on 1,100 desert acres pumped water by windmill, as did many. (RM.)

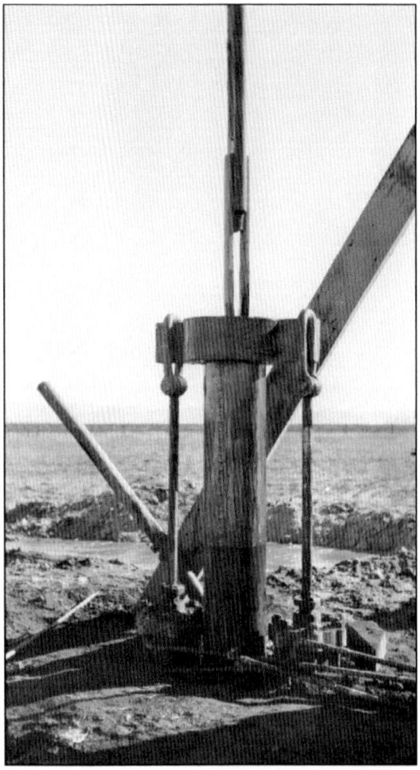

DEVELOPING WATER IN 1919. The picture at left shows a hydraulic unit pushing a well casing into the earth. Desert well-drilling and water redirection has always been a challenge. Below, three men stand at the gates of the headwaters of the Hesperia water ditch. Desert dwellers who have access to this kind of natural water are fortunate, even when taming it is difficult. By 1919, huge trenching machines had replaced men with shovels to dig water ditches for some free-flowing water or lay underground water pipes. Water was transferred from the east side of the Mojave River to Hesperia by inverted siphon. (Both, MHS/VVM.)

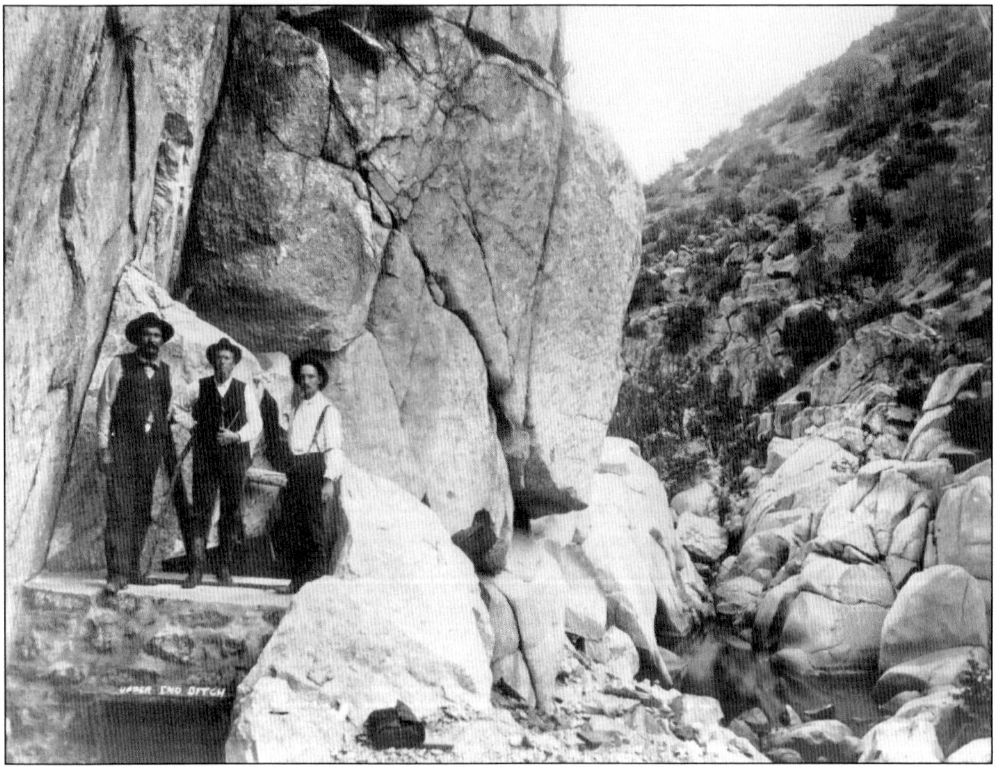

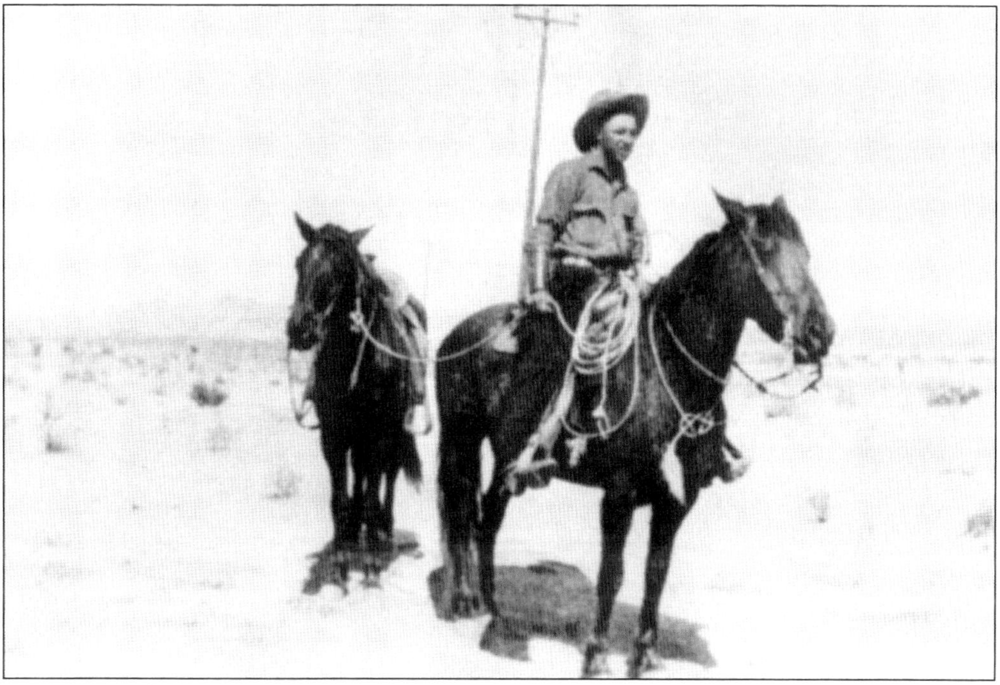

Power Line Construction. Because Cajon Pass is the easiest way over two mountain ranges, it is a natural corridor for all kinds of transportation—migrating geese, buzzards, and butterflies, ground vehicles, airplanes, and trains—and communication wires and cables. This photograph shows power line construction in 1922 near Victorville. (MHS/VVM.)

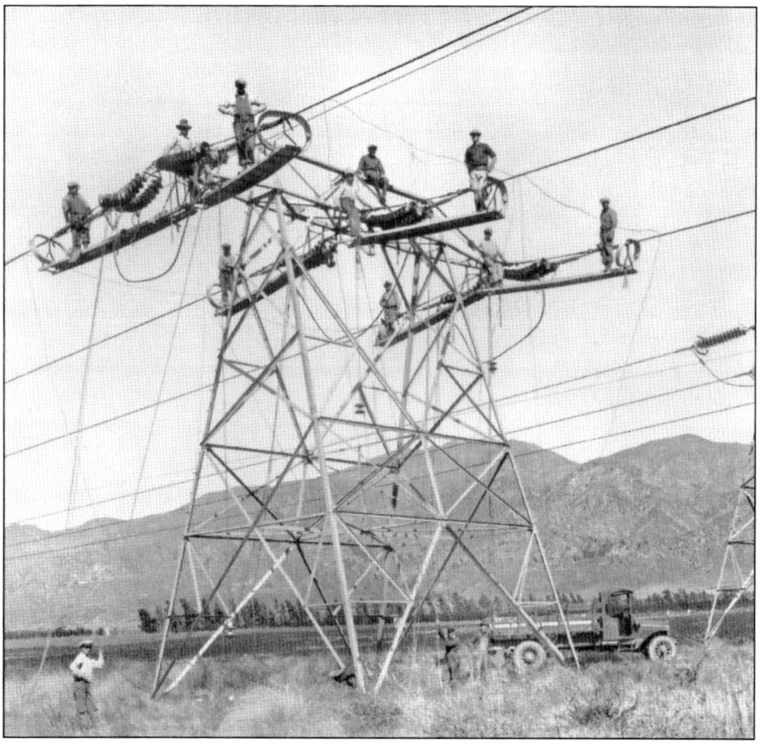

Major Power Lines. Cajon Pass is a corridor for major power lines. In 1912, Southern Sierra Power Company brought electricity over Cajon Pass from the east side of the Sierras to San Bernardino, where it had a plant. Southern Sierra Power Company became California Electric, which succumbed to an unfriendly takeover by Edison. This construction was done in the early 1930s. (MHS/VVM.)

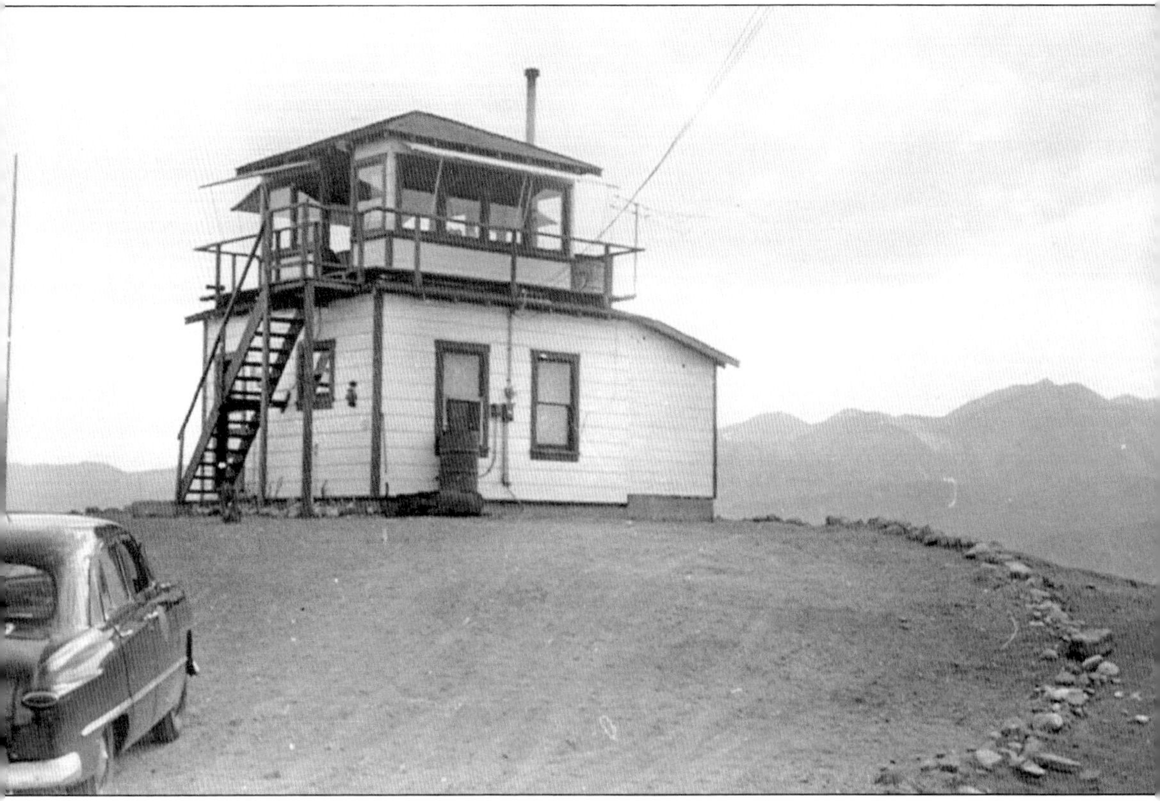

U.S. Forest Service/California Department of Forestry. Forestry lookouts, this California Division of Forestry (CDF) one near Cajon Summit west of Summit Inn, used to be seen from Cajon Pass, most of which is within the confines of the national forest. Manned by forestry personnel and volunteers, they were important in early reporting of fires. In 1886, the Board of Forestry report indicated the need for supervision and preservation of the forest and brush lands of California. The Forest Reserve Act, giving presidents power to set aside public land in preserves, was passed in 1891. CDF started in 1900, and the San Bernardino Forest Reserve became San Bernardino National Forest (SBNF) in 1907. U.S. Forest Service is responsible for federal lands, and CDF is responsible for private property within federal boundaries. SBNF contains 671,686 acres, as well as 71 animal and 85 plant endangered, sensitive, or threatened species. The land on the north side of the summit is within the Mojave Desert Resource Conservation District, which contains over 11 million acres of both urban and rural land. The purposes are to control wind erosion on cropland, stabilize stream channels and water quality, conserve water, and encourage proper range management and land stewardship. (CDFM.)

Two

ROADS

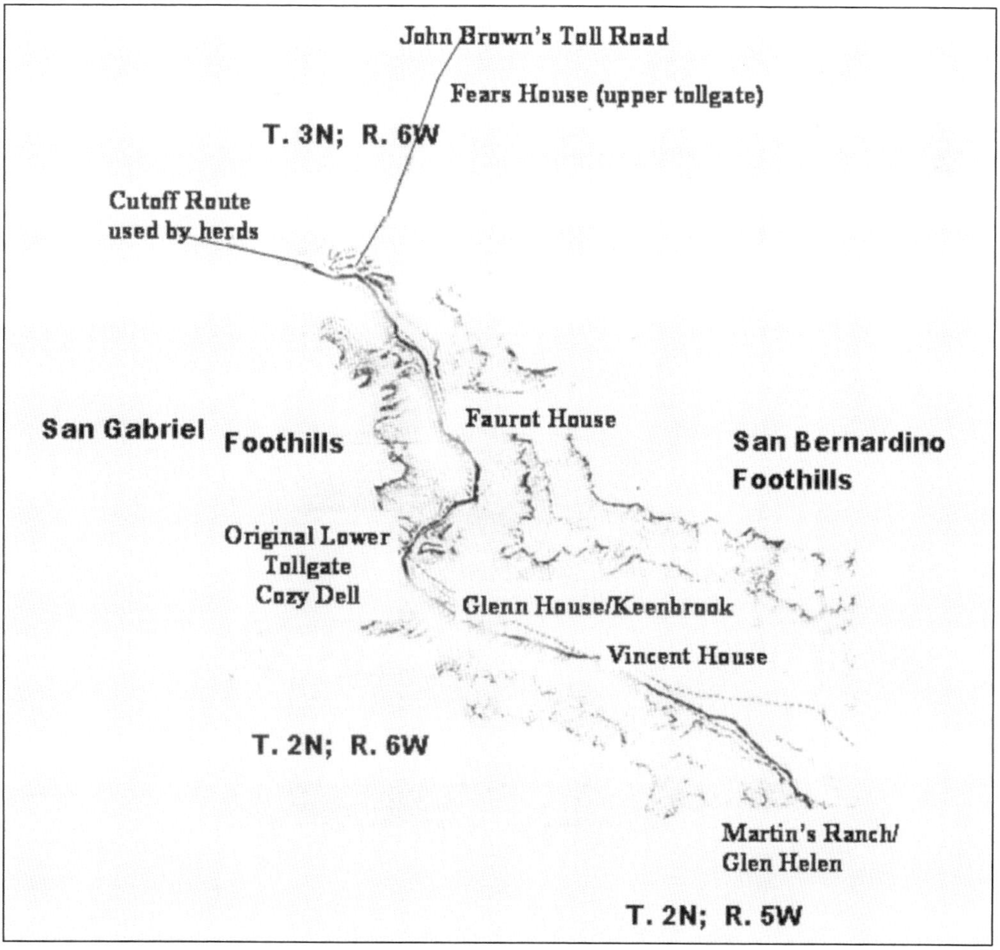

OLD SPANISH TRAIL. This road followed Native American paths through the pass. John Brown Sr. improved part of it for his toll road, which remained open for over 20 years starting in 1861. John Brown's Toll Road began north of Martin's Ranch, now Glen Helen Regional Park, and extended to the Cajon summit, encompassing the most difficult to maintain portions of the public road. Pass residents opened way stations for travelers' comfort. (AH.)

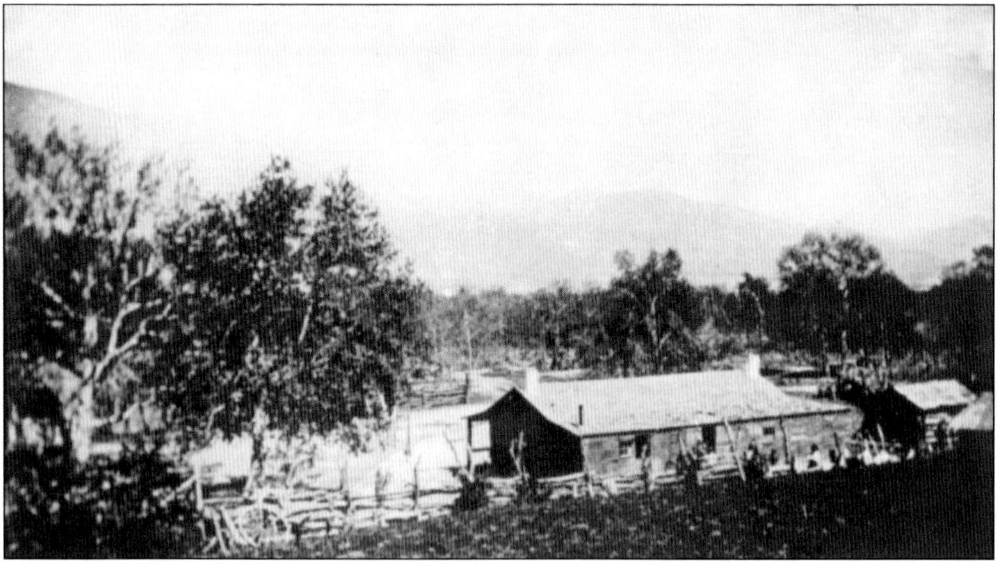

Martin's Ranch/Glen Helen. During the Civil War, Glen Helen was home to a Union army post under the command of Col. William Hoffman. George and Sarah Martin opened their home on the 2,700 acres they farmed as a way station for travelers near the start of John Brown's Toll Road in the 1870s. Horses and humans found rest and refreshment to help them continue their journey. (MHS/VVM.)

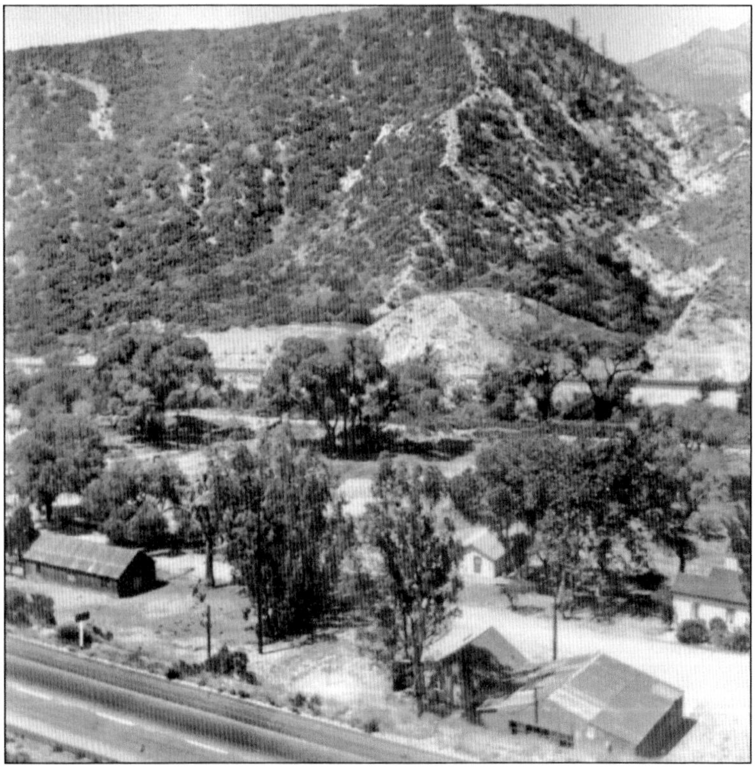

Cozy Dell/Bear Flats. Bear Flats way station was leased to Jesse Tay and Charles Lawrence in 1879 and renamed Cozy Dell. It remained an important traveler oasis with buildings on both sides of the road even through Route 66 years. Philip Hanf, the cook, became owner by 1902. The road followed the foothills on the west side for a short distance before it crossed Cajon Canyon to wend through Cozy Dell. (MHS/VVM.)

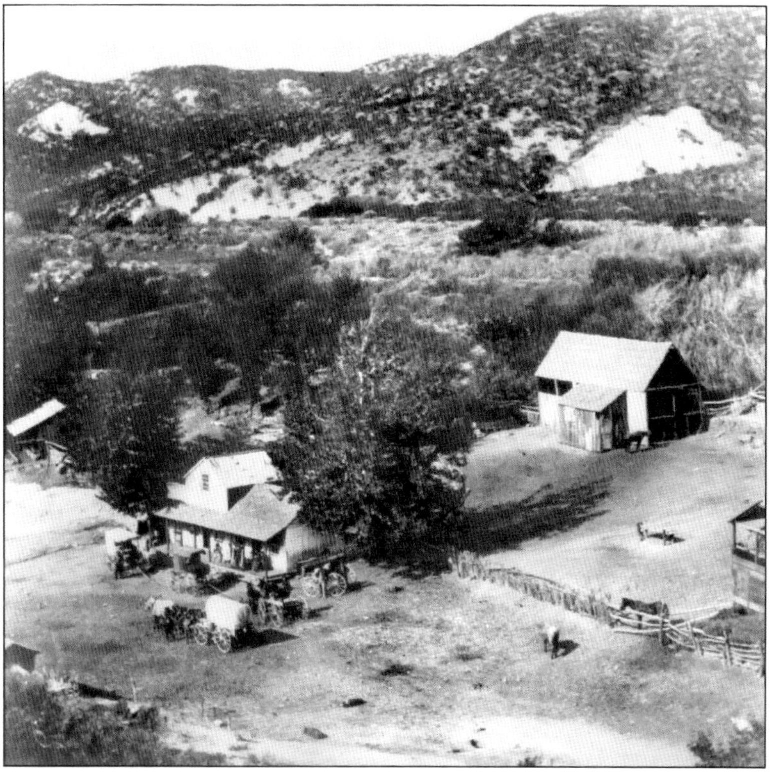

Fear's Way Station. James and Naomi Fears also modified their homestead in the east branch of Cajon Pass to serve travelers at the toll gate. James and Naomi Fears were well respected, and Naomi's meals were highly praised. Their daughter Rebecca, after her first husband died, married Jeremiah Vincent and helped him with his homestead by Cajon Creek between Glen Helen and her parents' place. (MHS/VVM.)

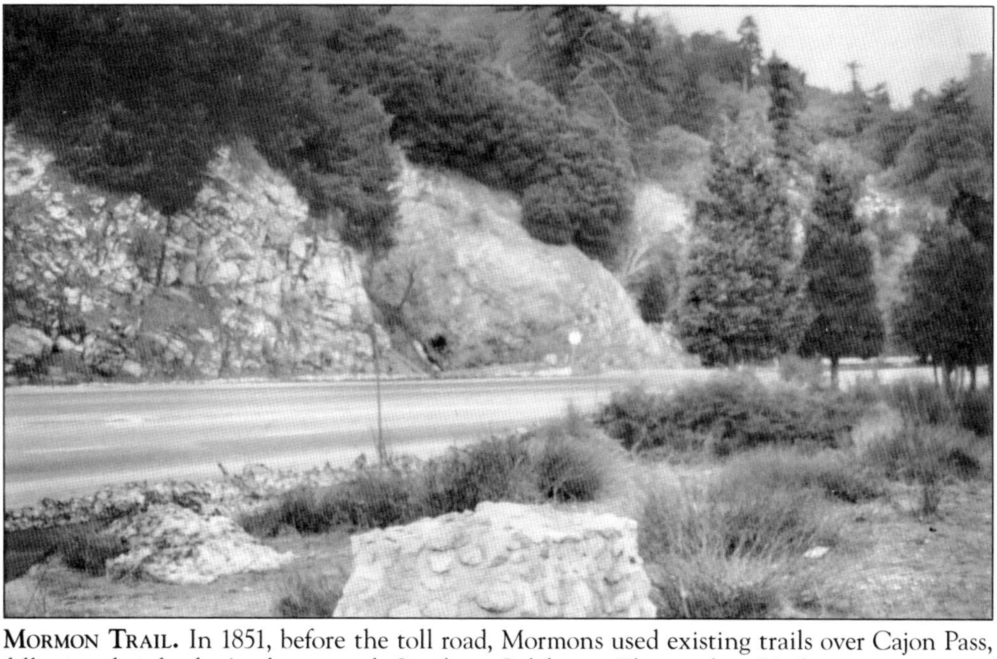

Mormon Trail. In 1851, before the toll road, Mormons used existing trails over Cajon Pass, following their leaders' orders to settle Southern California. The trip from Utah was excruciating. At the point pictured above or one like it in West Cajon Valley along Route 138, they had to dismantle their wagons and lower them and their loads down cliffsides by rope to be reassembled and repacked at the bottom. (MHS/VVM.)

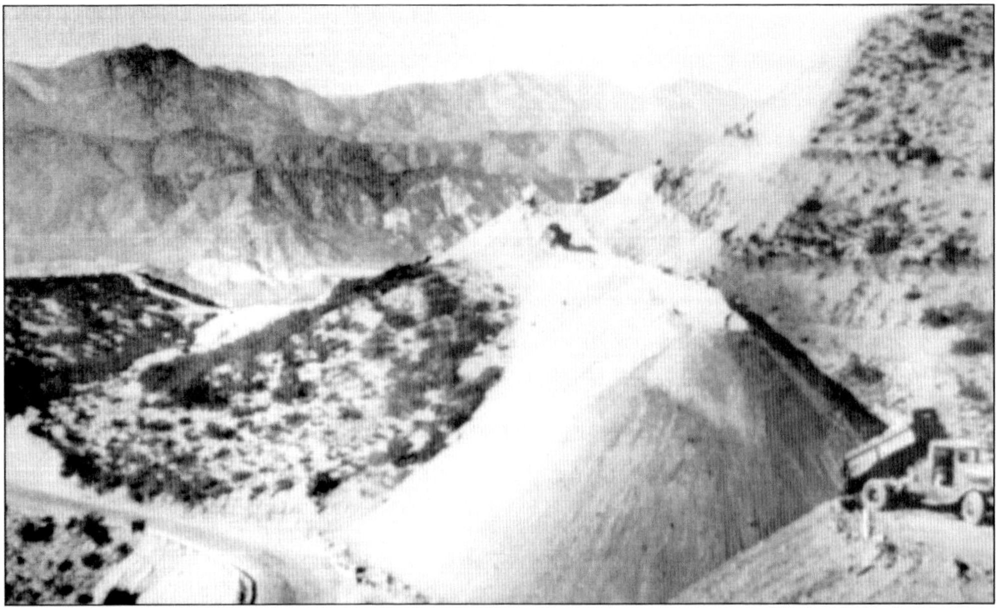

HIGHWAY CONSTRUCTION AT SUMMIT. Conquering the rugged terrain of Cajon Pass for the National Trails Highway, Route 66, was no easy task before 1930. The roughed-out highway wends its way around hills (lower left) while construction crews move mounds of rock and soil for the new highway on the right. (MHS/VVM.)

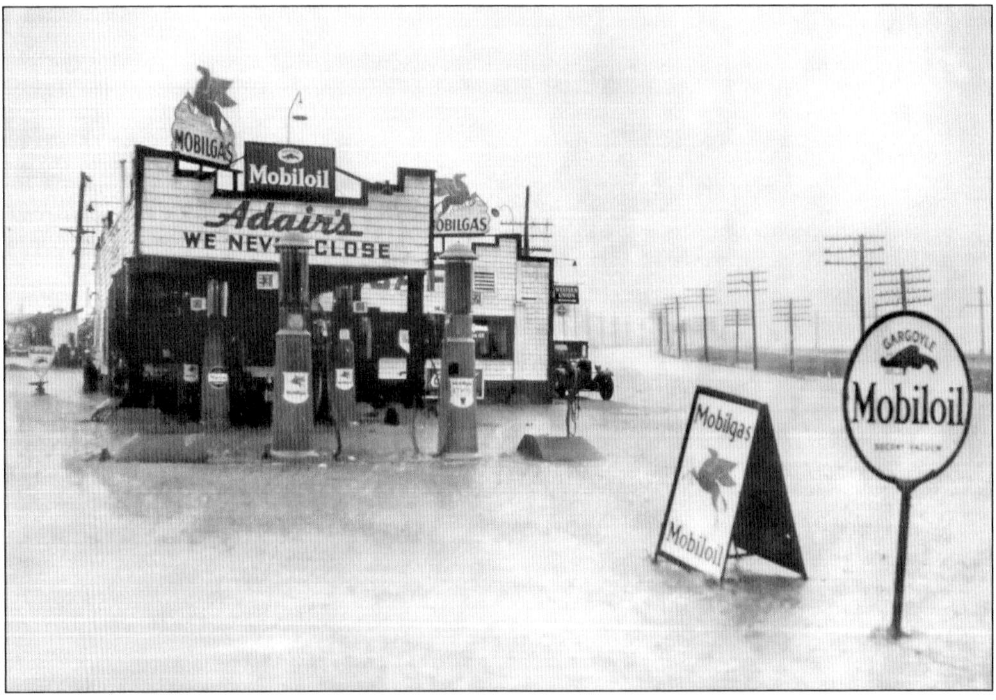

DOES THE PASS BEGIN HERE? Route 66 left San Bernardino at this intersection of Highland and Mount Vernon Avenues, where Adair's Mobile station once reigned. The corner is not well defined in this photograph taken during the flood of 1938. The highway paralleled the railroad tracks from this point to Verdemont, a few miles south of Devore. (SBHPS.)

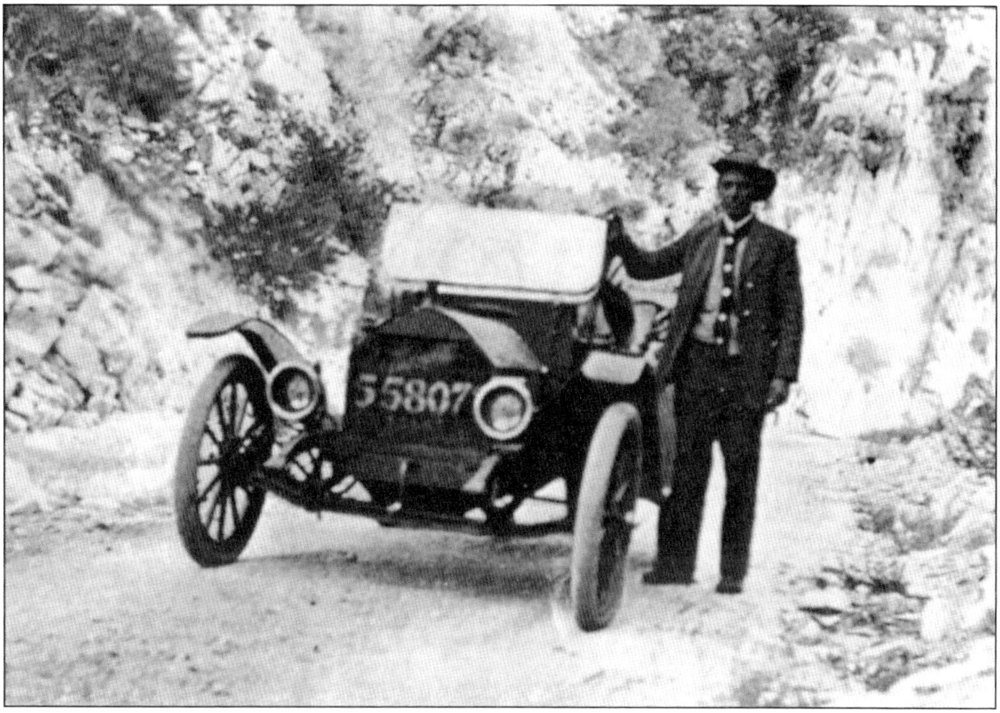

HUPMOBILE IN PASS. Charlie Morrow and his Hupmobile on Cajon Pass were featured in the first issue of *Kingdom of the Sun*, a magazine started in 1912 by the women of Oro Grande to introduce America to its "Sahara." The first issue described Cajon Pass as "unexcelled for rugged beauty and is a pleasant trip for an auto. The roads are excellent." (MHS/VVM.)

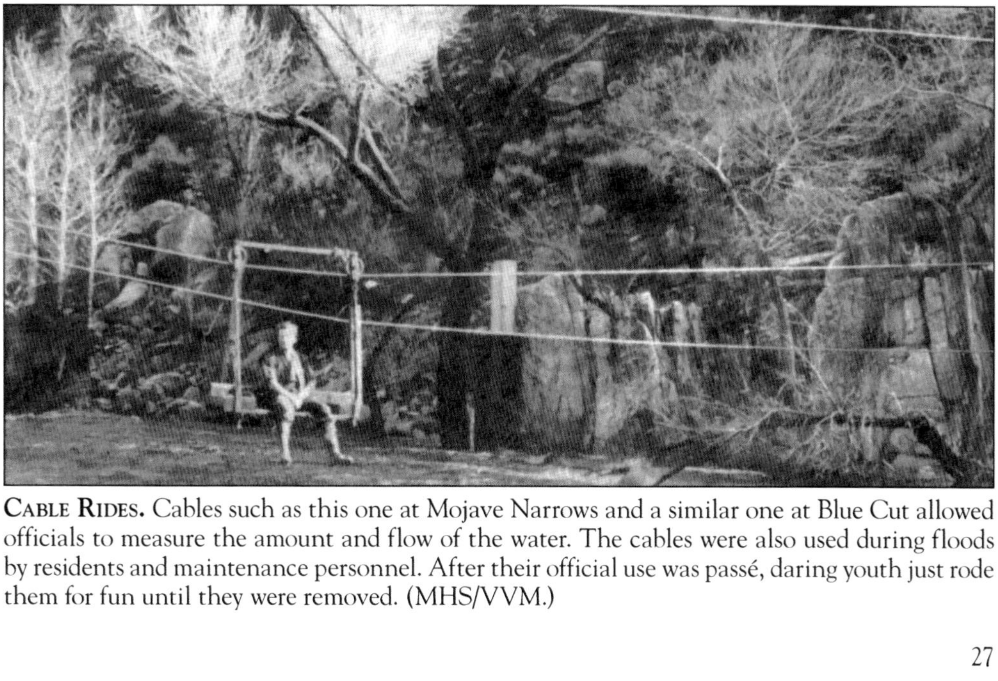

CABLE RIDES. Cables such as this one at Mojave Narrows and a similar one at Blue Cut allowed officials to measure the amount and flow of the water. The cables were also used during floods by residents and maintenance personnel. After their official use was passé, daring youth just rode them for fun until they were removed. (MHS/VVM.)

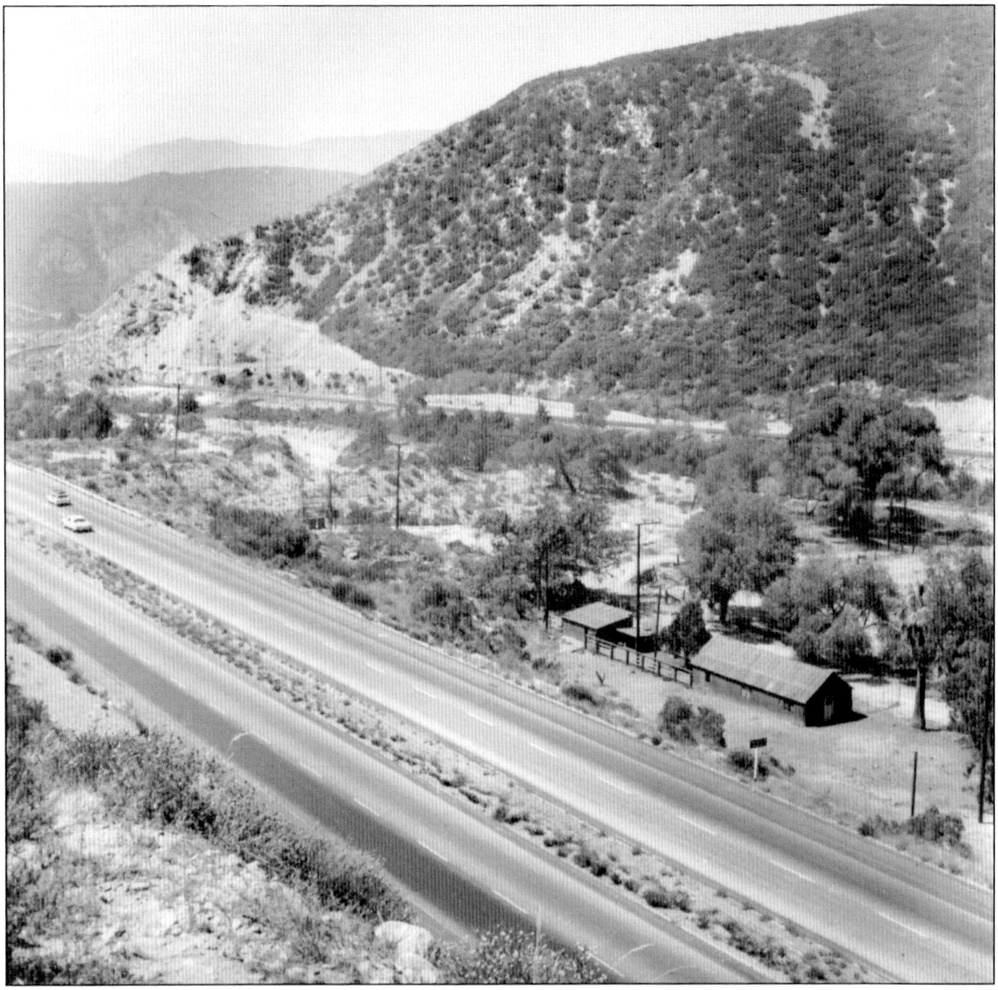

The Multiuse Highway. Route 66 over Cajon Pass in 1954 also claimed the names Route 91 and Route 395. On the right, behind the Cozy Dell buildings, lined by trees, is the older Route 66. The original route was paved in 1916 to Devore by May with macadam, continuing to Cozy Dell by summer—the first paved highway. Highway 91 originated in Sweetgrass, Montana, and ended at Highway 101 in Los Angeles. Now Highway 91 ends in Barstow. Highway 395 also began near the Canadian border north of Laurier, Washington, and extended to San Diego. Now it ends at the I-15 near Hesperia. (MHS/VVM.)

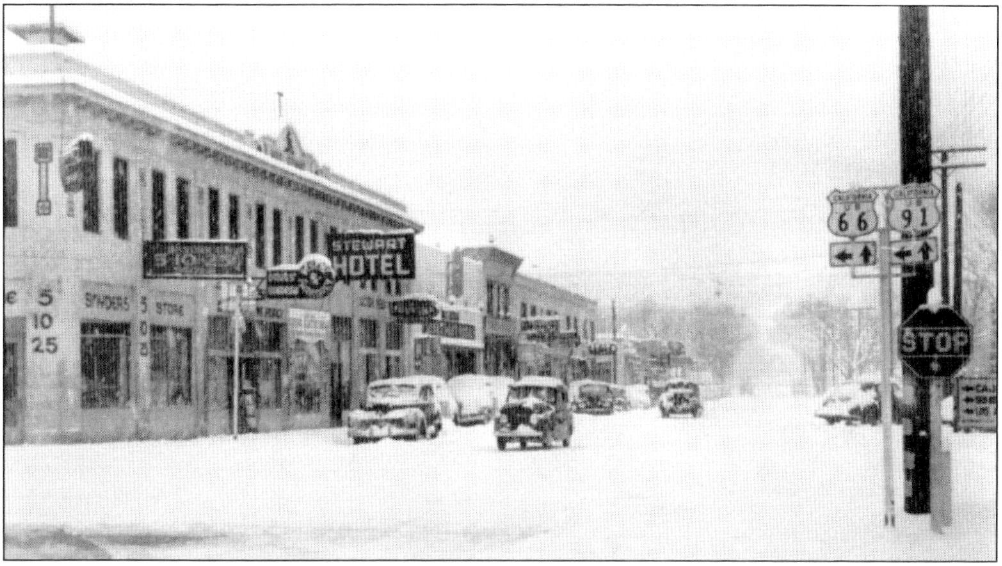

The High Desert Mother Road. Routes 66 and 91 made the main street, D Street, in Victorville. This photograph was taken after the road was named Route 66 in 1926. Today Route 66 still follows D Street north, where it takes the name National Trails Highway. D Street south is Highway 18 into Apple Valley. (MHS/VVM.)

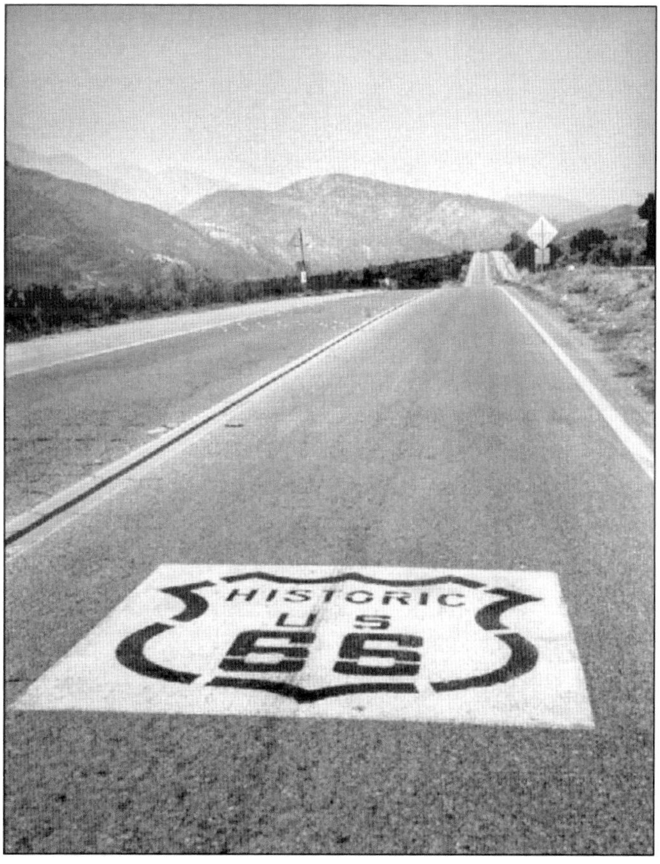

The Mother Road. In 1926, the Old Trails Highway was renamed Route 66 and became "the Mother Road," linking Chicago, Illinois, with Santa Monica, California. Route 66 fans enthusiastically celebrated the highway's 75th anniversary in 2001. San Bernardino County participated by marking usable stretches of Route 66. This particular symbol is in Cajon Pass just north of Kenwood Avenue not far from the old Devore Garage. (AH.)

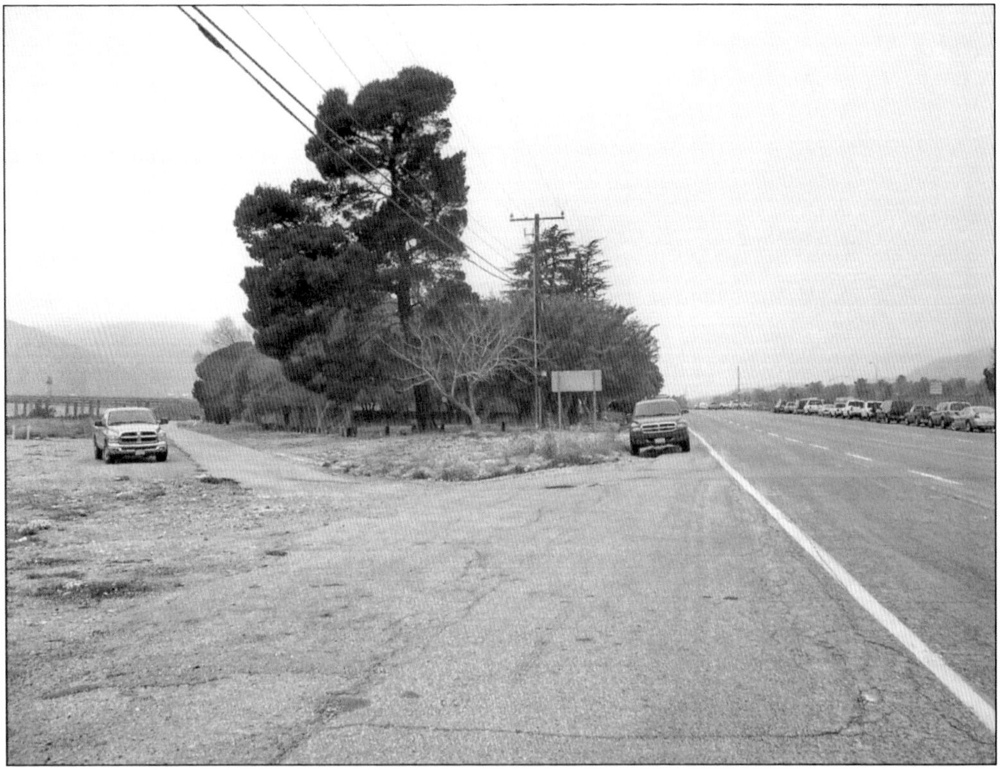

Two Mother Roads. The California Division of Forestry Devore station nestles in the trees between old macadam Route 66 on the left and the 1939 Route 66 on the right. The original followed the wash and had to be moved and straightened in 1931. It was rebuilt again after the flood of 1938. The figure in the picture below points at the old macadam Route 66. The 66 that was widened to four lanes in 1953 runs between the box culvert and the large tree. The trucks to the left of and behind the tree travel southbound on I-15 near Kenwood Avenue in Devore. (Above, AH; below, RH.)

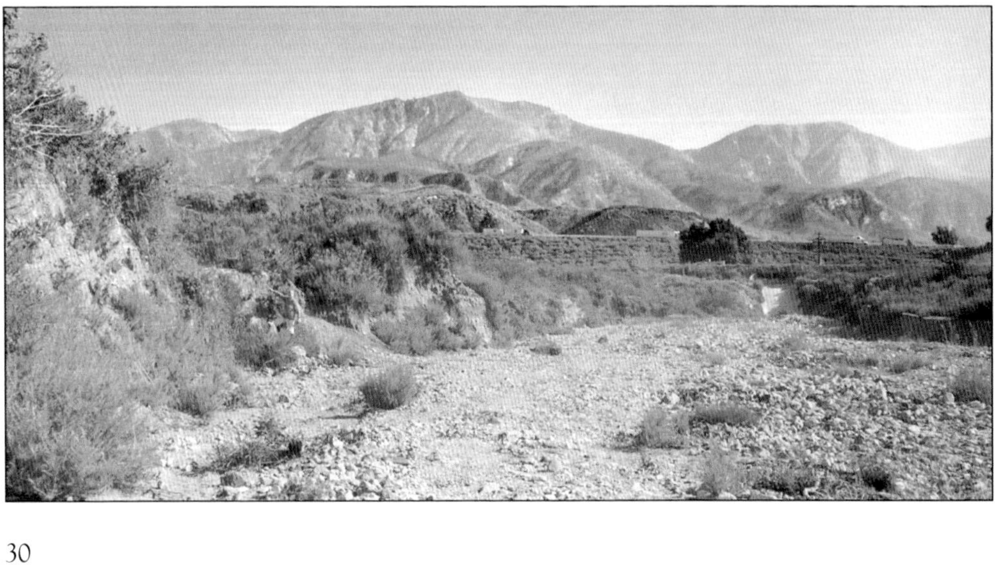

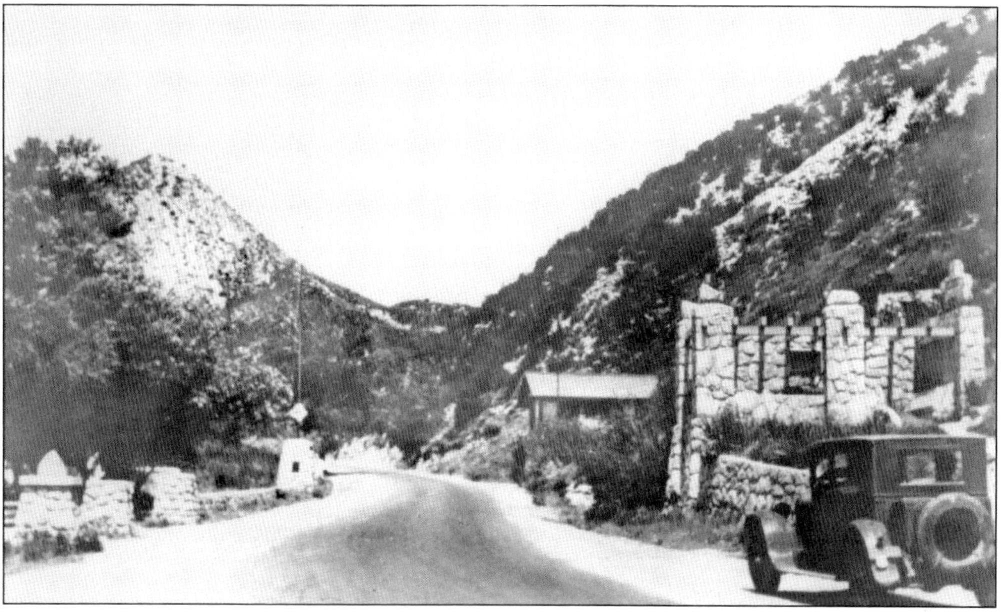

Route 66 through Cajon Campground. William Bristol conceived and designed Cajon Campground in 1919, and the camp offered free picnicking, camping, and other amenities until the flood of 1938 washed it away. Various communities sponsored heavy concrete picnic tables, and organizations subsidized rock buildings and monuments. This was the location for Cajon Post Office, and there were rooms for travelers and a small store. The photograph is from 1930. (AHCRFL.)

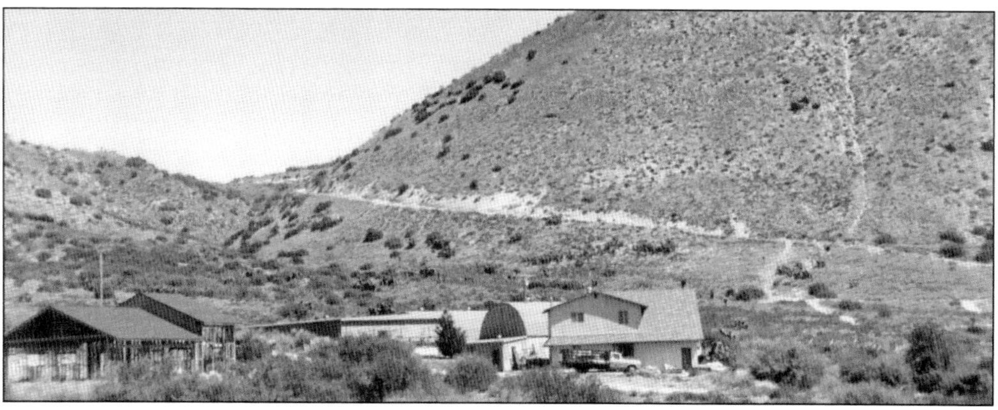

The Sanford Grade. This road can be seen from Highway 138 in West Cajon Valley. It is the route William Sanford, a teamster from Banning, created in 1850 because it was better for freight wagons than trails in East Cajon Valley. Mormon trail monument No. 577 commemorates this development. (MHS/VVM.)

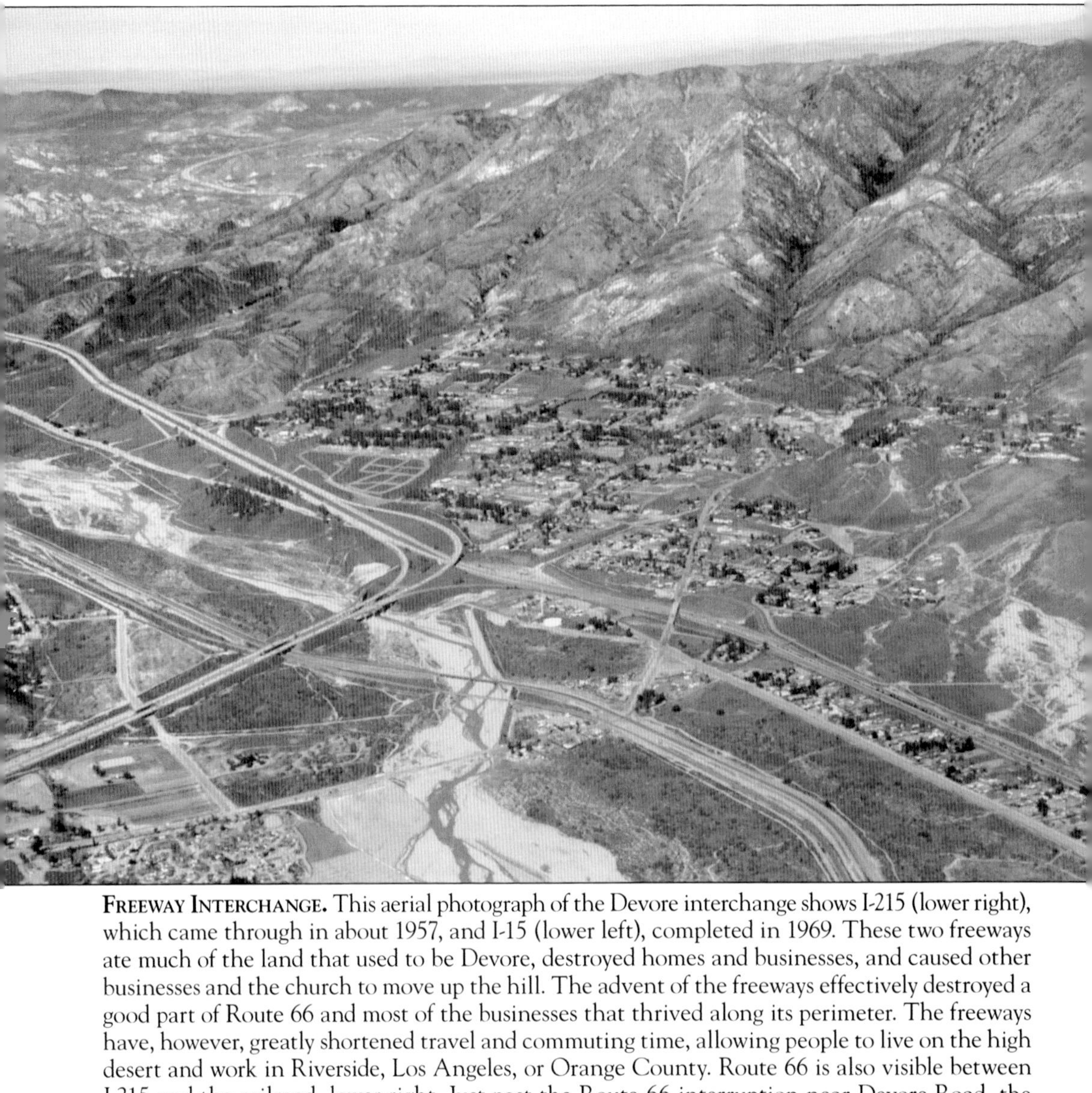

Freeway Interchange. This aerial photograph of the Devore interchange shows I-215 (lower right), which came through in about 1957, and I-15 (lower left), completed in 1969. These two freeways ate much of the land that used to be Devore, destroyed homes and businesses, and caused other businesses and the church to move up the hill. The advent of the freeways effectively destroyed a good part of Route 66 and most of the businesses that thrived along its perimeter. The freeways have, however, greatly shortened travel and commuting time, allowing people to live on the high desert and work in Riverside, Los Angeles, or Orange County. Route 66 is also visible between I-215 and the railroad, lower right. Just past the Route 66 interruption near Devore Road, the two Route 66 roads are visible immediately beyond the center of the photograph (as shown on page 30). Both end where Kimbark Creek empties into Cajon Creek. The newer Route 66 goes north again from where Kenwood Avenue intersects with it. South of Kenwood, it is blocked. By 2016, the interchange will have been enlarged and Route 66 reconnected, according to Cal Trans. (DNM.)

Three

RAILROADS

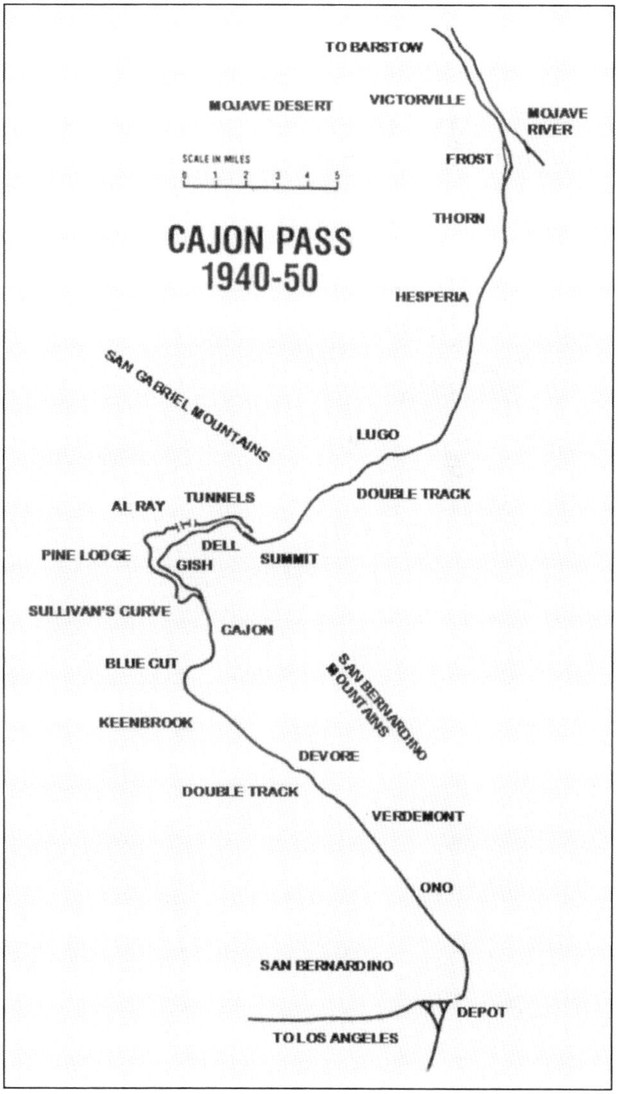

SPECIAL IDENTITY. The railroad gave Cajon Pass a special identity. Yes, it carved up some homesteads and stole some pasture and cropland, but necessary railroad stops encouraged little communities to develop along the tracks. The communities south of the summit dwindled when the freeways went through. The communities north of the summit flourished when the freeways tied into them. Cajon Pass still draws rail fans from near and distant places. (AH.)

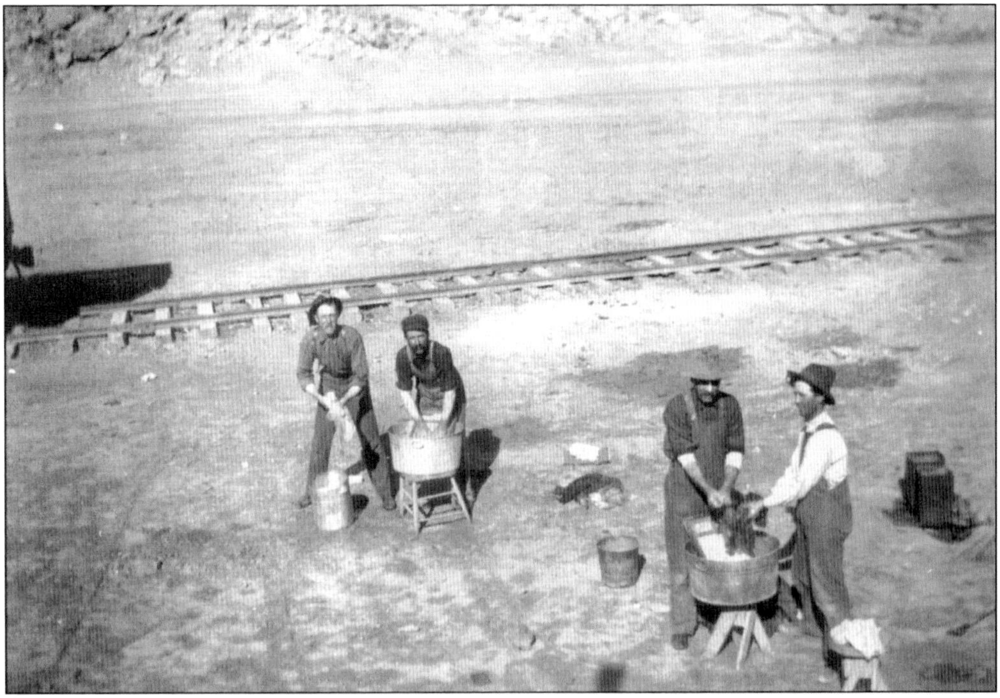

RAILROAD SURVEYORS. Railroad surveyors mapped out Cajon Pass in 1884. A chief surveyor on the railroad project was Fred T. Perris, and Jacob Nash Victor was the general manager or superintendent of California Southern Railroad and oversaw the construction of that track from Colton through Cajon Pass, one of the busiest rail freight routes in the nation. Surveyors and other workers lived in tent cities and performed domestic chores. (SBHPS.)

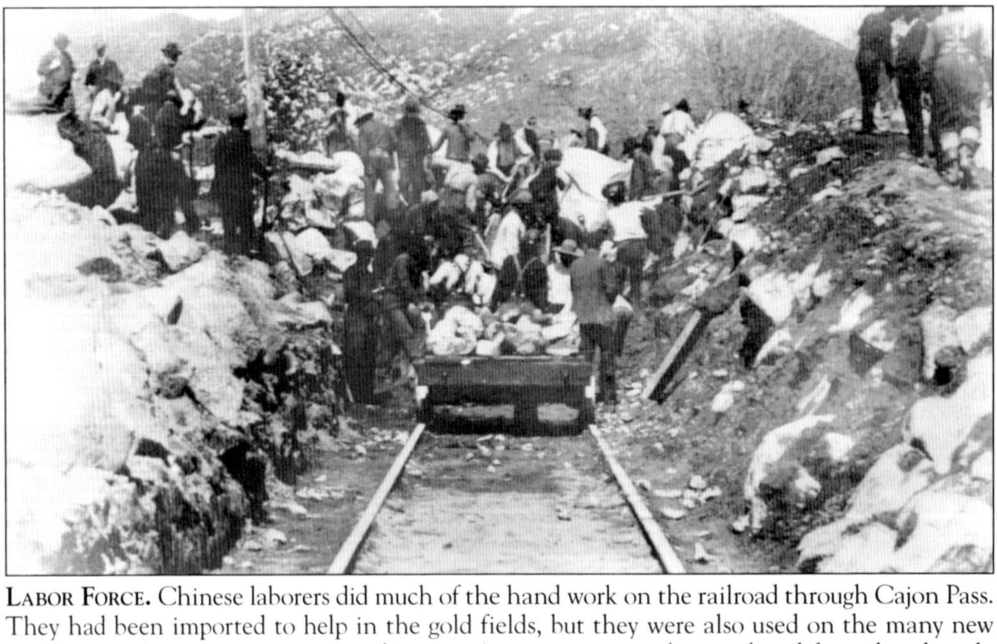

LABOR FORCE. Chinese laborers did much of the hand work on the railroad through Cajon Pass. They had been imported to help in the gold fields, but they were also used on the many new railroads in the West. Mexicans and Native Americans were also employed for railroad work. (MHS/VVM.)

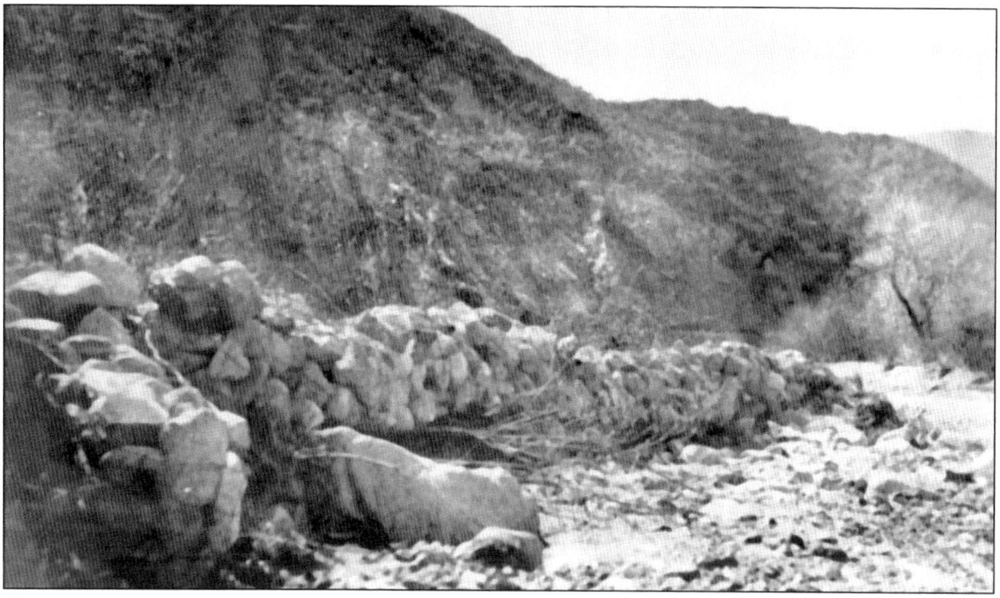

TERRACING AND SAUSAGING USED. Because of the unstable hillsides throughout Cajon Pass, elaborate terracing and installation of "sausages" (pictured) were done to cut down on landslides or flooding that might destroy newly laid railroad tracks. This photograph was taken during the original construction in 1884–1885, but even today, landslides and washouts threaten the tracks, and railroad crews patrol and work often on the Cajon Pass railroad tracks. (MHS/VVM.)

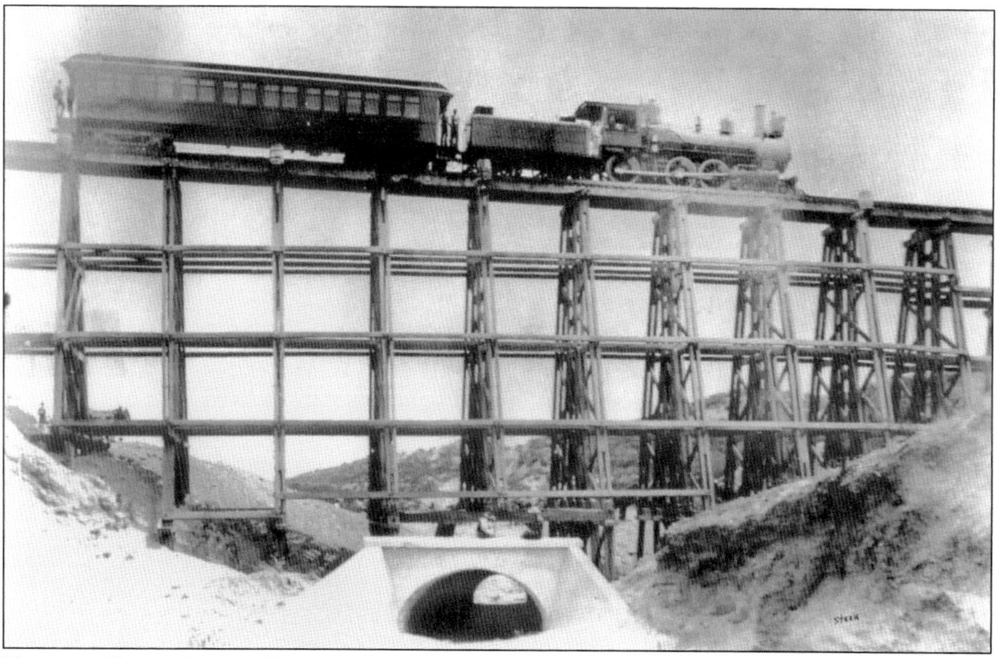

TRESTLES SHORT-LIVED. Terracing continues on new cuts today, but the magnificent trestles on which trains traversed rough areas of Cajon Pass were later filled. This allowed the tracks to be laid on solid ground, giving more stability than wooden, or even metal, trestles would. Fire threatened wooden trestles. (SBHPS.)

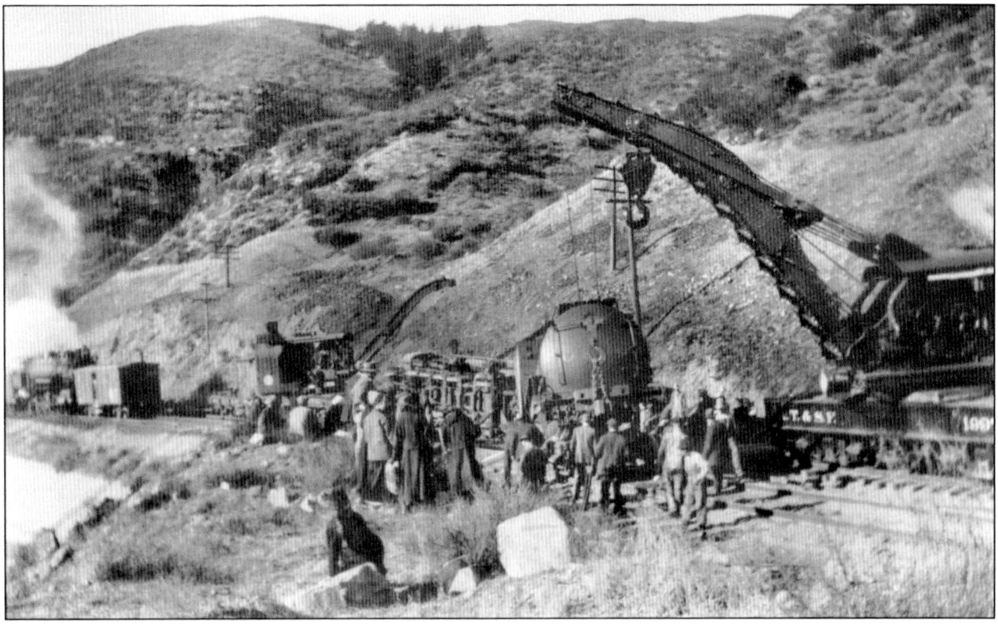

HAZARDS. Because of the steep grade of the tracks in Cajon Pass and because of landslides, flooding, and even earthquakes and fires, railroad accidents have occurred regularly and frequently. Righting derailed engines and cars usually presented a terrible dilemma for railroad workers, and tracks often washed out. Even today, that is a concern, and railroad personnel patrol the pass constantly during stormy weather. These photographs were probably taken by Edward Ehwegen, telegrapher at the Cajon Depot from 1910 to 1937. (RB.)

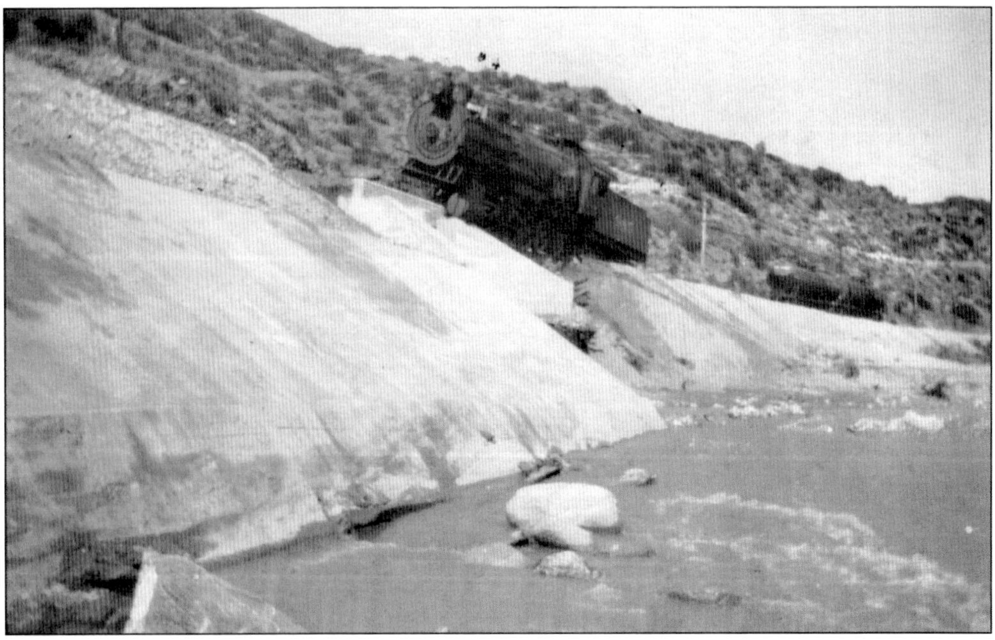

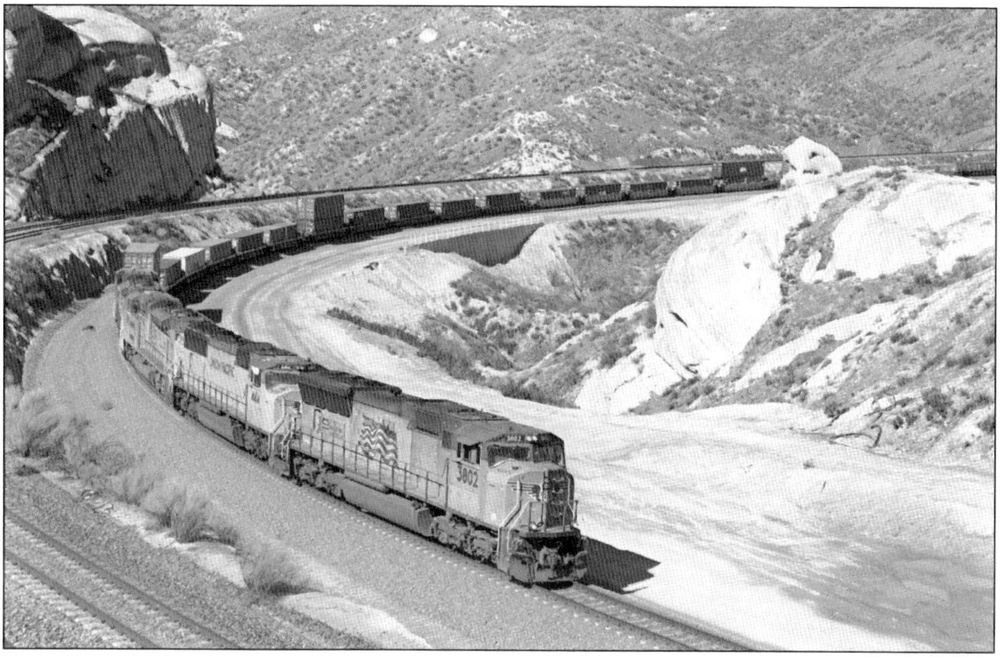

Sullivan's Curve. Sullivan's Curve is one of the larger, more graceful arcs in the tracks designed to improve the grade through Cajon Pass. Sullivan's Curve was named for a photographer from Placentia who frequently visited the pass for pictures. Chard Walker, pass and railroad historian, was partly responsible for the name. (GG.)

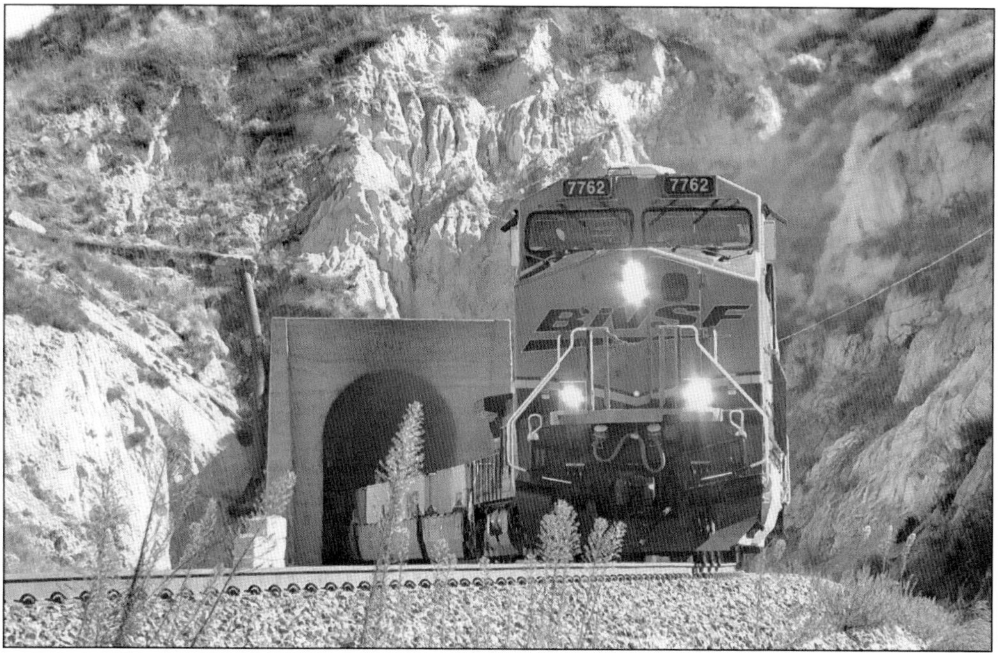

Alray. An important and necessary railroad siding was positioned at Alray, which is seldom seen anymore on most maps. Alray is also where tunnels helped to smooth the way through impossible grades. During the world wars, armed guards were posted at Alray and sometimes on railroad bridges through the Cajon Pass to protect this vital link with eastern states. (DT.)

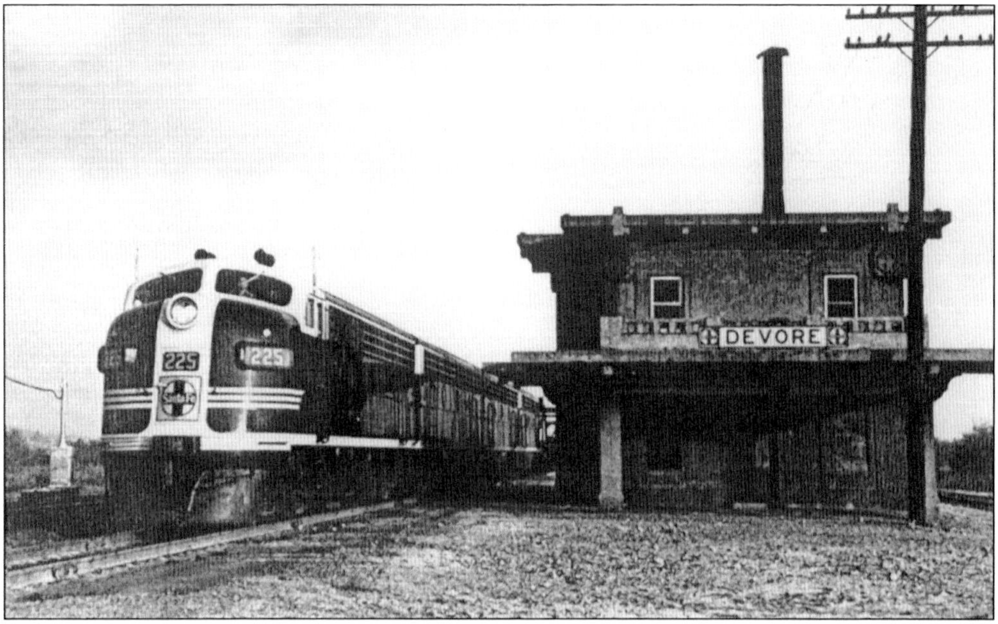

Devore Depot. To honor John A. Devore, who had generously contributed land easements to Santa Fe, the depot at Devore was built more sturdily and ornately than any of the other depots in Cajon Pass. The Devore Depot opened in 1908 and remained under the care of Herbert Benton Davis until 1930. The depot reopened for a time during World War II and was torn down in the early 1950s. (AG.)

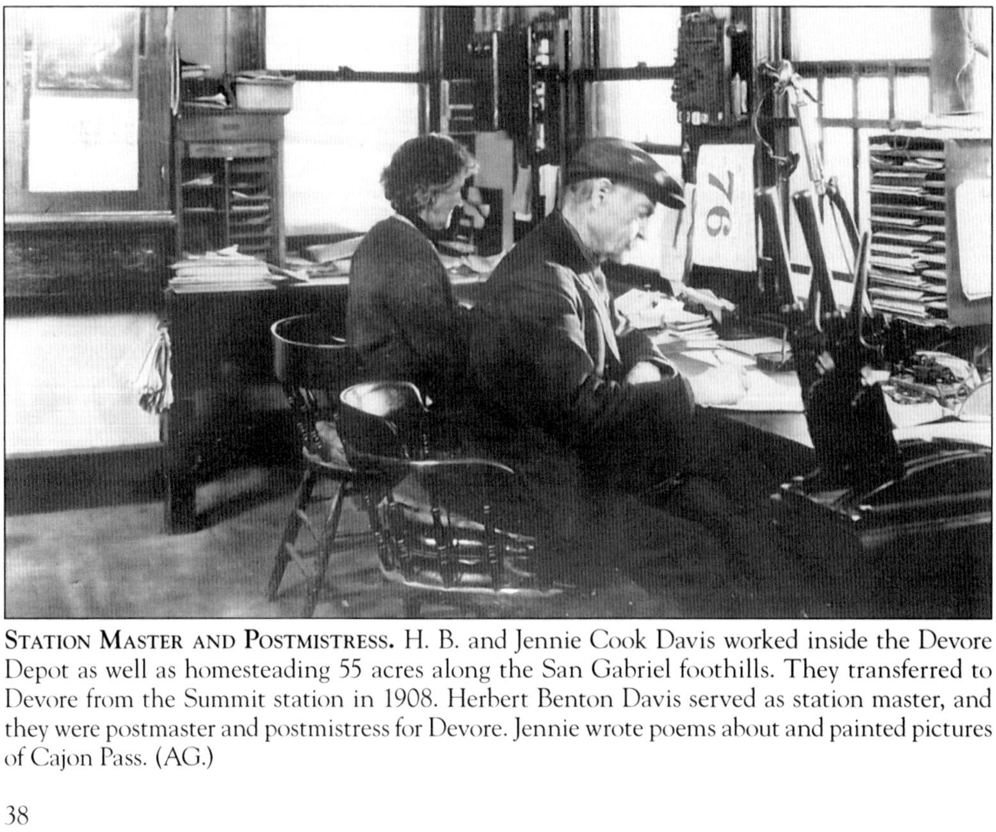

Station Master and Postmistress. H. B. and Jennie Cook Davis worked inside the Devore Depot as well as homesteading 55 acres along the San Gabriel foothills. They transferred to Devore from the Summit station in 1908. Herbert Benton Davis served as station master, and they were postmaster and postmistress for Devore. Jennie wrote poems about and painted pictures of Cajon Pass. (AG.)

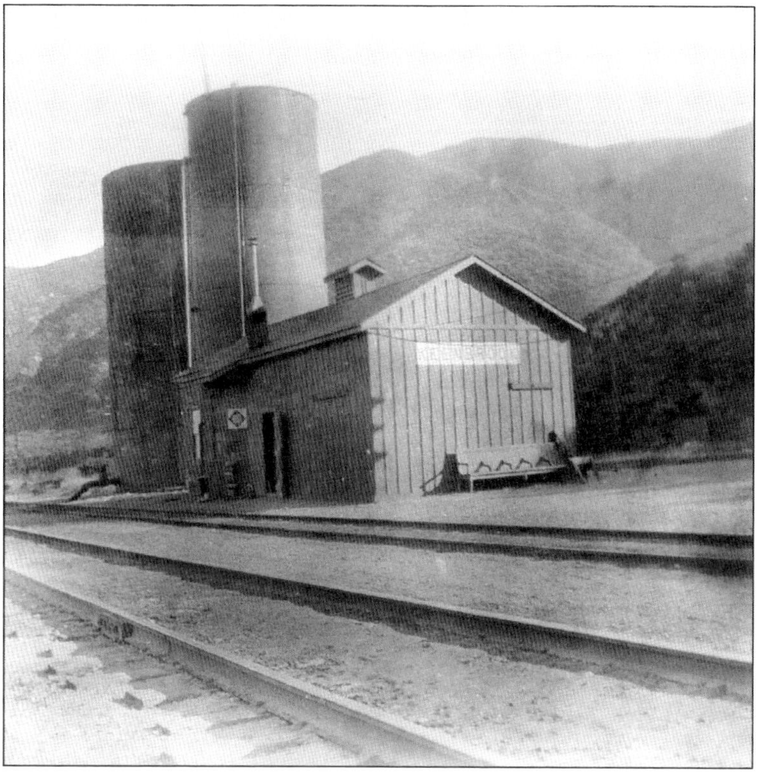

KEENBOOK STATION. Railroad stations were placed only a few miles apart, as the steam locomotives needed water frequently to make the climb up Cajon Pass. On the way down, they had to stop often to cool brakes and wheels. The Keenbrook station, only a few miles from Devore, also served residents north of Devore as a place to catch the train to San Bernardino for shopping and doctor visits. (HS.)

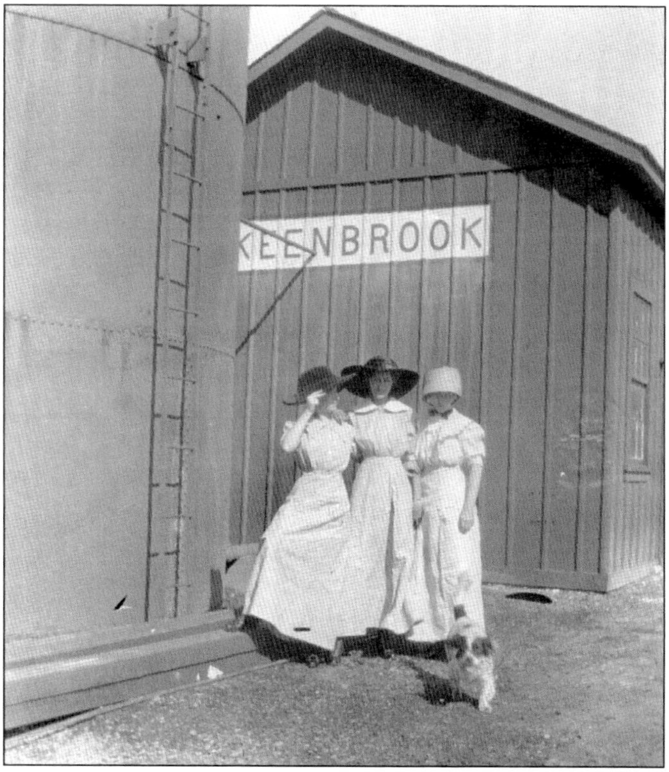

BESIDE HER NAMESAKE. Mrs. G. H. (Sarah) Keene stands at the left near the Keenbrook towers. The Keenes, William Gould Bailey, and another party bought the land in 1883 from James and Ruth Ellen Applewhite, the son-in-law and daughter of the previous owners, Silas and Mourning Dove Glenn, who moved to Lytle Creek and established a successful resort. (RB.)

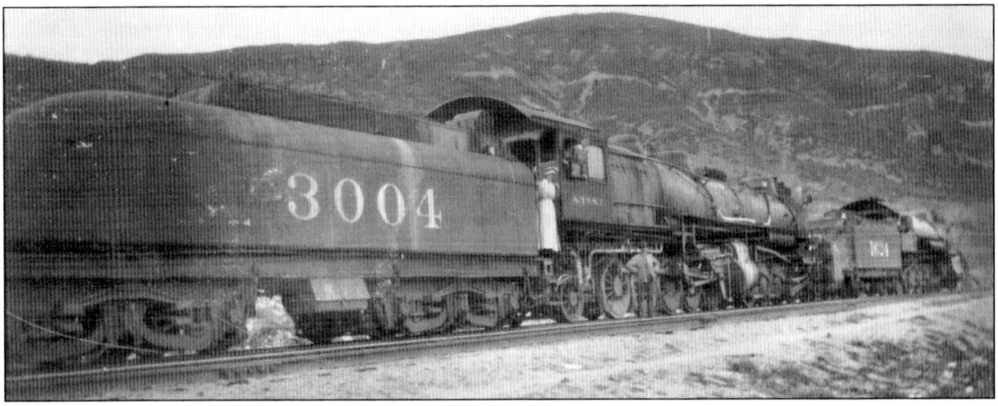

Posing at Keenbrook. Londa Bailey and Stella Ehwegen became well acquainted with this engine during a stop at Keenbrook. Londa stands in the doorway, and Stella leans out the window. The huge 3000 class ATSF 2-10-10-2 steam locomotives were built in 1911 specifically for the slow-speed freight service between San Bernardino, Barstow, and Bakersfield (Cajon Pass). They were rebuilt as two 2-10-2 engines each between 1915 and 1918. (RB.)

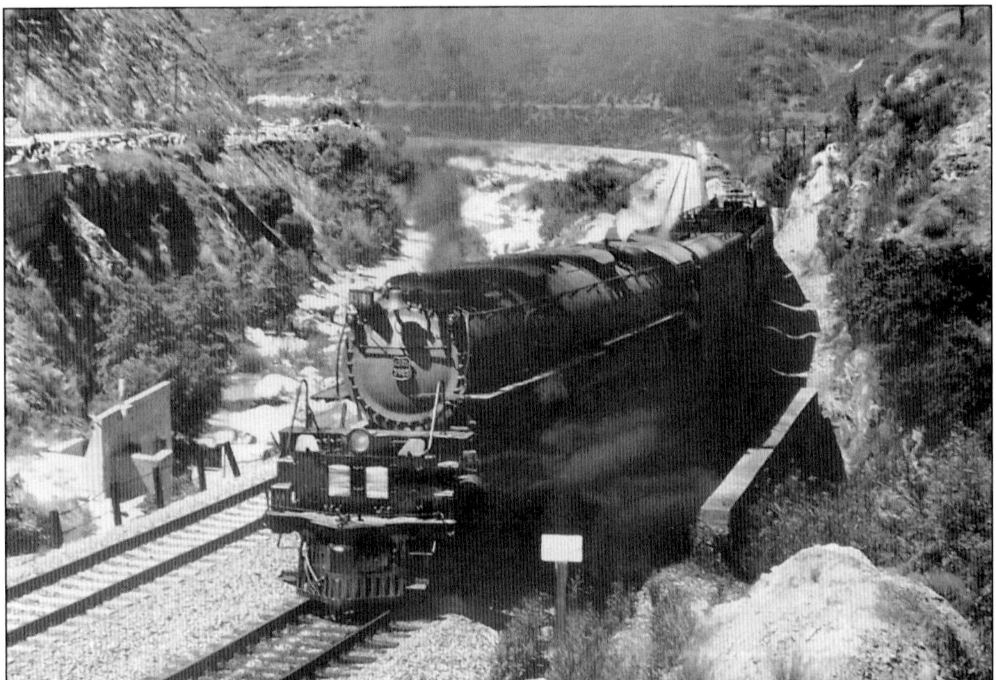

Rail Fan Opportunity. Rail fans seldom have a chance to see the old steam locomotives any more except on special occasions. In 1993, this old Union Pacific steamer made a showy run up Cajon Pass. Here it is at Blue Cut. At left are the remains of what might have been part of Wilson's Muscoy Water project. (LB.)

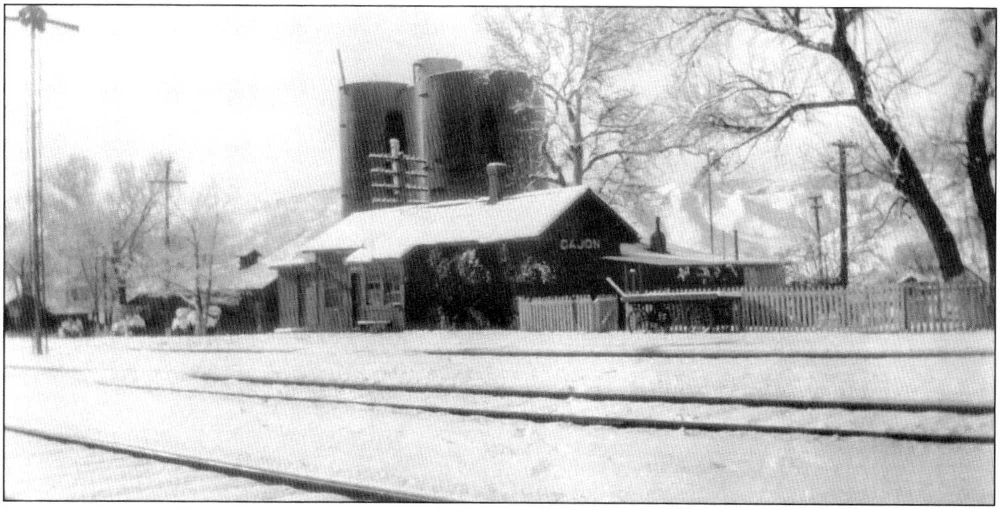

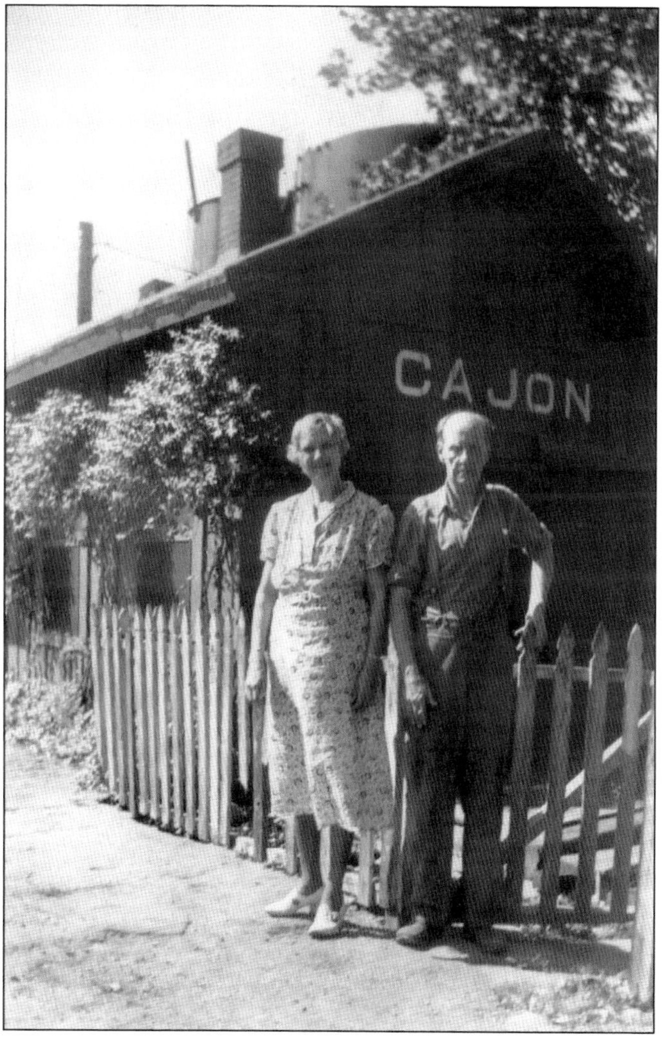

CAJON AND THE EHWEGENS. Edward Ehwegen was the telegrapher at Cajon station from about 1910 to 1937. His wife, Stella Zula, was the sister of Londa Bailey, the wife of Hervey Bailey, the son of William Gould Bailey, who bought his Keenbrook land from the Glenns and Applewhites. Stella also served as postmistress of the Keenbrook Post Office for a few years. These connections served to make available a treasure trove of photographs of the Cajon and Keenbrook stations. The Ehwegens lived at Cajon the entire time they worked there. (RB.)

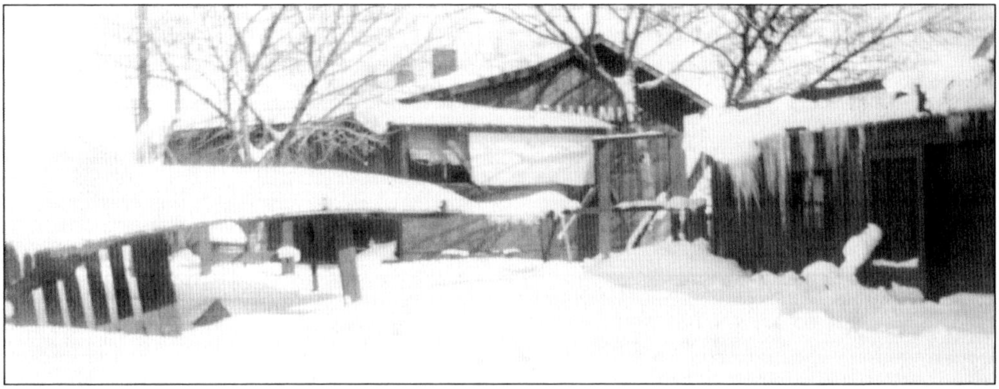

Summit Station. While the main highway travels more northerly to the Cajon Summit before it turns east, the railroad curves west into West Cajon Valley before it travels east through Summit Valley and into Hesperia. This route, also taken by Highway 138, is one of the three branches of Cajon Pass. The Summit station was manned by H. B. Davis before he transferred to Devore in 1908. Summit Valley is the location of the famous Las Flores Ranch, and Cedar Springs was there before it was buried under Silverwood Lake, part of the California Aqueduct project. The above photograph was taken from the rear by the Ehwegens when the station was in use, and the photograph below was taken in the 1960s and also shows the homes of the operators, foreman, and agent. Chard Walker, pass and railroad historian and author, worked at Summit station from 1953 to 1968 when it closed. (Above, RB; below, AHCRFL.)

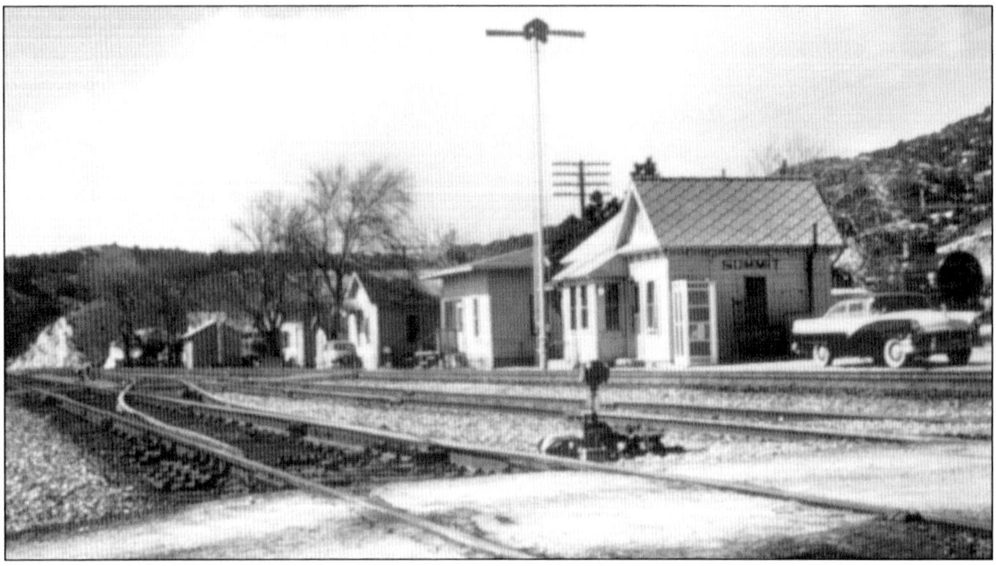

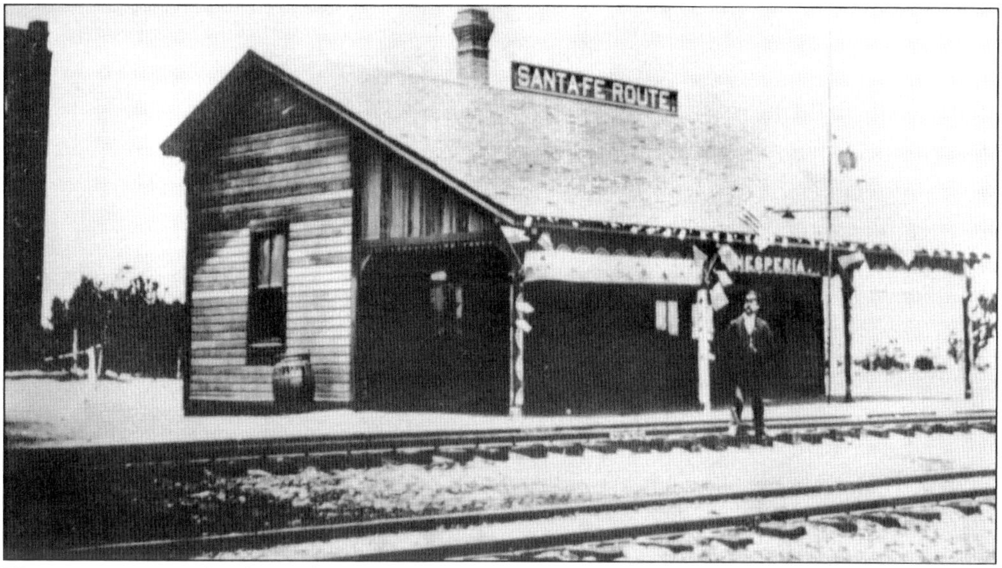

Hesperia Depot. This frame depot, built in 1887, was donated to Hesperia for a temporary railway depot. An addition was built in 1905. The loading platform next to the depot was removed in 1941, and the depot was moved to Victorville for a locomotive maintenance facility the following year. (MHS/VVM.)

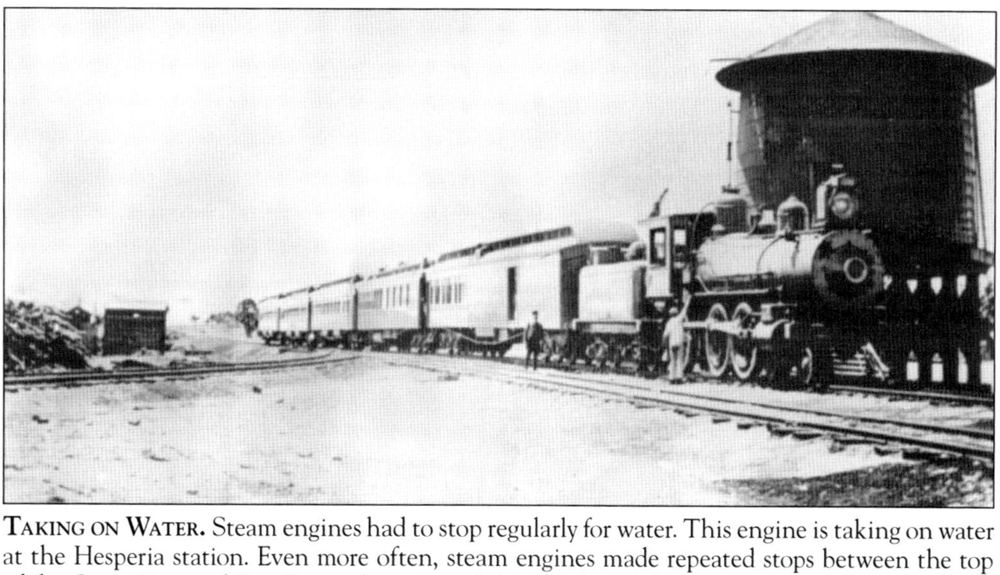

Taking on Water. Steam engines had to stop regularly for water. This engine is taking on water at the Hesperia station. Even more often, steam engines made repeated stops between the top of the Cajon Pass and San Bernardino to cool their brakes and wheels. Constant braking down the steep grade caused wheels to glow, so it was necessary to make use of the Cajon Pass railroad stations for cooling. (MHS/VVM.)

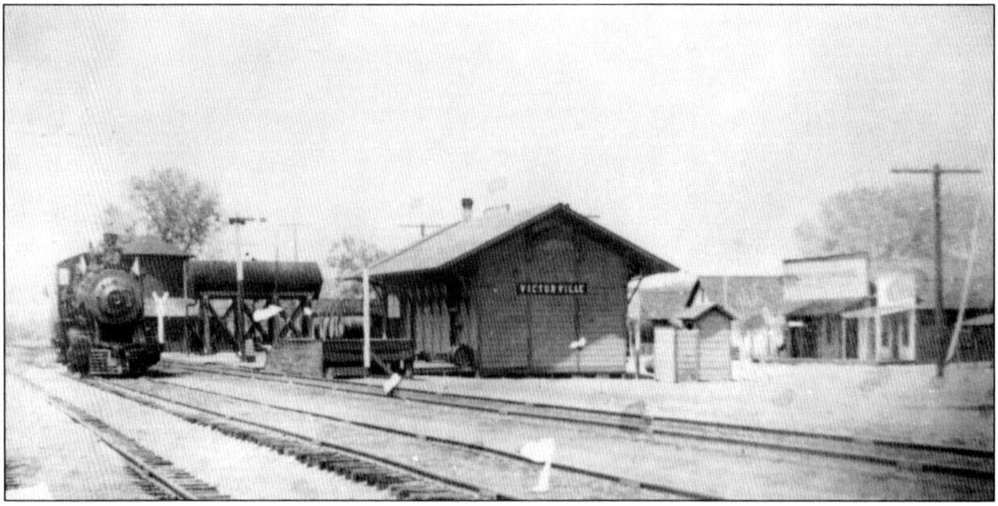

VICTORVILLE DEPOT. Victorville used a boxcar as an interim depot from 1885 to 1887. The new frame depot was built in 1887 with four later additions built through 1943. By 1924, when the depot was jacked up and moved to the side of the tracks away from the river, it had been enlarged to 178 feet. Between 1943 and the early 1960s, there was also a 20-foot waiting room. (MHS/VVM.)

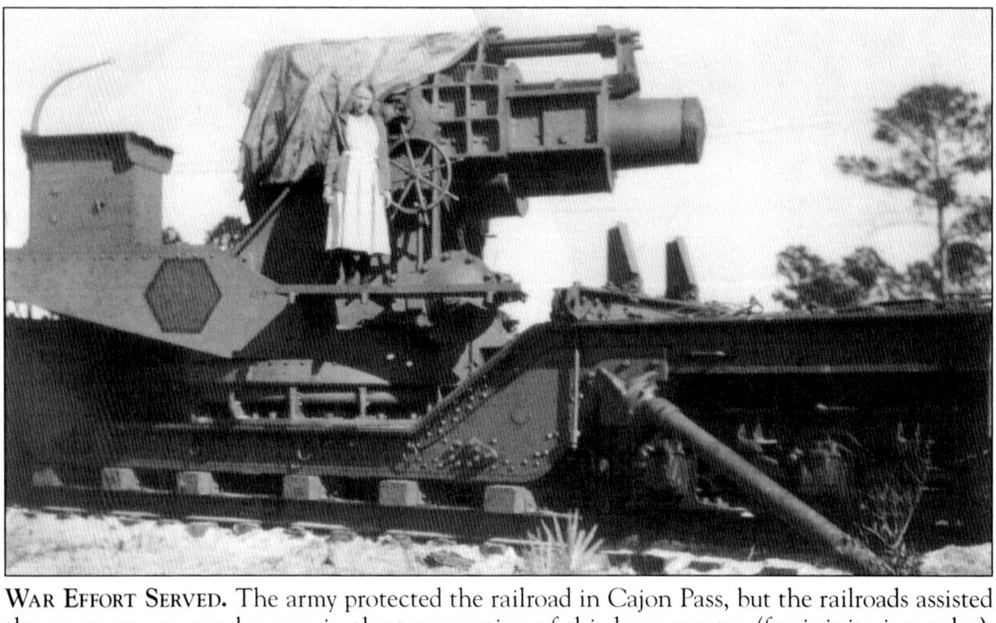

WAR EFFORT SERVED. The army protected the railroad in Cajon Pass, but the railroads assisted the army, too, as can be seen in the transporting of this huge mortar (femininity is surplus). (MHS/VVM.)

Diesels Arrived. Union Pacific's M-10000, made by the Pullman Standard Company in February 1934, was the first diesel engine to travel over Cajon Pass on its publicity tour. It was followed in April by the *Pioneer Zephyr*, made by the Budd Company and owned by the Chicago, Burlington, and Quincy Railroad (or Burlington Route). So both evolutionary trains came out at about the same time. The M-10000 probably does not still exist, but the *Pioneer Zephyr* is on display in the waiting hall of Chicago's Museum of Science and Industry. The arrival of the diesel phased out use of steam locomotives by 1958, and that spelled the death of all communities that had built up around watering stations in Cajon Pass. (Both, RB.)

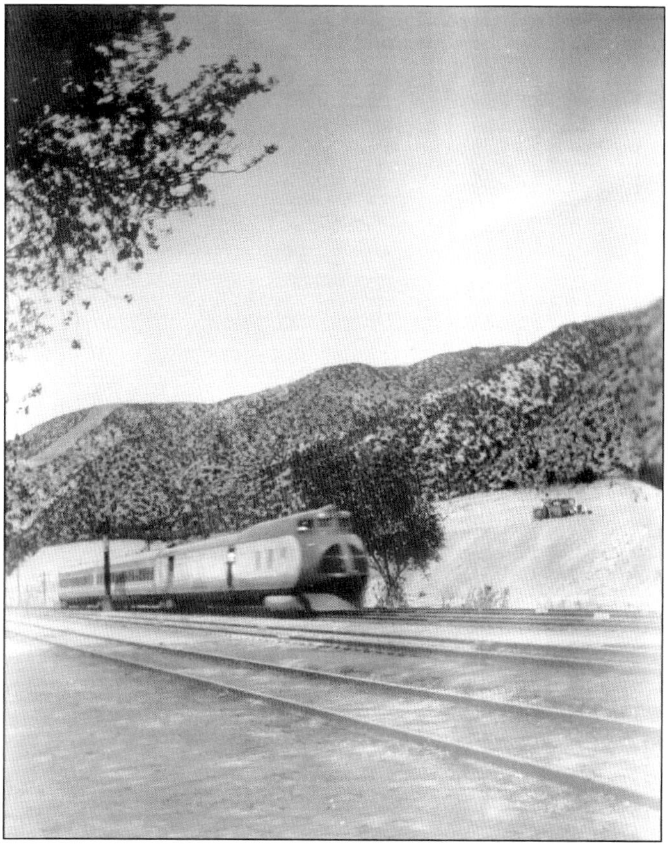

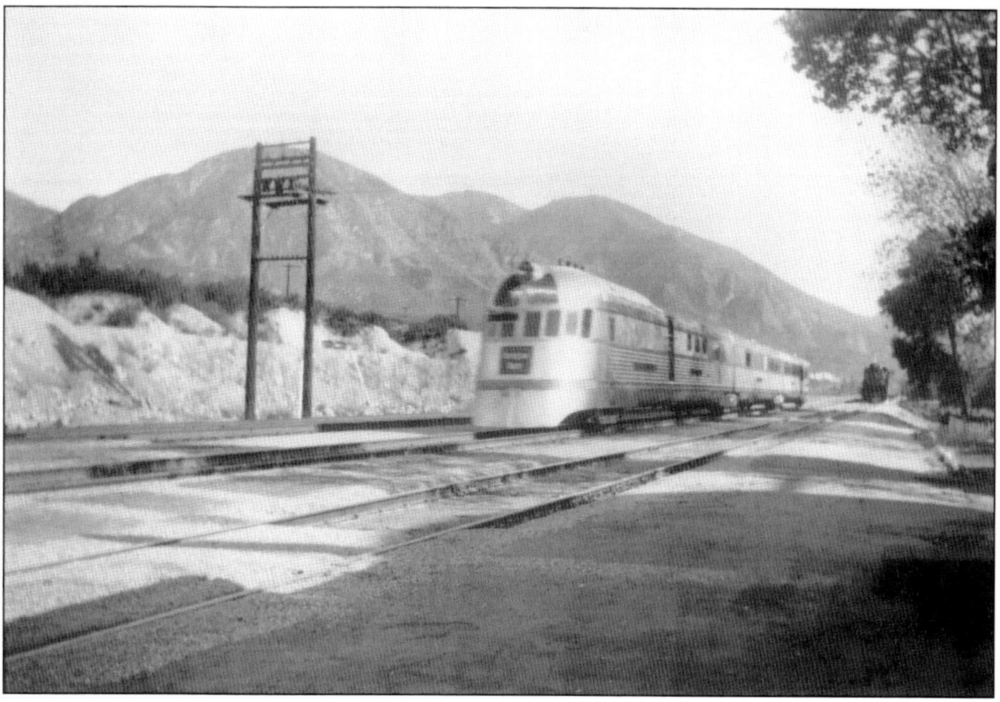

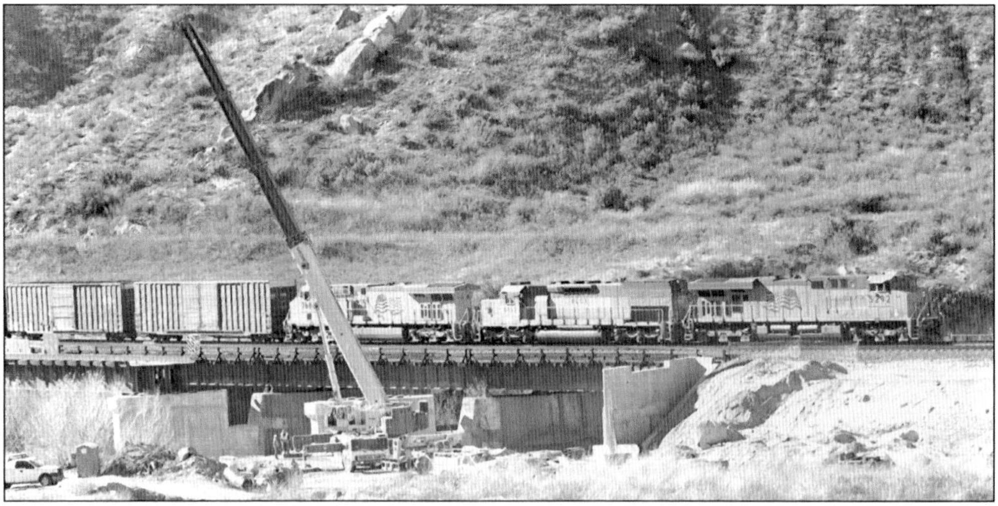

Capacity Increased. The third main rail line, the first Burlington, Northern, and Santa Fe (BNSF) main track through Cajon Pass since 1913, went into use at the end of 2008. The BNSF hopes the track will increase capacity on the Chicago–to–Los Angeles transcontinental route from 100 to 150 trains a day. The new track extends 16 miles, cost $90 million, and involves moving over a million tons of dirt and laying 42,000 concrete railroad ties and over 30 miles of steel rail. Each intermodal train can reduce big rig truck traffic on local highways by more than 250 long-haul trucks, which should save on fuel, as a modern train can haul a ton of freight for over 400 miles on one gallon of diesel fuel, according to BNSF publicity. Maintenance of the Cajon Pass line is "critical to supporting the growth and vitality of local, regional, and national economies." (Above, GG; below, DT.)

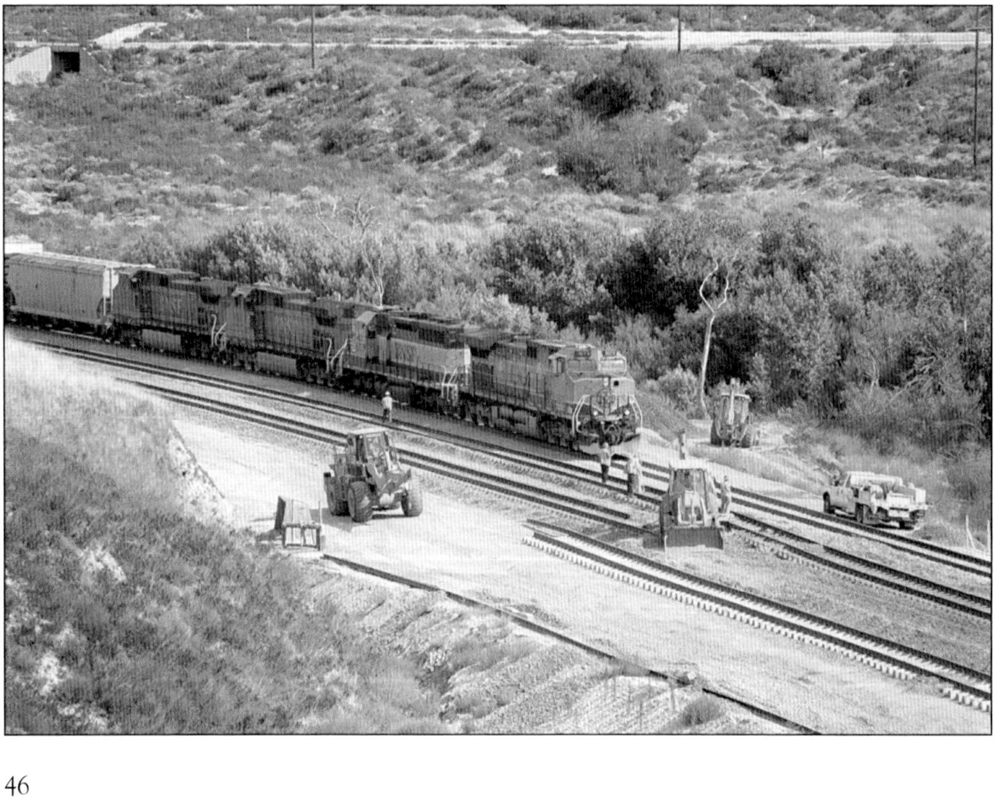

Four

South of the Summit

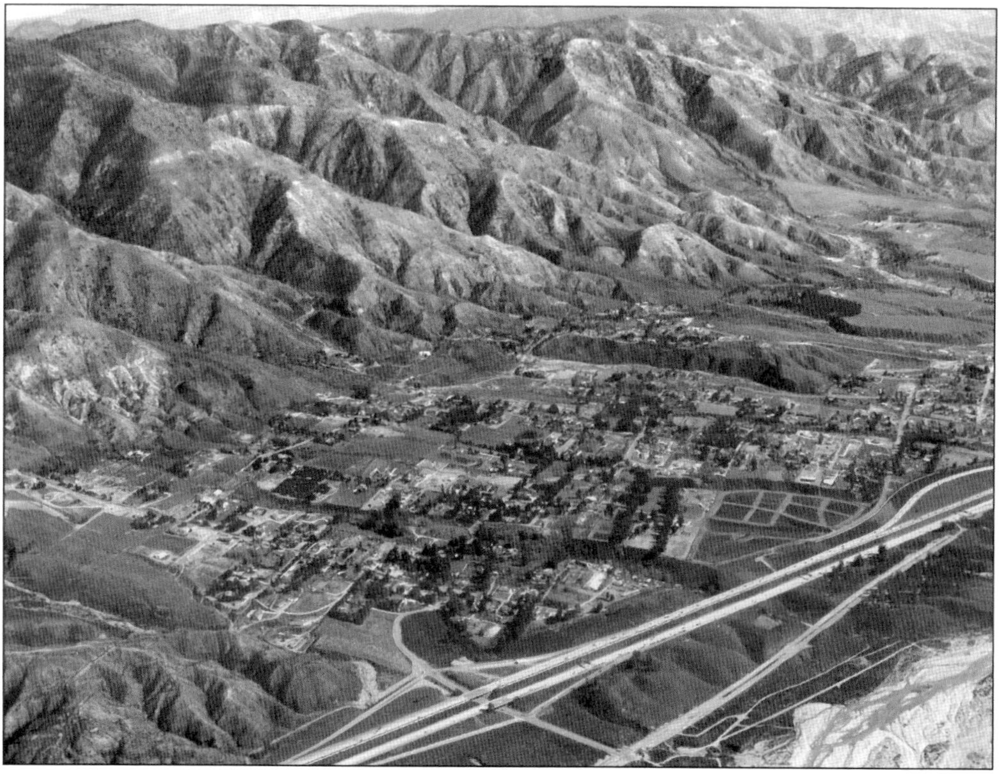

Aerial View of Devore from the West. Devore is the southern portal to Cajon Pass. In the days of Camp Cajon, Devore labeled itself "Home of the Muscat Grape," but those days of Devore spreading from the San Bernardino Foothills to the San Gabriel Foothills are long past. Expansion of Glen Helen Regional Park; easements for railroads, highways, freeways, gas lines, and petroleum pipelines; and encroachment by San Bernardino have taken such massive chunks out of the community that little of it remains except what is on the hill on the San Bernardino (east) side. Devore's motto is "Rural Living at its Finest." (DNM.)

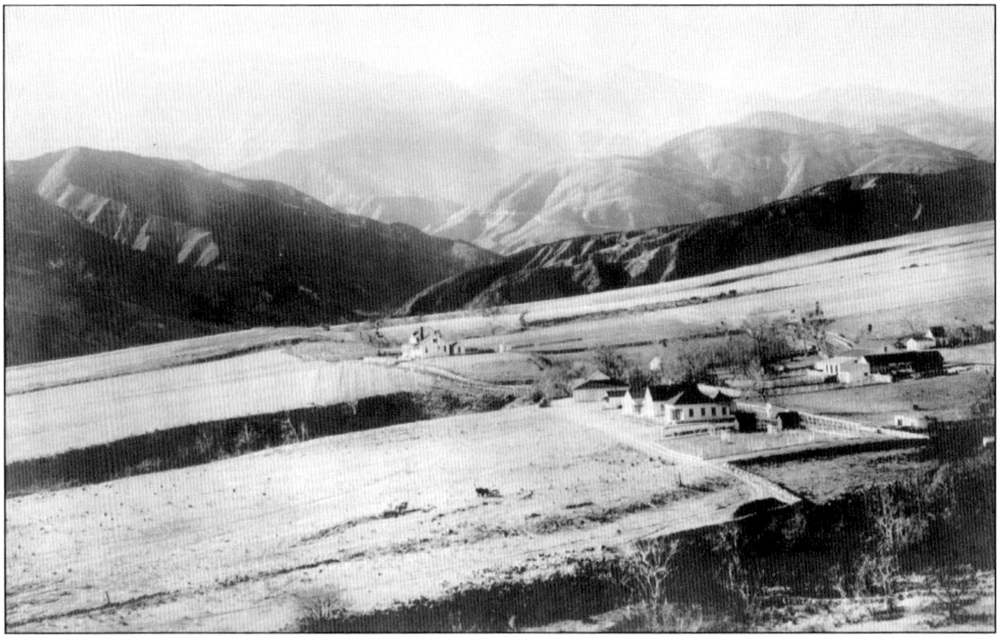

KENWOOD IN 1904. For most of 1904, Kenwood was the name of the hilly 1,800 acres that later became Devore. This Mendenhall photograph shows the Devore farmhouse toward the rear and the farm manager's house closest to the camera, next to the cookhouse and workers' bunkhouse. Two teams of horses plow the field, and Applewhite Road can be seen crossing the distant hills into Lytle Creek. (SBHPS.)

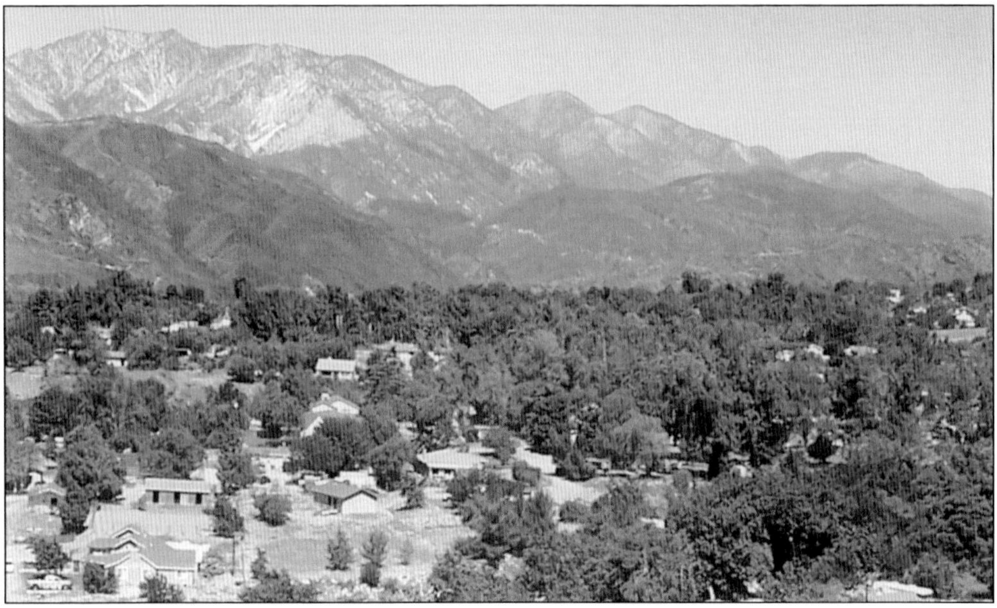

DEVORE TODAY. The same view as the one above over a century later shows little change in the mountains. Even Applewhite Road, now a forestry road, can still be seen. But there is a lot more congestion composed of residences, trees, walls, and fences. Applewhite Road was never maintained as a county road, even though 114 residents, landowners, and interested parties petitioned for that in the 1860s. (RH.)

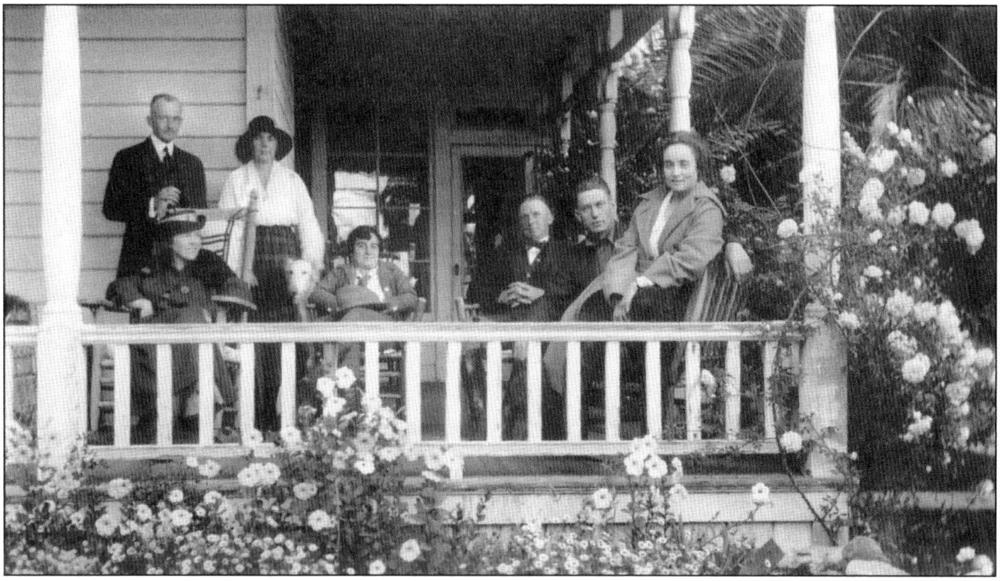

DEVORE HOUSE PORCH. John A. Devore died in 1907 after only seven years in the vicinity of the depot and community that bear his name. In 1920, Devore farm owners Robert B. and Florence Walker Peters along with farm manager Leon Lamson and his fiancée, Edith Hutchinson, entertain guests with the spectacular view from the porch of the Devore house. (GLM.)

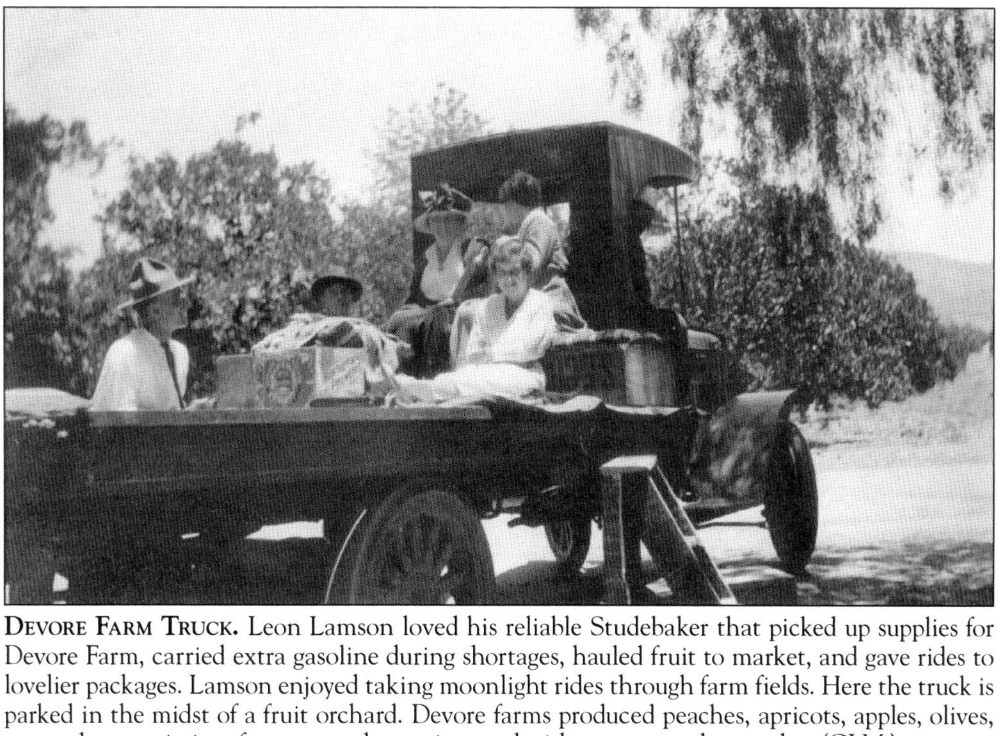

DEVORE FARM TRUCK. Leon Lamson loved his reliable Studebaker that picked up supplies for Devore Farm, carried extra gasoline during shortages, hauled fruit to market, and gave rides to lovelier packages. Lamson enjoyed taking moonlight rides through farm fields. Here the truck is parked in the midst of a fruit orchard. Devore farms produced peaches, apricots, apples, olives, pears, three varieties of grapes, and experimented with oranges and avocados. (GLM.)

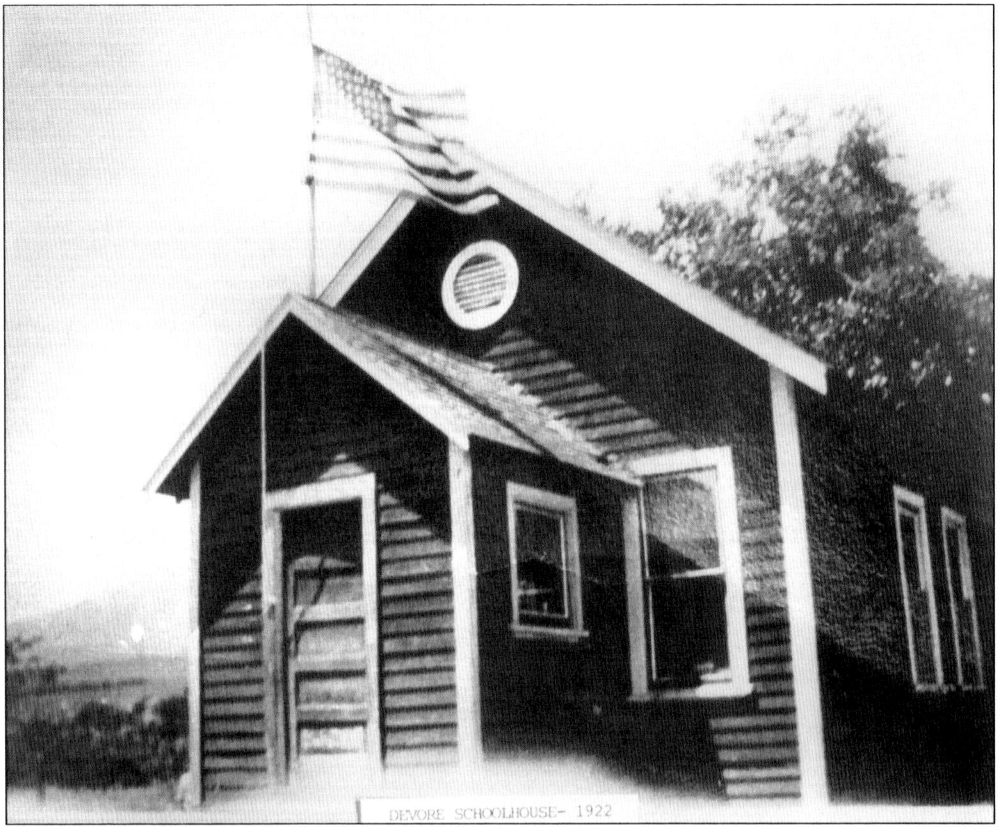

DEVORE SCHOOLS. The first Devore school was built in about 1870. It was called Cajon School and served lower Cajon Pass along with other one-room schoolhouses at Verdemont, Keenbrook, and Clear Springs near the Cajon station until 1924. Students reportedly arrived via horse and buggy or on foot. Average daily attendance was usually only 50 percent in most of these schools, and teachers decried the dangers students faced to attend. Cajon School, across Old Trail Highway from the first Cajon School, was built in 1924 of native stone by local residents on land donated by Robert and Florence Peters and/or Tom and Myrtle Coverston. The one large room could be divided in two so that two teachers could instruct four to six classes. Students came from Verdemont to 5 miles west of Route 66 up Highway 138. (Above, AG; below, GLM.)

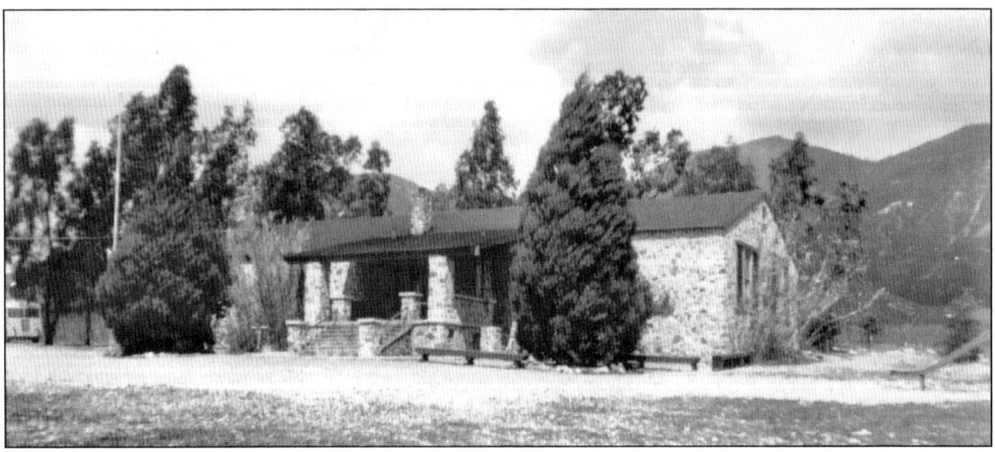

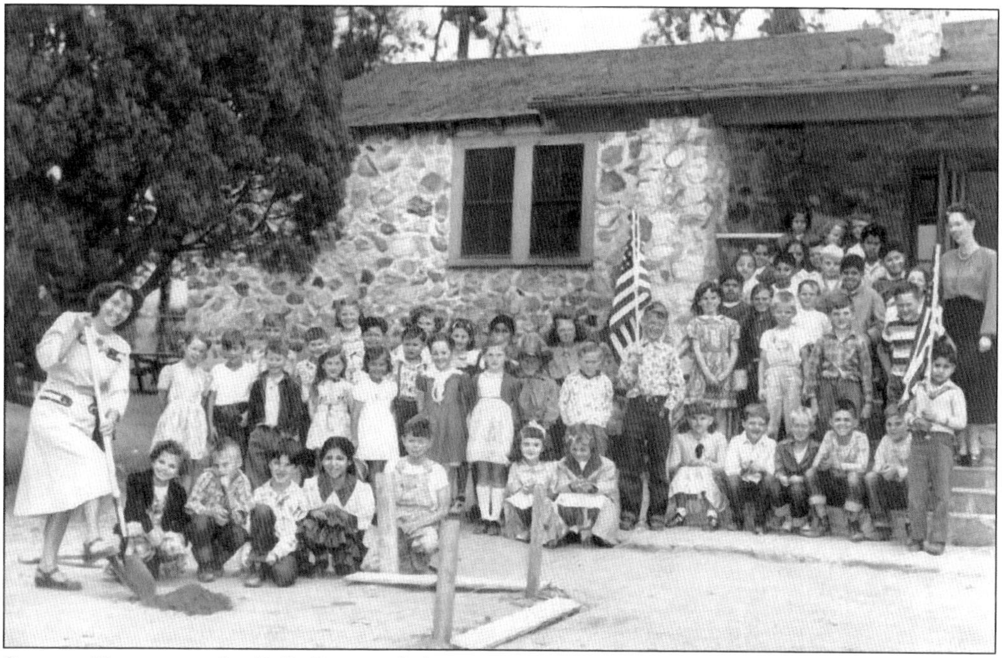

SCHOOL EXPANDED. In 1949, Principal Anna Marie Houghton broke ground for an additional two classrooms at Cajon School. Before that time, area students in grades five and six had to ride Jake Roesch's bus down to San Bernardino for school. With the new addition, all area elementary students attended the local school. (AH.)

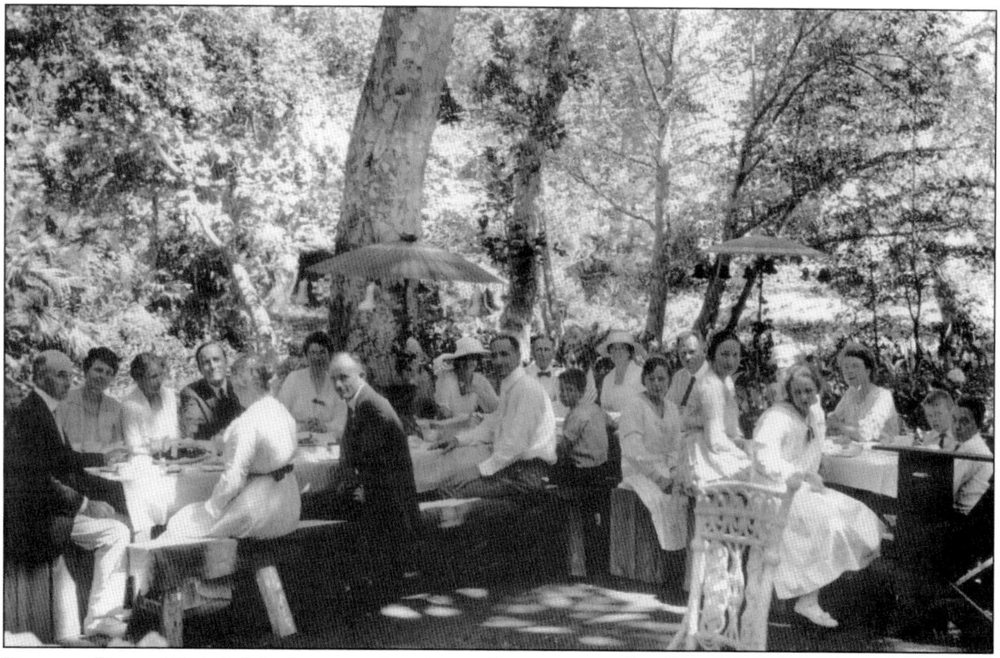

DEVORE PARK. This 1920 photograph taken of a picnic in the Devore Park includes Theodore and Harriet Walker and their daughter and son-in-law Florence and Robert Peters; Leon Lamson; Devore landowners Calendars, Bates, and Wilmot; and Mabel Smith. Their guest is Merle Smith, pastor of the largest Methodist church in Pasadena. (GLM.)

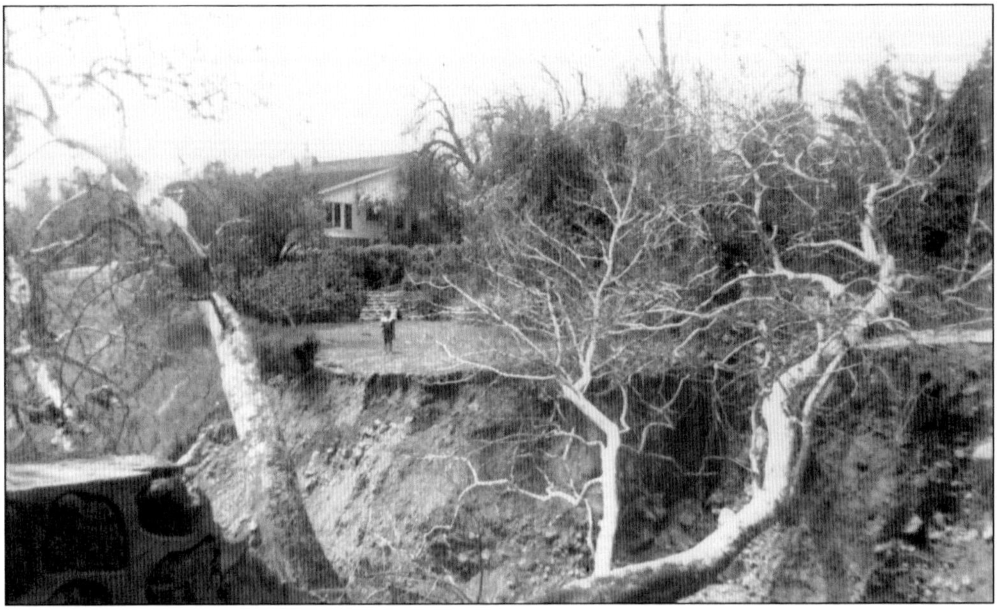

Park Destroyed. John Devore planned a picturesque community, and he was especially proud of Devore Park. The beautifully sloping lawns, sunken pools, exotic plants, and exquisite rose garden were appreciated almost every Sunday afternoon by picnickers and concert attendees from the local area and Los Angeles. The park was demolished by the flood of 1938, during which even giant sycamore trees floated away. (GLM.)

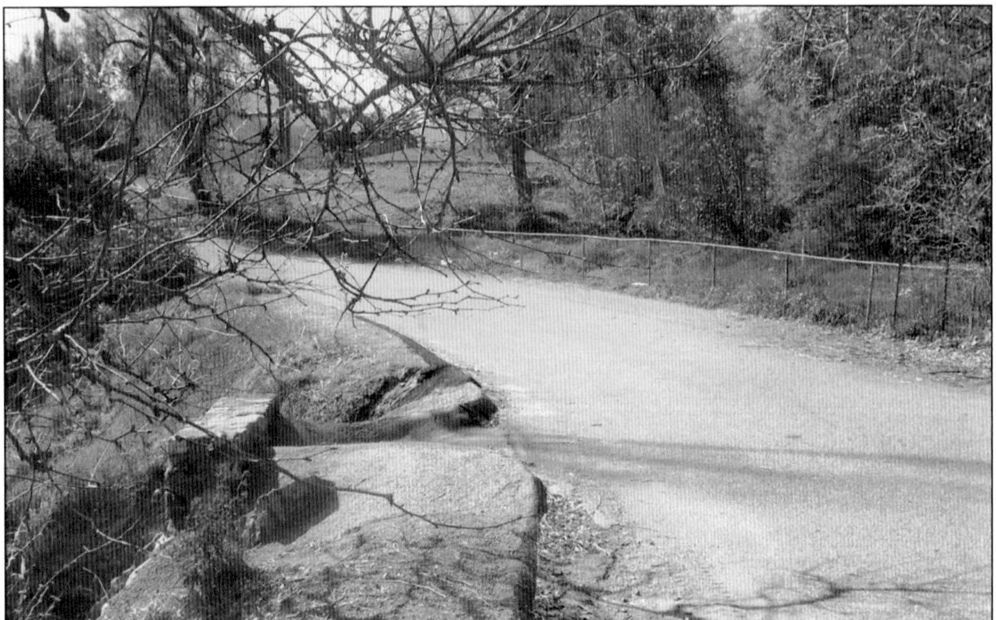

Devore Today. Muriel Street is the existing Devore street that borders the previous park and meanders past the houses built by Leon Lamson and John Devore. It still exudes the charm its planner envisioned for it, although less romantic modern residents pulled out the old sycamore tree that used to divide the street not far from the silo. The rock work on the culvert at left was done by the WPA in 1940. (KH.)

Devore Silo. The old silo appears as if it is crumbling under a rainbow, but its condition has not changed appreciably in the past 60 years. It is located near Muriel Street and Redwood Lane, downhill from the water company on land that is called the "Devore Farm," just west of the house that was built for farm managers in 1901. (KH.)

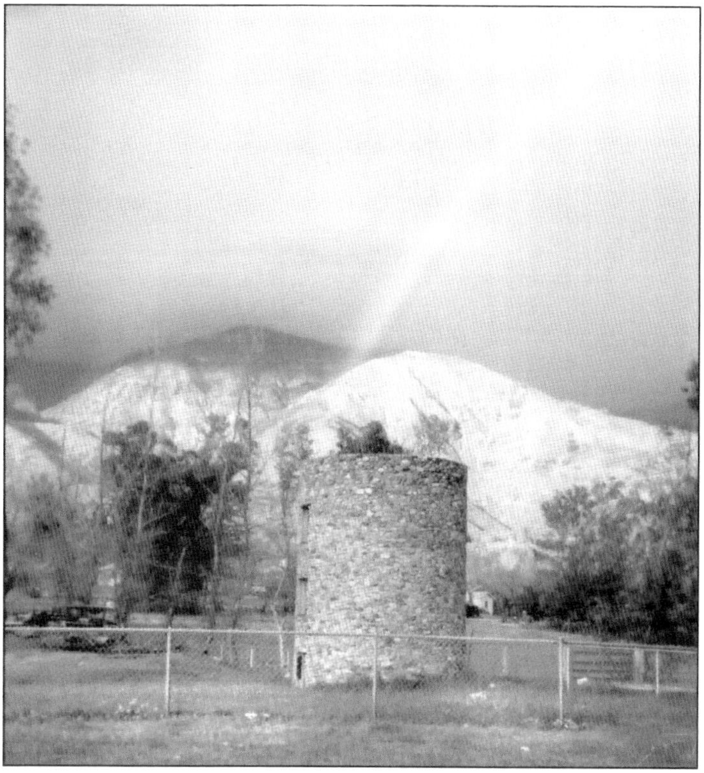

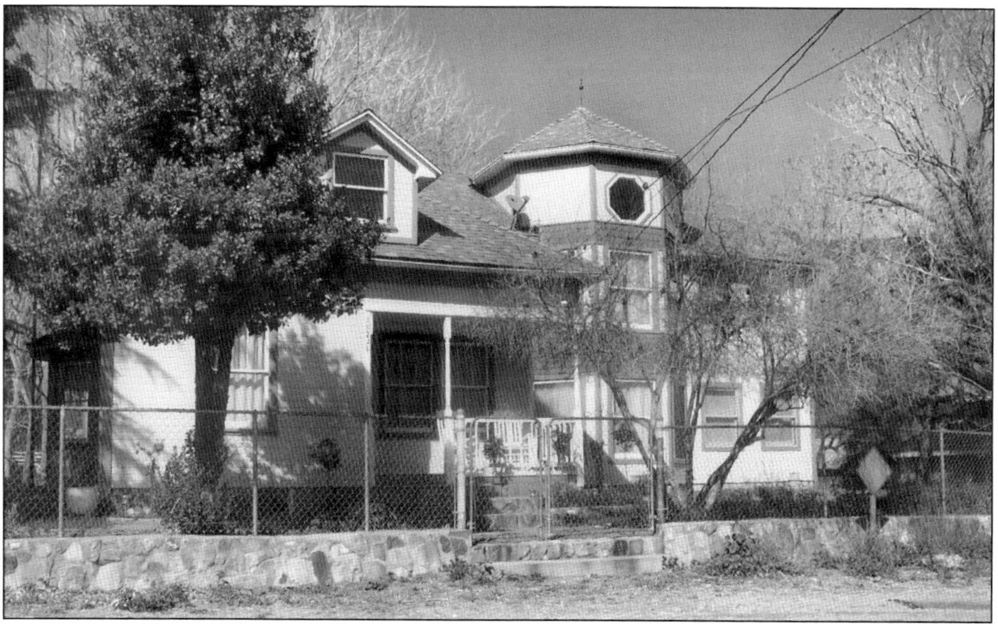

Manager's Home. Tom and Sarah Gladwill bought the Devore farm manager's house in 1944 and strongly supported the community for almost three decades. The house may have been damaged in the 1920 fire that took the adjoining cookhouse and laborers' housing as well as the barn, but subsequent owners rebuilt and added on to the original structure while maintaining the style of the old home. (KH.)

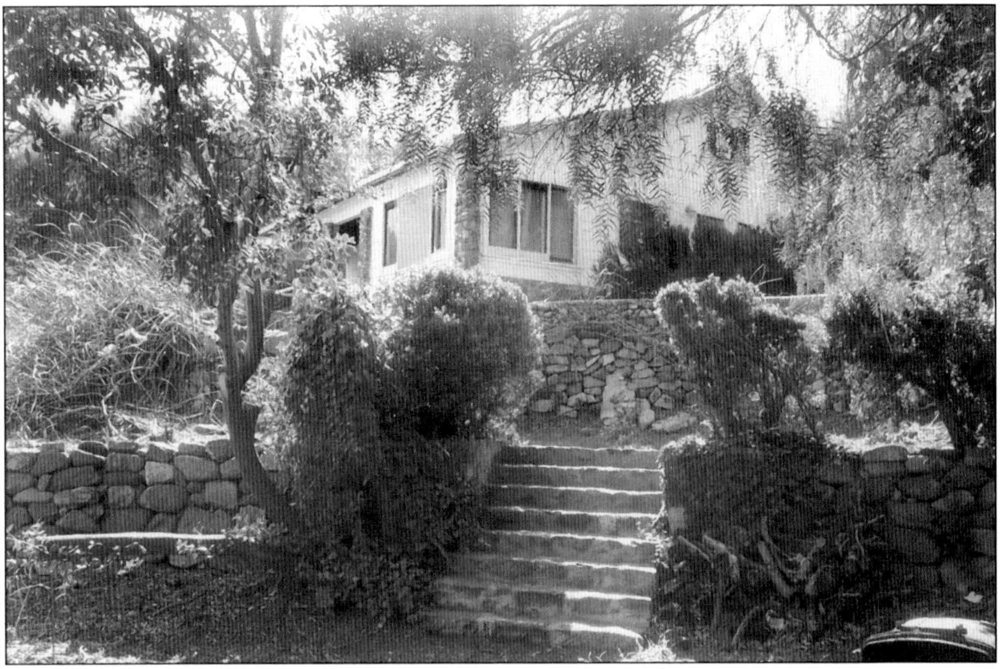

Lamson House. Leon Lamson built this house in 1918 in an olive grove, and olive stumps still exist under it. Leon and Edith Lamson were active community supporters until Leon's death. Their son Phillip, an aeronautical engineer, bought the house from his mother and lived there until 2004. He expanded the carriage house to accommodate the prototype glider he designed and built. (KH.)

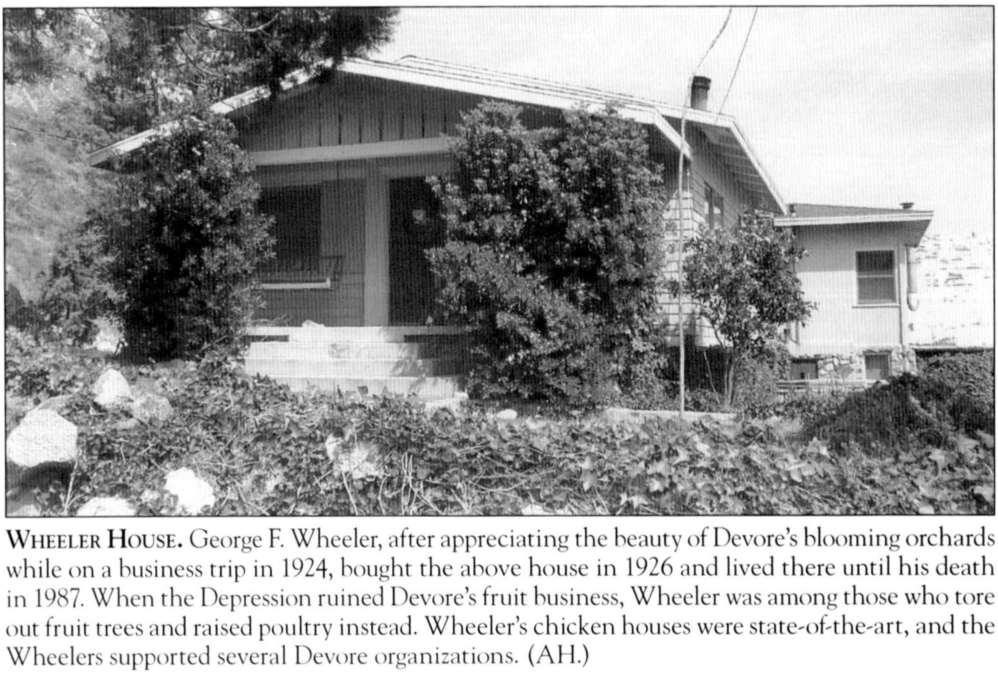

Wheeler House. George F. Wheeler, after appreciating the beauty of Devore's blooming orchards while on a business trip in 1924, bought the above house in 1926 and lived there until his death in 1987. When the Depression ruined Devore's fruit business, Wheeler was among those who tore out fruit trees and raised poultry instead. Wheeler's chicken houses were state-of-the-art, and the Wheelers supported several Devore organizations. (AH.)

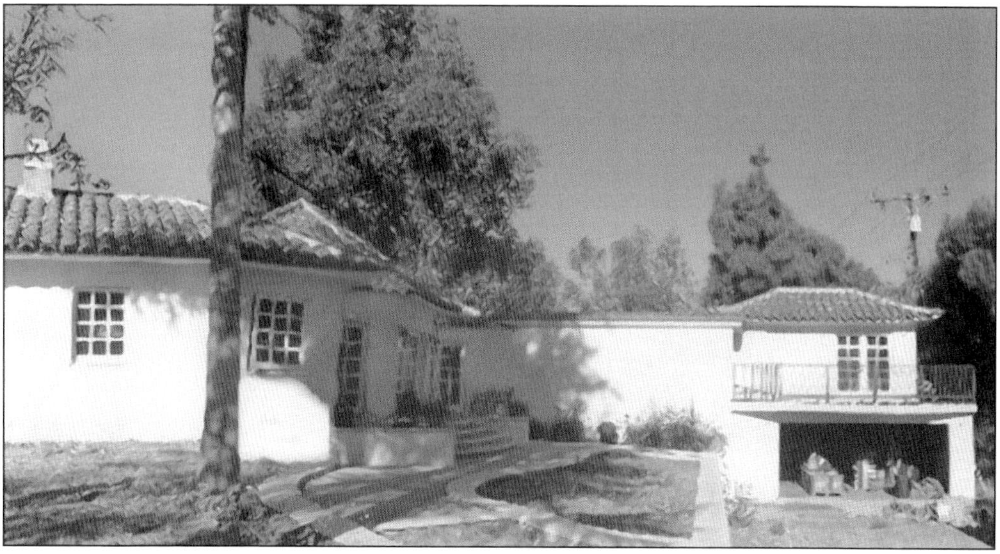

Hearst House. Local lore indicates William Randolph Hearst had this house built, although his name does not appear on any of the deeds. Actor Dean Jaeger told Devore resident George Sneed that he had spent his 1926 wedding night in this house with Hearst's permission. Jaeger said they did not spend their entire honeymoon in the house because the Santa Ana winds drove them crazy. (AH.)

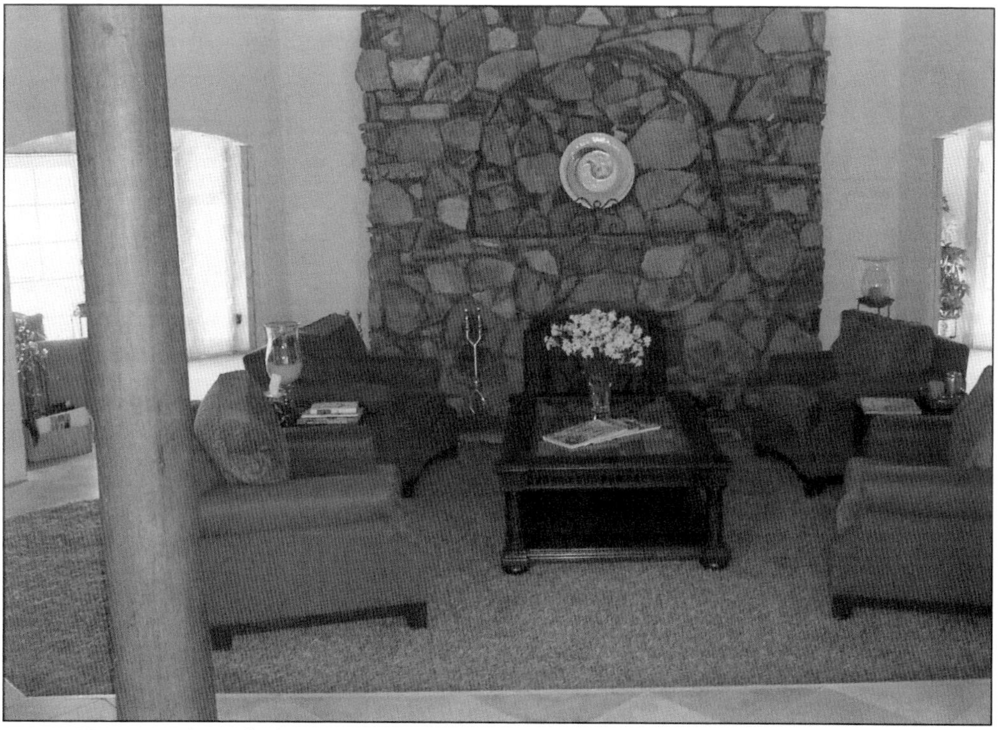

Inside Hearst. Through the 1950s, the house was owned by Otto and Frieda Stearn. Otto raised hogs and butchered them so Frieda could serve pork in her German restaurant. Guests ate either in this sunken living room, converted into a dining room, or on the wraparound porch with a lovely view. Frieda, an artist, sold her paintings of Switzerland that graced the restaurant walls. (AH.)

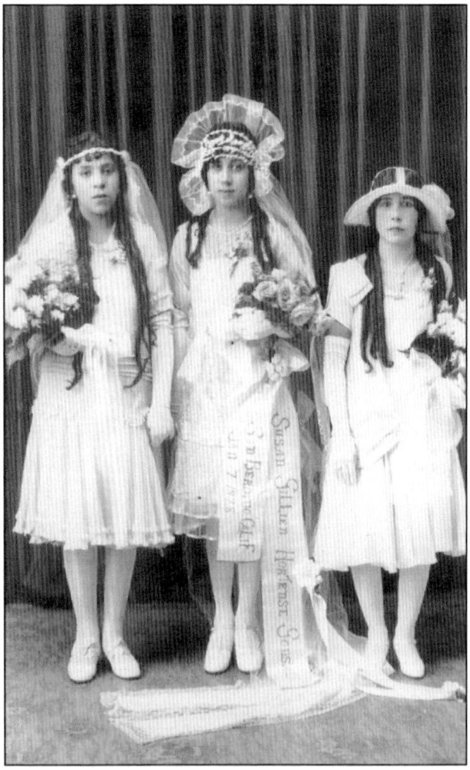

A Mexican Wedding. In 1939, Andres Gonzalez bought the 1,000-foot-long chicken house that Robert Peters had built on the Devore farm and ran his poultry farm there until 1970. A bachelor, Andy employed family members and participated in family events like the wedding of his niece, Susan Gonzales. Left of her is Julia Gonzales Parra, and on the right is Andy's sister, Marcos Gonzales. (GLM.)

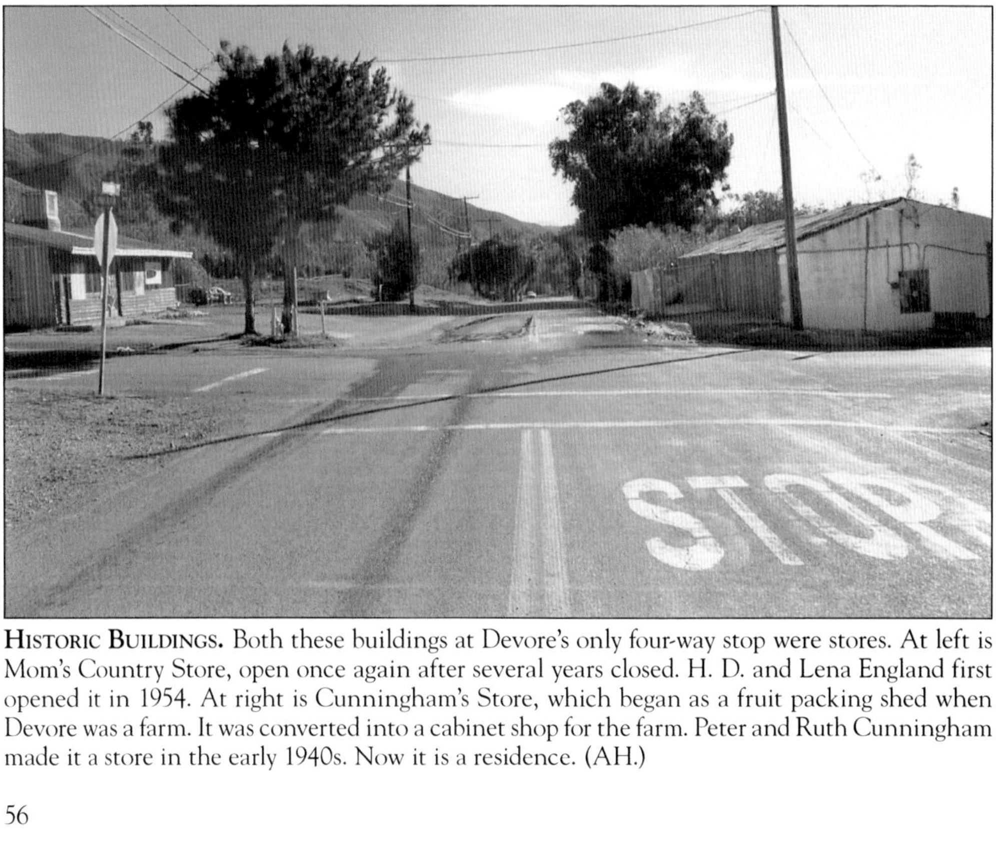

Historic Buildings. Both these buildings at Devore's only four-way stop were stores. At left is Mom's Country Store, open once again after several years closed. H. D. and Lena England first opened it in 1954. At right is Cunningham's Store, which began as a fruit packing shed when Devore was a farm. It was converted into a cabinet shop for the farm. Peter and Ruth Cunningham made it a store in the early 1940s. Now it is a residence. (AH.)

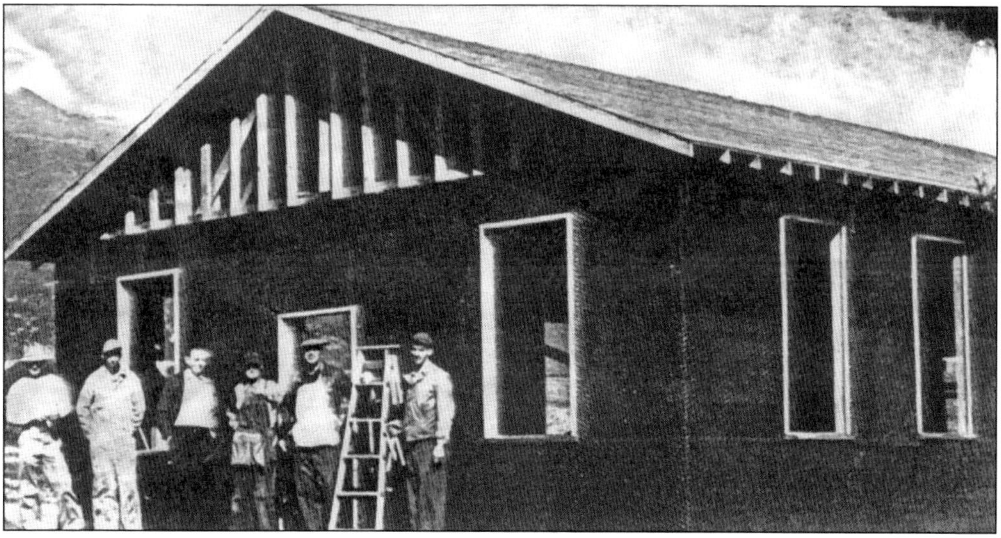

Church Built. In 1947, construction of a church was begun in Devore under the patronage of First Baptist Church of San Bernardino. Devore residents John Finn, E. G. Willie, Harry Hall, and others who worked for the Devore Water Company are shown here during pipe installation. The first service was held August 22, 1948. Freeway construction demanded that the church be moved farther up Devore Road (Main Street) in 1957. (RH.)

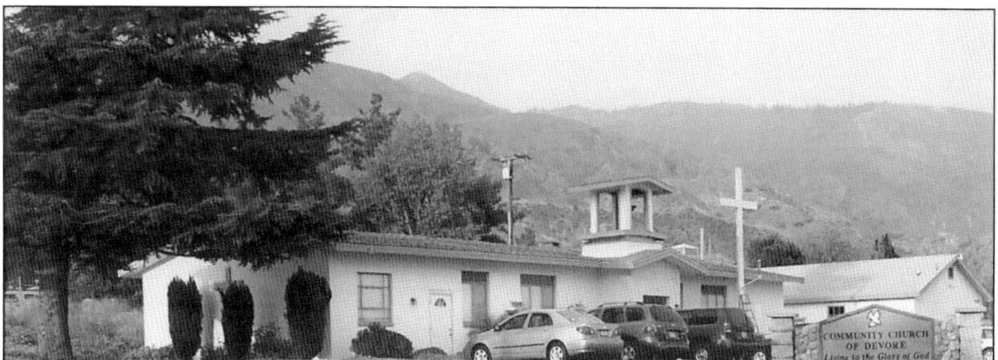

Name Changed. The old church building, behind the newer structure that opened in 1962, is still used for youth activities. The name was changed to Community Church of Devore in 1974 in the hopes it would appeal to more people. (AH.)

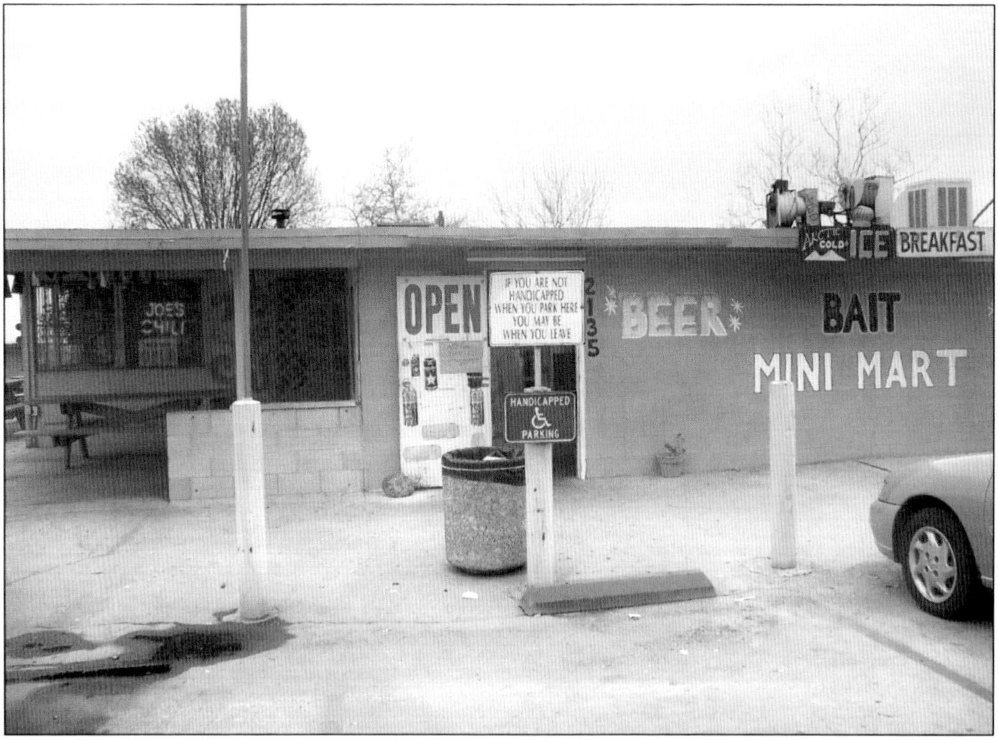

COUNTRY CORNERS CAFÉ. Country Corners Café sits right beside the railroad tracks, across the street from where Devore Depot used to stand. It opened in 1960 as the Pink fruit stand, followed by Pablo's and Joe's. Through the years, this little café has been popular among rail fans, who can watch trains, hear their rumble, and enjoy a snack at the same time. (AH.)

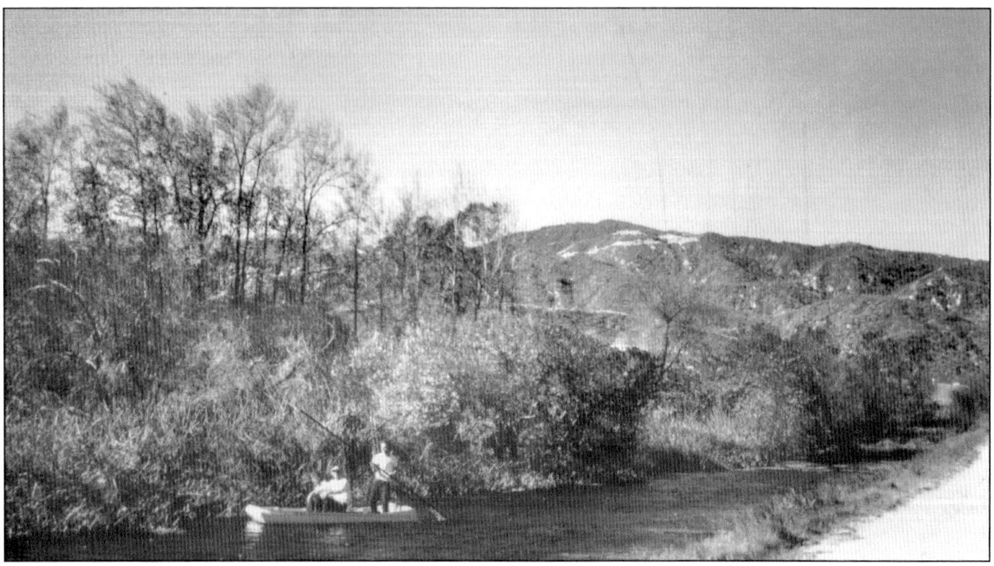

NATURAL LAKES GONE. Glen Helen boasted natural springs, streams, and small ponds or lakes. The one pictured being enjoyed by the Grogan family was covered and the pavilion/amphitheater built over it. These amenities of nature survived during regional park years but disappeared when Renaissance Faire and the pavilion began using park space. (EG.)

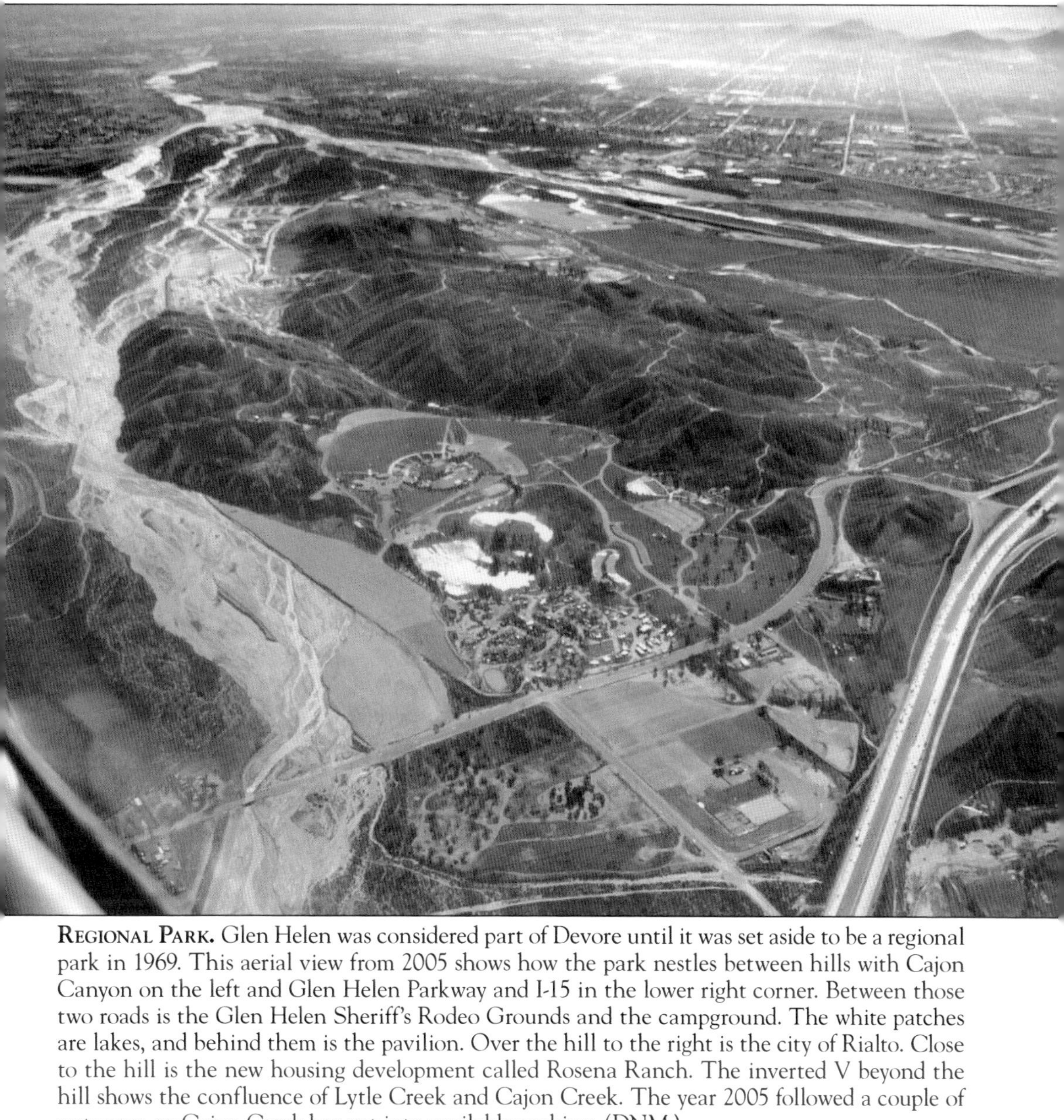

Regional Park. Glen Helen was considered part of Devore until it was set aside to be a regional park in 1969. This aerial view from 2005 shows how the park nestles between hills with Cajon Canyon on the left and Glen Helen Parkway and I-15 in the lower right corner. Between those two roads is the Glen Helen Sheriff's Rodeo Grounds and the campground. The white patches are lakes, and behind them is the pavilion. Over the hill to the right is the city of Rialto. Close to the hill is the new housing development called Rosena Ranch. The inverted V beyond the hill shows the confluence of Lytle Creek and Cajon Creek. The year 2005 followed a couple of wet years, so Cajon Creek has cut into available parking. (DNM.)

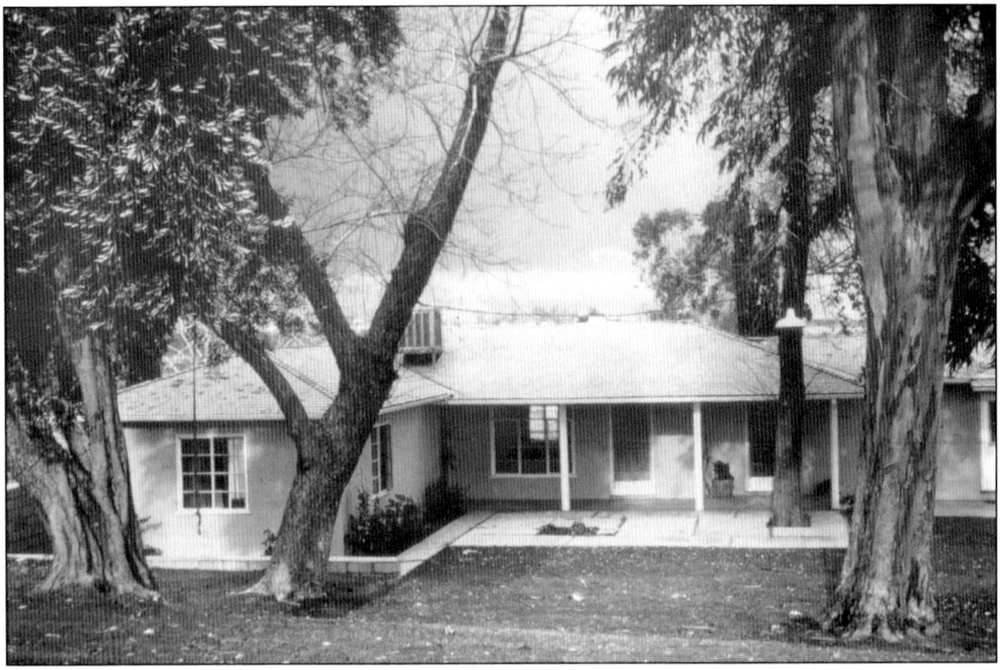

Glen Helen. After George Martin's death, John A. and Nettie Cole co-owned Glen Helen with Robert N. C. Wilson as a Jersey cow breeding farm in the 1890s. The Terribilini brothers ran a dairy there in the early 20th century. By 1952, Glen Helen County Farm utilized 2,000 acres for crops and cattle. Manager Tony Giannini lived in the house. Inmates from Chino Men's Prison supplied labor. (EG.)

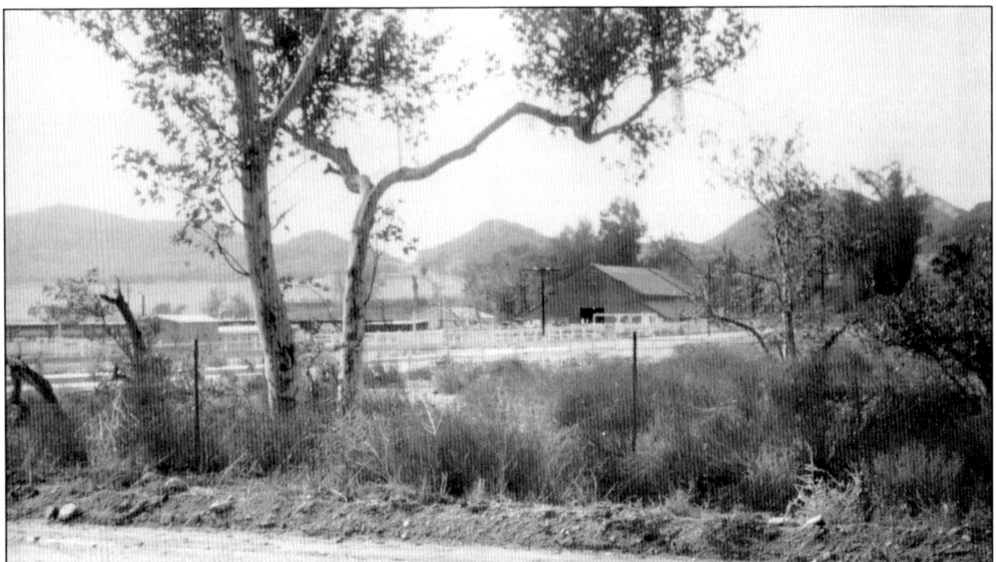

Big Red Barn. Glen Helen cattle and horses, as well as their hay supply, were housed in the big red barn through the 1950s, when it was the county farm, and 1960s, when Liz Grogan trained horses for Billy and Thelma Beardsley. "Doc" and Belle Davis kept their horses at Glen Helen until the county turned it into a regional park. (EG.)

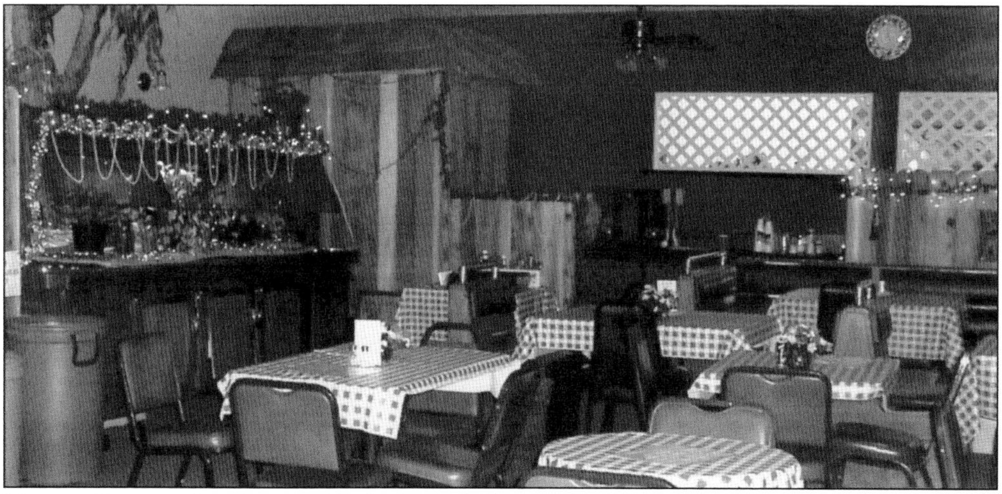

Nudist Resort. Between Terribilini's and Glen Helen, the Deer Park has nearly a score of acres. Valley o' the Sun moved from today's Gem Ranch around 1936 and became Oakdale. The name changed in the early 1970s to Tree House. It became the Deer Park in 1993 and has lovely amenities for its guests: two swimming pools, hot tubs, tennis, volleyball, and basketball courts, and the buffet restaurant pictured. (AH.)

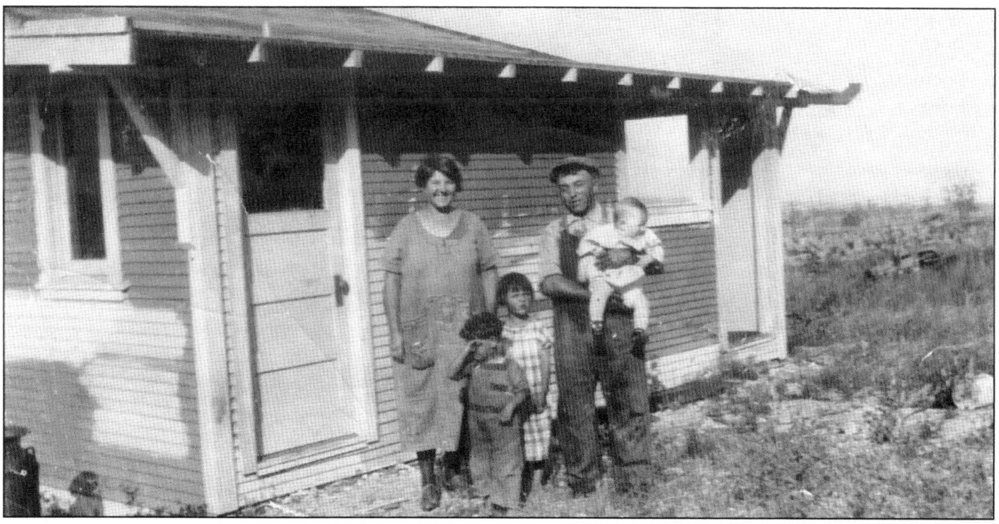

Terribilinis. John Terribilini, former Glen Helen dairyman, married Lily Bubier, whose family also lived and farmed in the area. They moved up the pass on the San Gabriel side and raised eight children. Here they are pictured with their first three children in 1925. Their youngest child, Earl, lived in Devore until 2002, when he moved to Hesperia. (AlG.)

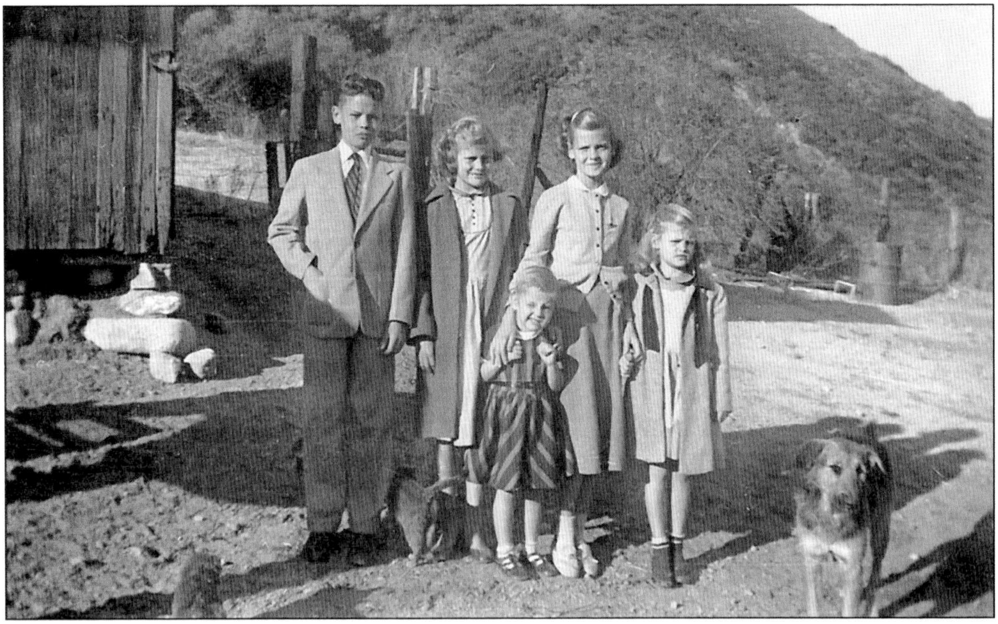

Ruddell Hill. On forestry and some railroad maps, Ruddell Hill is labeled. Ardo and Vivian Ruddell bought the hill north of the Terribilinis in 1944 and raised five children in a tiny house with no power. The children loved open acreage and a reservoir for swimming. The Ruddells sold to Lee and Joanna Price in 1959. Joanna and her two sisters spent their childhood on the hill as herdsmen for the Lenhardts. (LRH.)

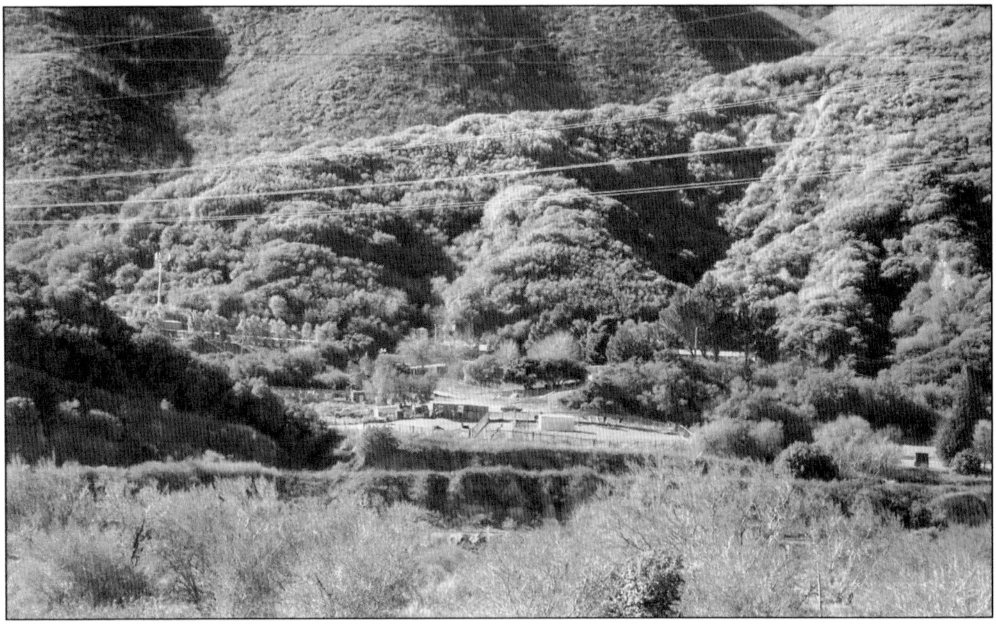

Times Have Changed. Today Ruddell Hill contains less acreage because of additional railroad tracks, and it is owned by Joe Camp, who trains wild animals for movies and commercials. Brush conceals pens, but training arenas can be seen from Route 66 and I-15. The tower is for training African fishing eagles that are used in place of bald eagles, which are illegal to own. Pass residents can hear lions roar. (AH.)

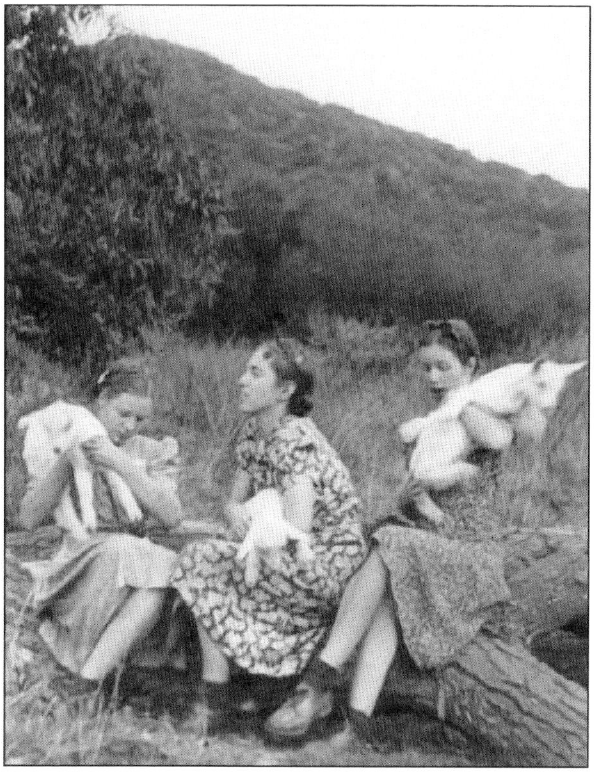

DAIRY GOATS THRIVE IN CAJON PASS. At right, from left to right, Hilda, Judith, and Joanna Wharton cuddle kids Mine, Yours, and Hers, from the herds they cared for through the 1930s and 1940s at the Lenhardt (later Ruddell) and Obst (later Anna Mills' Freedom Acres) places in Keenbrook. Below, Edward Ehwegen helps Mrs. Loomis with her milking while the doe and buck kids eat grain. Either Saanens were the most popular breed at the time or the most photogenic. Pass people now have switched to long-eared Nubians. Their richer milk makes creamier cheese, which is often heated on wood stoves. Many in the pass still heat with wood and have their own wells or springs. And most milk their goats from the side rather than the rear. Another food producer still in the pass is the honeybee, but they spend part of their lives in Utah now. (Above, HS; below, RB.)

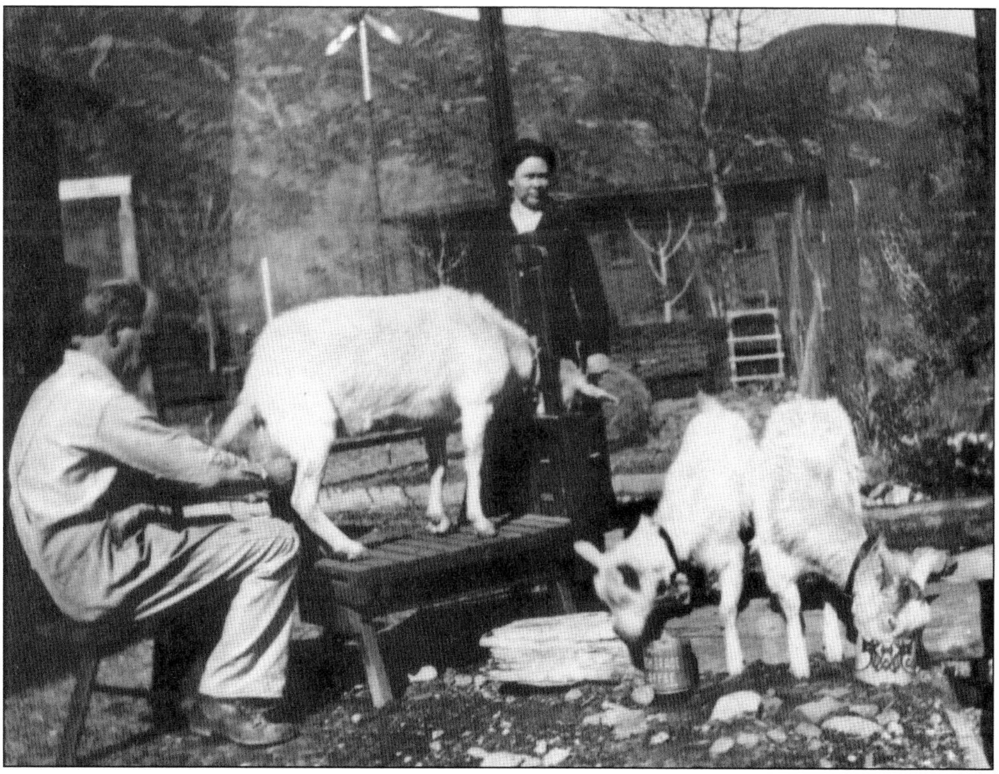

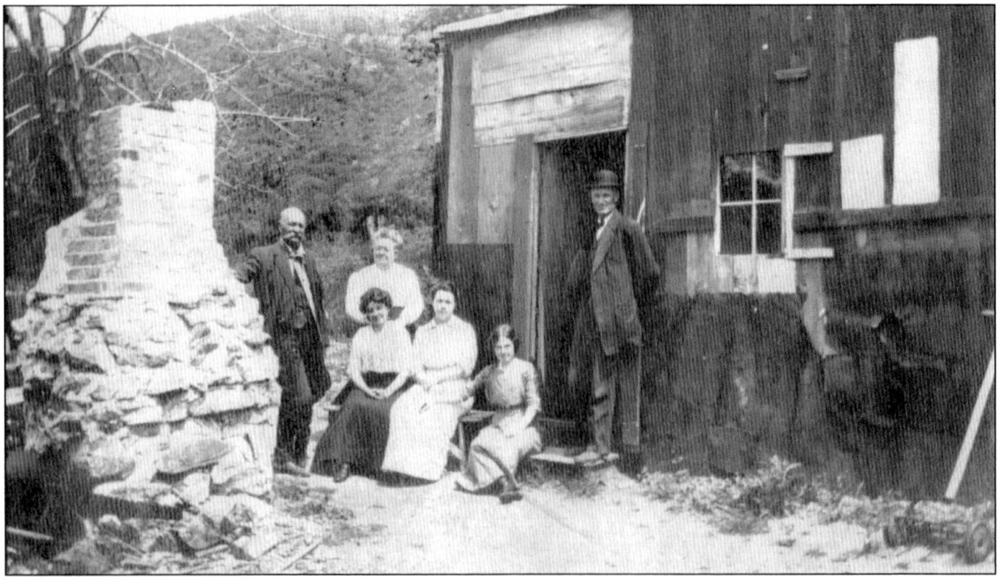

Christmas Trees. Curtis squatted on the east side of Cajon Canyon but lost his claim for homestead to Francisco Luna because of a medical trip east. In 1913, Dr. Henderson Pittman, county coroner (pictured), and his stepson Monte Mathews bought the Luna homestead and sold wood and peat. Monte's son Bob raised Christmas trees. Pictured are the chimney from the Curtis cabin and the Luna cabin. The author's ranch is just southeast. (RM.)

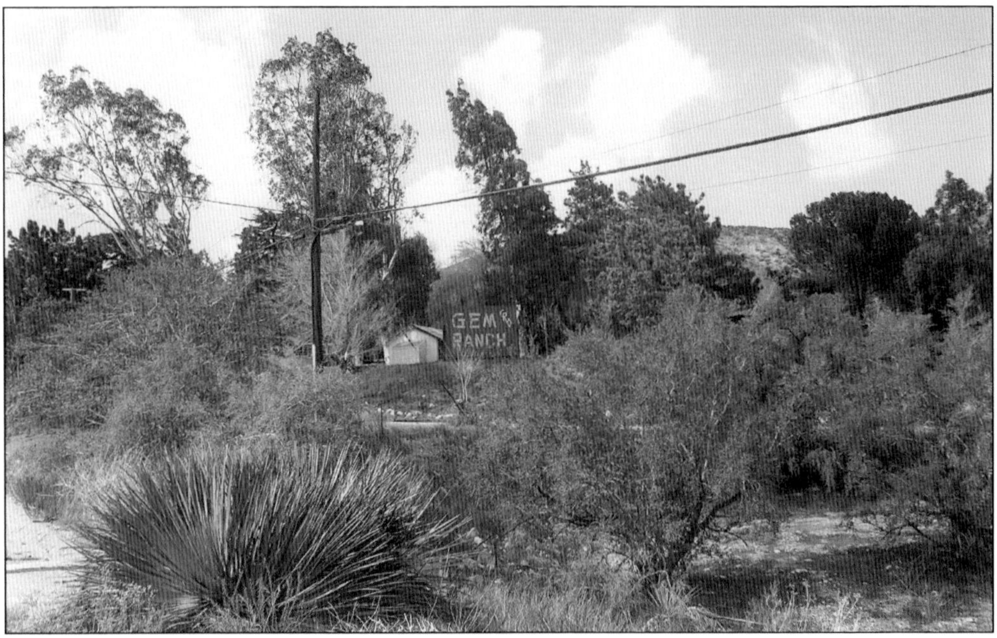

Gem Ranch. On this piece of property south of Blue Cut, Valley o' the Sun nudist resort dwelt in the 1930s. Three decades later, new owners considered another nudist camp and had cabanas built around the swimming pool. The big house was constructed with a large recreation room underneath, but current owners rent out all the little houses and host community meetings in the recreation hall. (AH.)

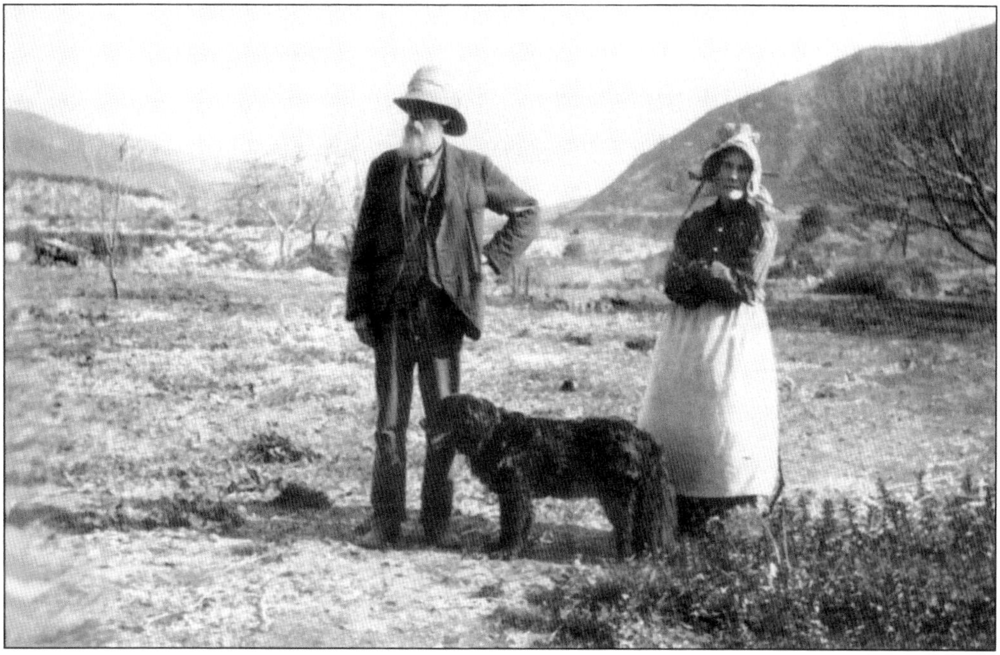

BAILEY'S AT KEENBROOK. William Gould Bailey, his wife, Cinderella, and dog Coaly stand on their Keenbrook land before the railroad came through in 1885. Bailey's bees were burned out of Bailey Canyon between Verdemont and Crestline, so at Keenbrook, he raised chickens. William's son Hervey and his son Raymond Gould took over until their deaths. Hervey willed the land to his stepson Frank Schultz. (HS.)

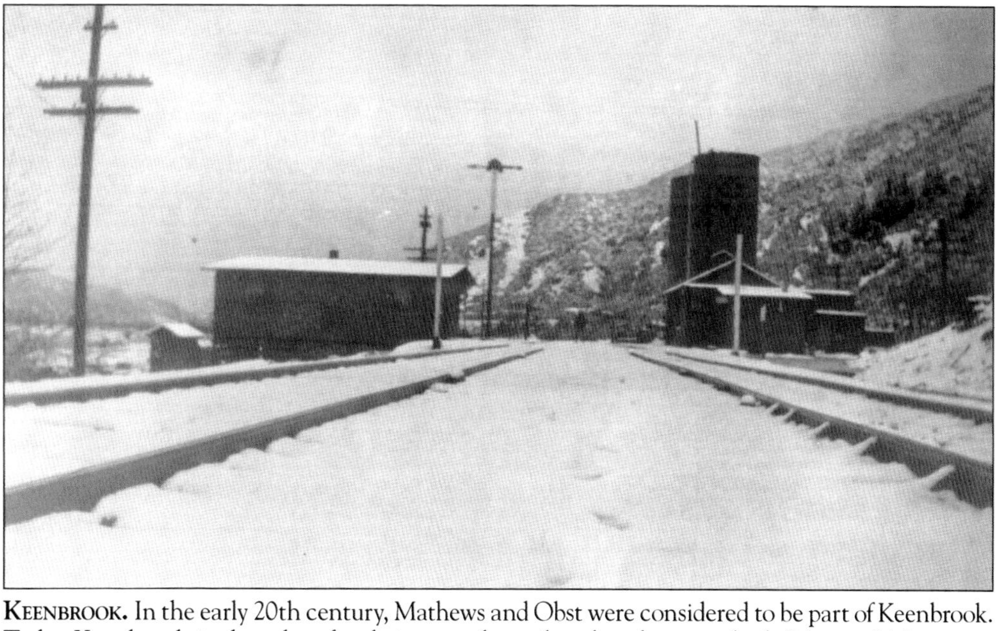

KEENBROOK. In the early 20th century, Mathews and Obst were considered to be part of Keenbrook. Today Keenbrook is thought of as being on the railroad and stream bed. Silas and Mourning Dove Glenn settled the area in the 1860s. They sold to their daughter and son-in-law, Ellen and James Applewhite, when they moved to Lytle Creek. Applewhites sold to the Keenes and Baileys in the early 1880s. (RB.)

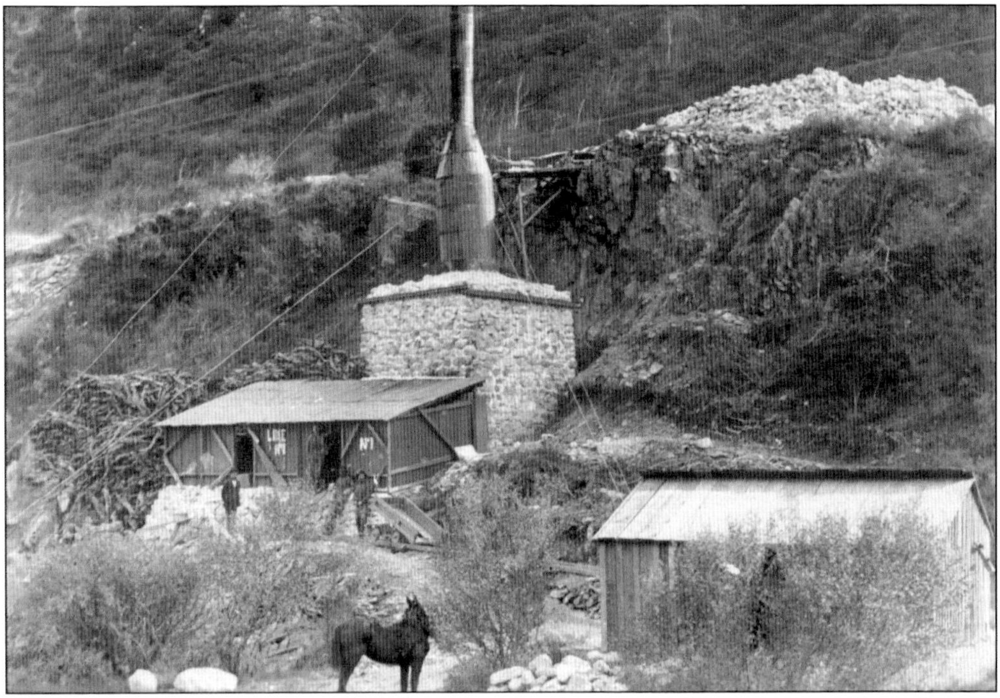

Limestone Was Big Business. The kiln at Keenbrook was one of many in Cajon Pass. Cement was not readily available, and lime was widely used in construction of pioneer cabins. This kiln was a thing of the past by 1917. The photograph above shows the kiln when it was in use, and the photograph below pictures the Keenbrook kiln as it looks today. It is located on the west side of the railroad tracks just north of Keenbrook Road. (Above, RB; below, RH.)

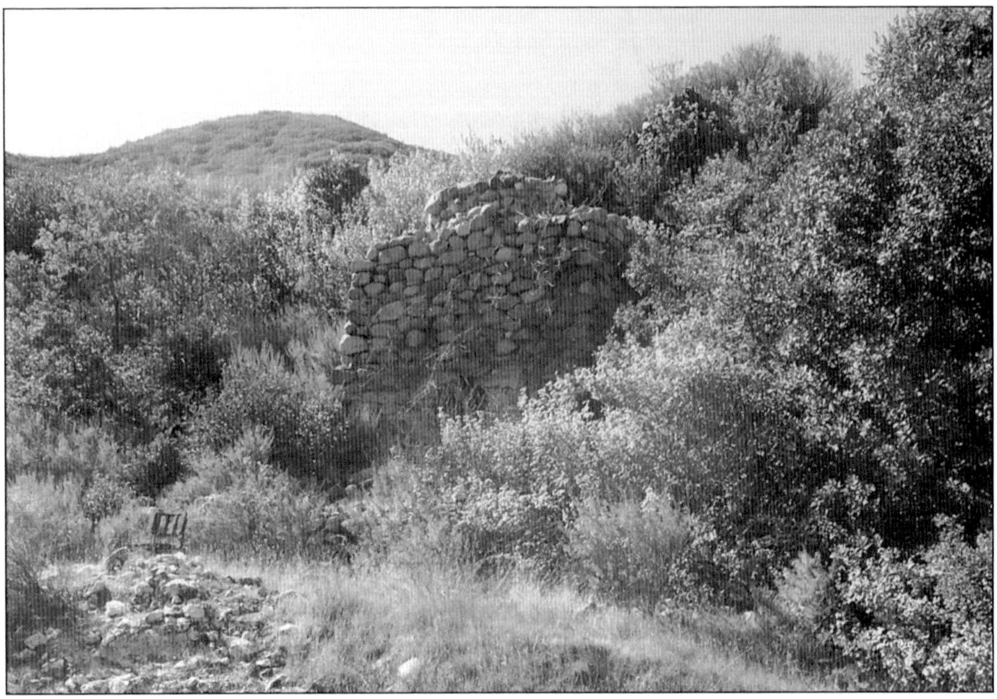

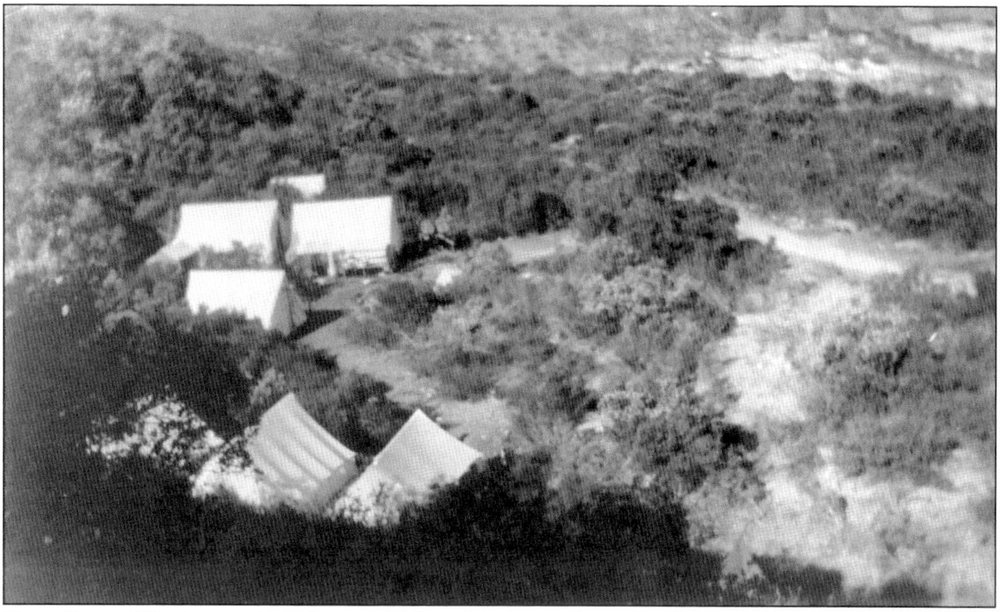

Kiln Camp. Workers at the kiln camped in tents near their Keenbrook work site. The kiln camp was not the only residential tent area in the Cajon Pass. Army camps, similar to this, were located near the Cajon Station and Blue Cut. A federal/state relief camp for 200 men was located at Camp Cajon in 1932. The Civilian Conservation Corps followed, the second of 16 in San Bernardino National Forest. (RB.)

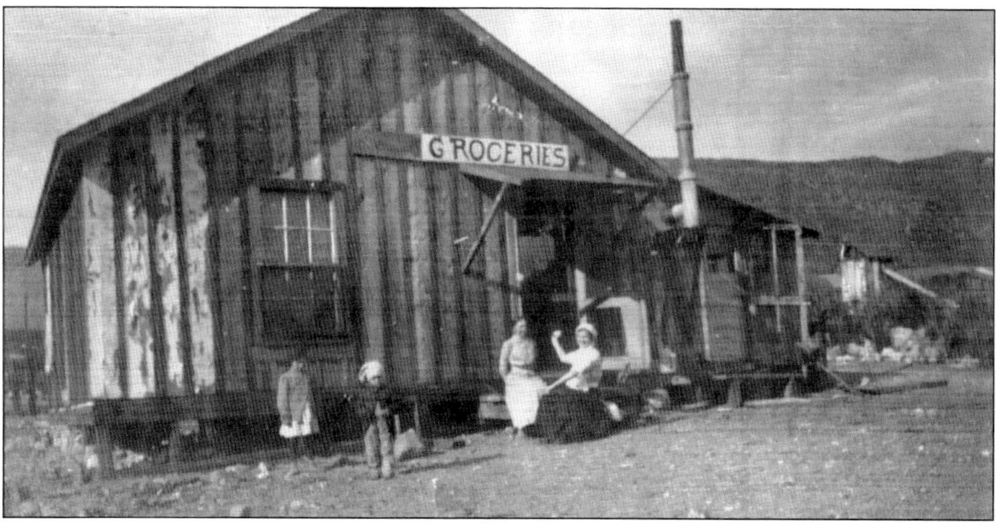

Keenbrook Grocery. Ben, Kathleen, and Mary Bess Verbryck visit with Londa Bailey at the local grocery store. The Verbryck family donated land for the construction of the first fire lookout platform in Cajon Pass in San Bernardino National Forest. Steam locomotives often started fires, which could burn ties and ruin a track. Residents cooperated with forestry and railroad personnel to build and man the first lookout in 1914. (RB.)

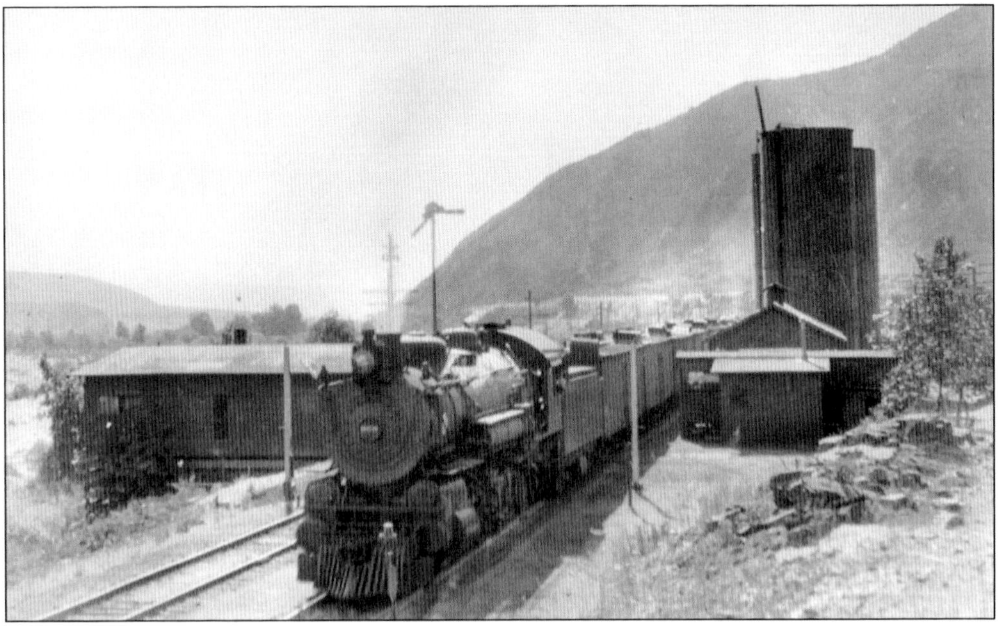

Steam Engine at Keenbrook. Keenbrook was one of several stations on the steep Cajon grade where steam engines had to stop to replenish their water supply or cool their wheels. From that stop, a small community developed, including a post office, which moved from homes to the store to the depot. (RB.)

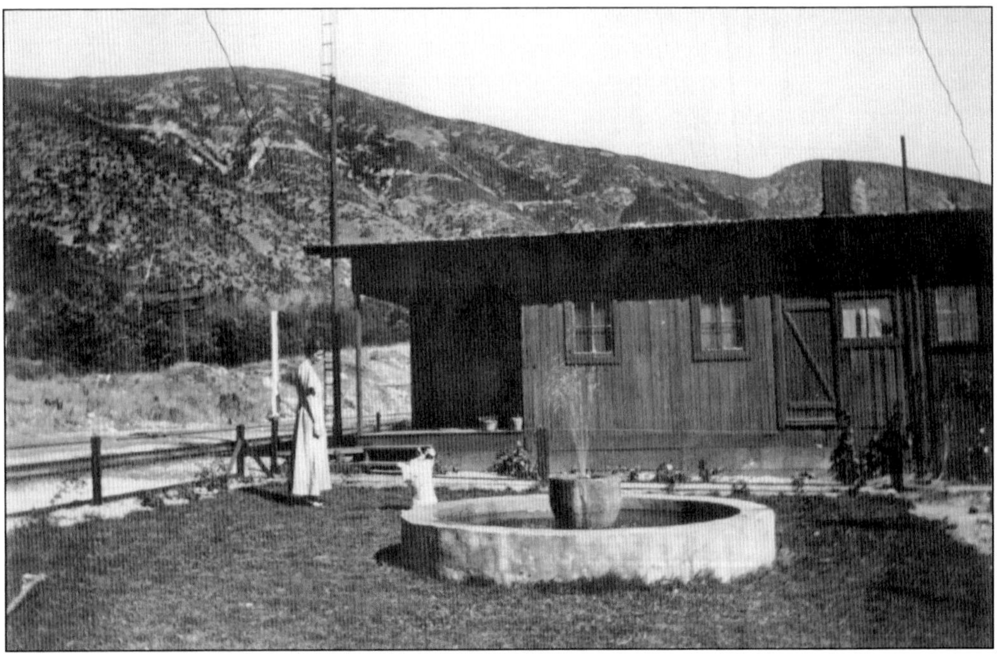

Private Lives Revealed. Railroading was important to residents at the stations, but they also tried to instill some beauty and fun into their daily lives. This scene is the backyard at Keenbrook with either Stella Ehwegen or Londa Bailey encouraging the dog. (RB.)

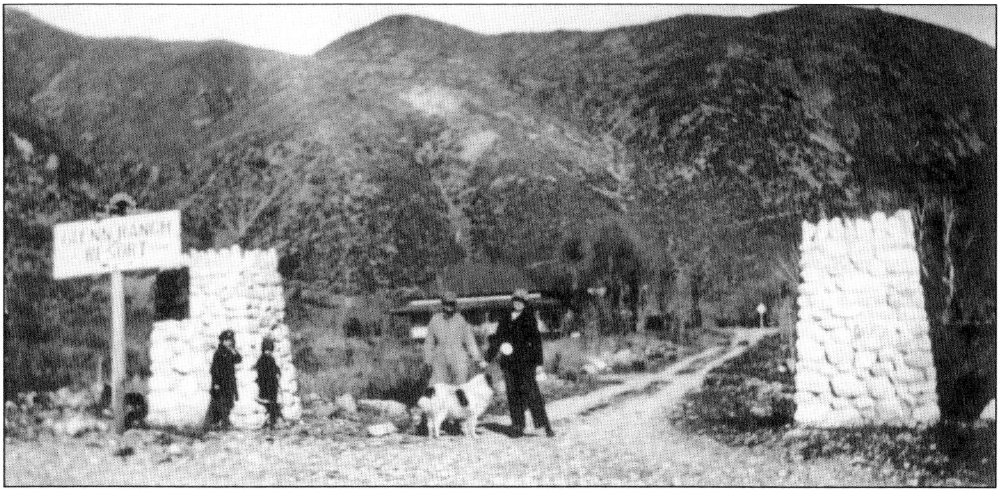

GLENN RANCH, LYTLE CREEK. After the Glenns sold their Keenbrook property in the 1860s, they started the famous Glenn Ranch in Lytle Creek. The Applewhites built a road over the hills between Keenbrook and Glenn Ranch so the guests could disembark from the train at Keenbrook and ride by stage, wagon, or later farm truck 2.5 miles over Applewhite Road to Glenn Ranch. Applewhite Road was never paved or improved by the county in spite of petitions signed by residents and interested parties. Today it is a forestry road. The building below served as a store for the 300–800 guests and campers Glenn Ranch entertained each summer. (Both, RB.)

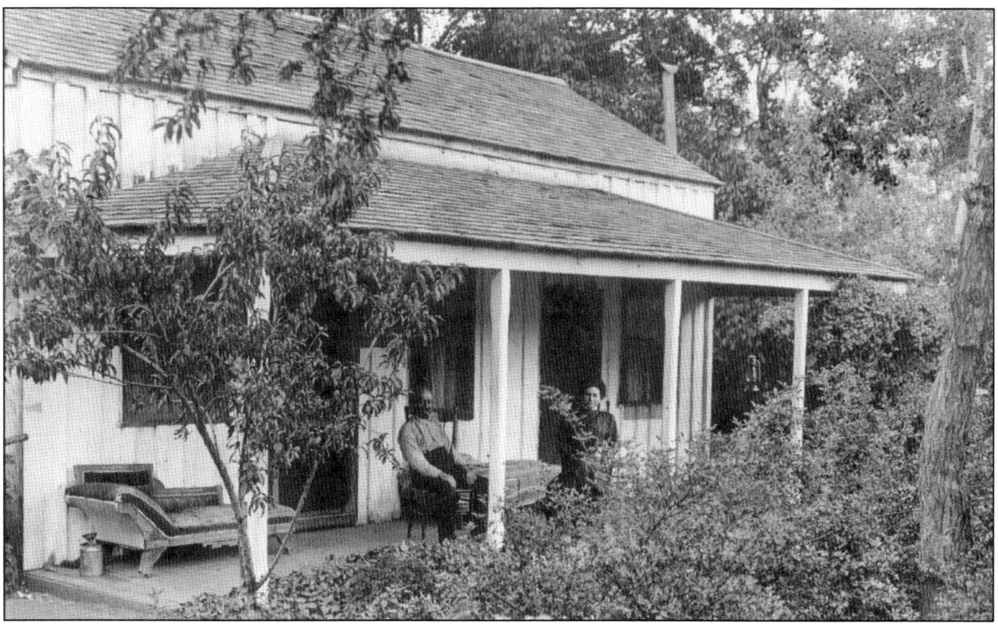

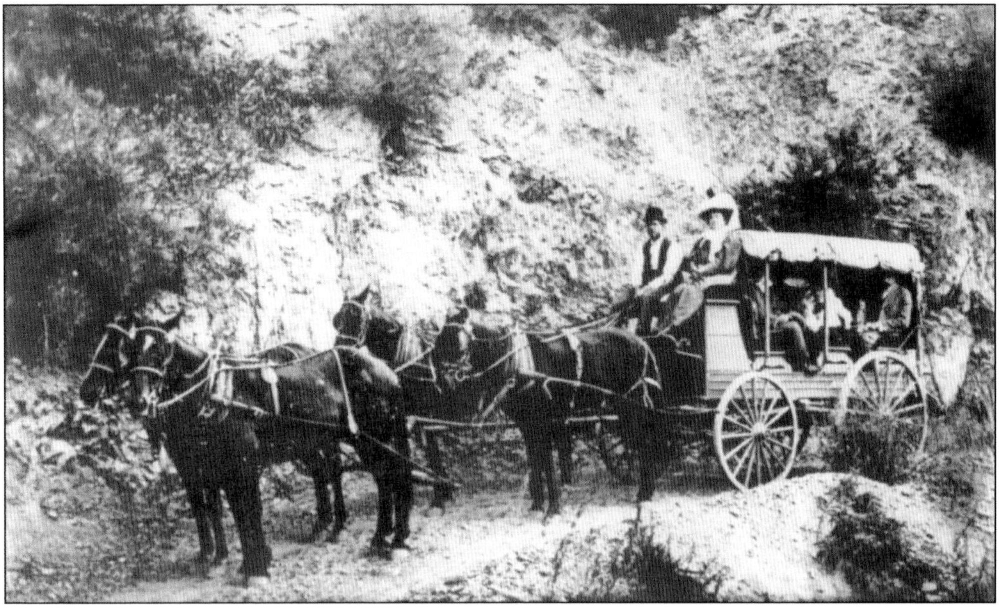

Keenbrook to Glenn Ranch. The "stage" from Keenbrook to Glenn Ranch was one rough ride. By 1913, Glenn Ranch had replaced horse and carriage with farm truck to transport guests from Keenbrook to the resort. When the truck was not used for ferrying Glenn Ranch guests, it held apple and peach packing boxes and was parked under the productive trees. (AHCRFL.)

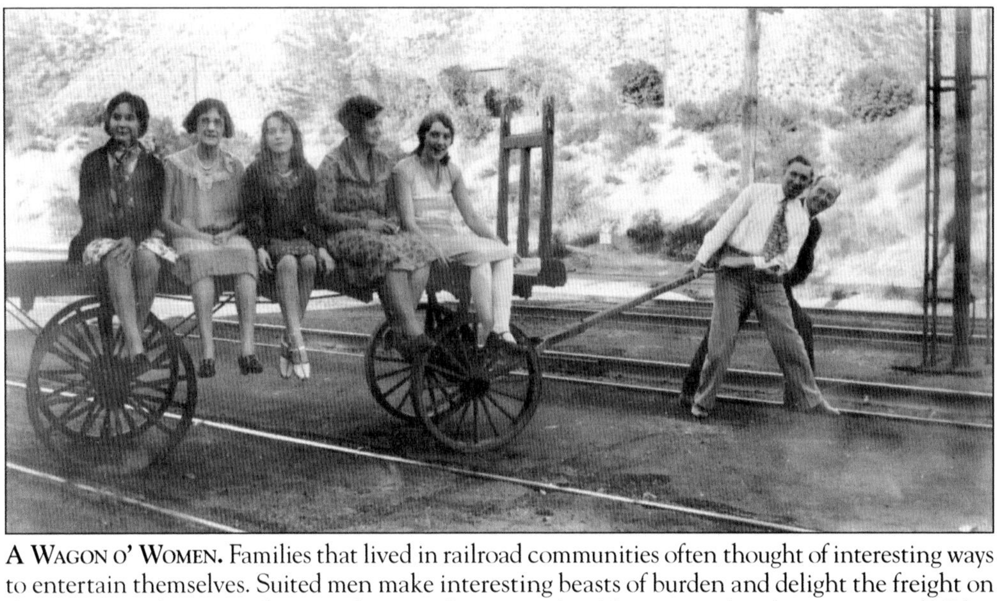

A Wagon o' Women. Families that lived in railroad communities often thought of interesting ways to entertain themselves. Suited men make interesting beasts of burden and delight the freight on their wagon. The cover photograph is another example of fun in a railroad community. (RB.)

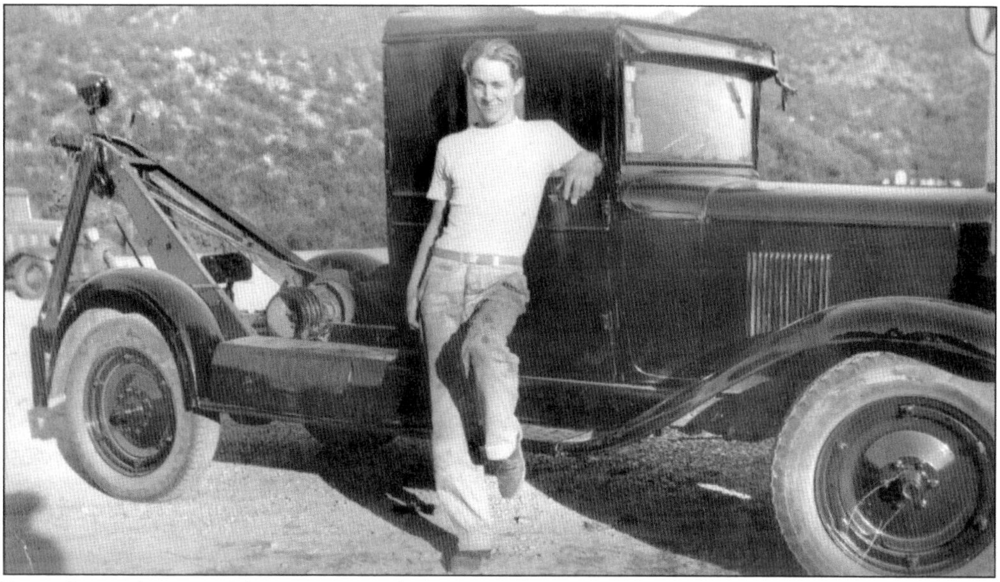

Blue Cut. The name Blue Cut comes from the color of the Pelona schist when highway or railroad construction cuts through the rocks. Prospectors see the blue color and surmise that other colors will be forthcoming. Theodore Jenkins leans on the 1929 Chevrolet ton-and-a-half tow truck he drove for his father-in-law, Hugh Hickman, in 1946. The Hickmans owned a gas station and restaurant in the Blue Cut business row. (TJ.)

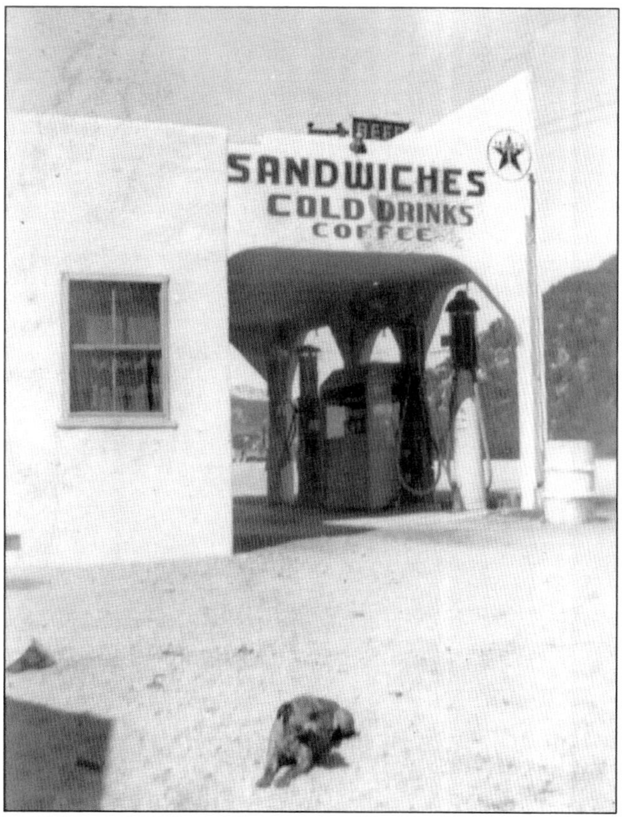

Blue Cut Businesses. In the Route 66 heyday, successful businesses lined the highway at Blue Cut. Cabins, restaurants, garages, and filling stations all did a good business until the freeway came through in 1957. Maude and Hugh Hickman bought their Blue Cut business in 1929 and moved it to the 395/66 junction in 1950 when they heard of freeway plans. Tom Shepherd bought the Blue Cut property. (TJ.)

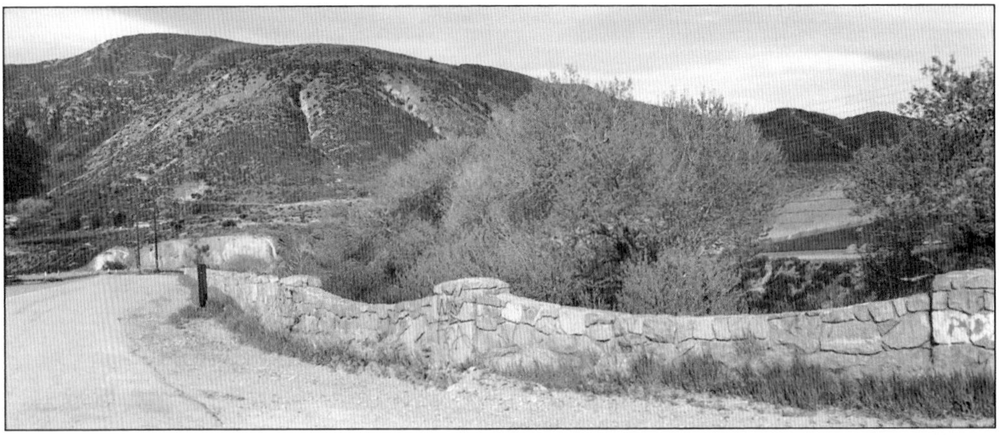

The Walls. The beautiful Blue Cut retaining walls that keep motorists from driving off into Cajon Creek were designed by B. A. Switzer and built by Olie Dahl, who also did much of the rock work for Camp Cajon. The Blue Cut in the hills is off the picture to the left. The creek is on the right. The Route 66 California Highway Patrol truck scales stood in this area. (AH.)

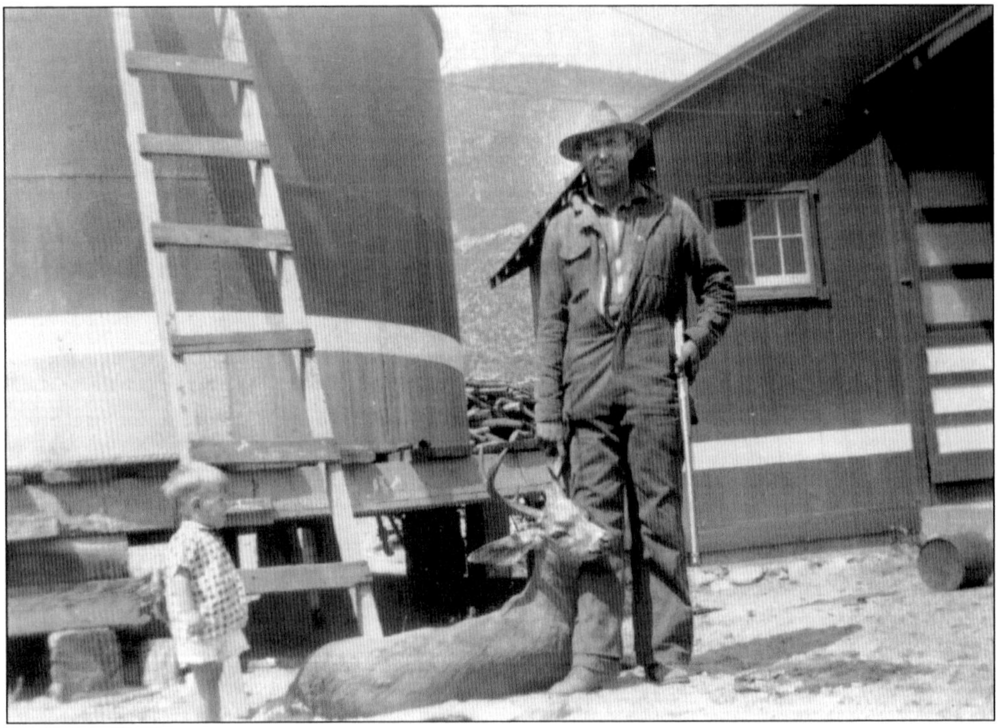

Water Tank. Water for Blue Cut business came from wells dug down near Cajon Creek. Windmills brought the water up to a tank and into barrels placed beside gasoline pumps so motorists could dip water into steaming radiators. In the days of Route 66, game was plentiful, and residents, as well as recreational hunters, took advantage of the abundance. (TJ.)

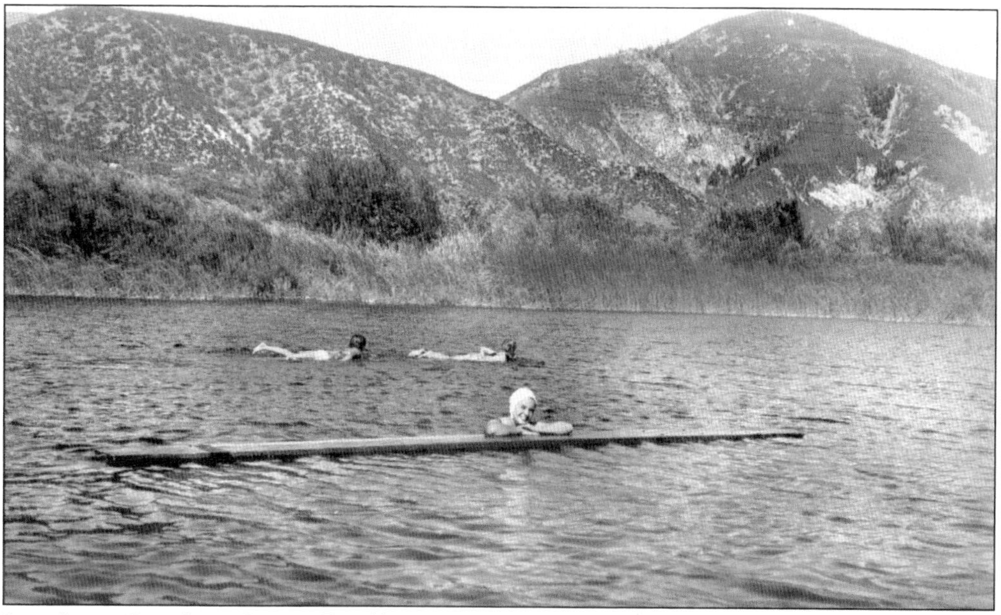

LOST LAKE. Swarthout Canyon Road leaves Route 66 where the old forestry station and camp were. It crosses Cajon Creek and passes residences between tracks, where a hungry Native American brave ghost haunts, before intersecting the railroad tracks. Lost Lake (formerly Mathis Lake) can no longer be seen from the road, but this "bottomless" sag pond on the San Andreas Fault is still attractive. It was dry for a year in the mid-1960s. (GLM.)

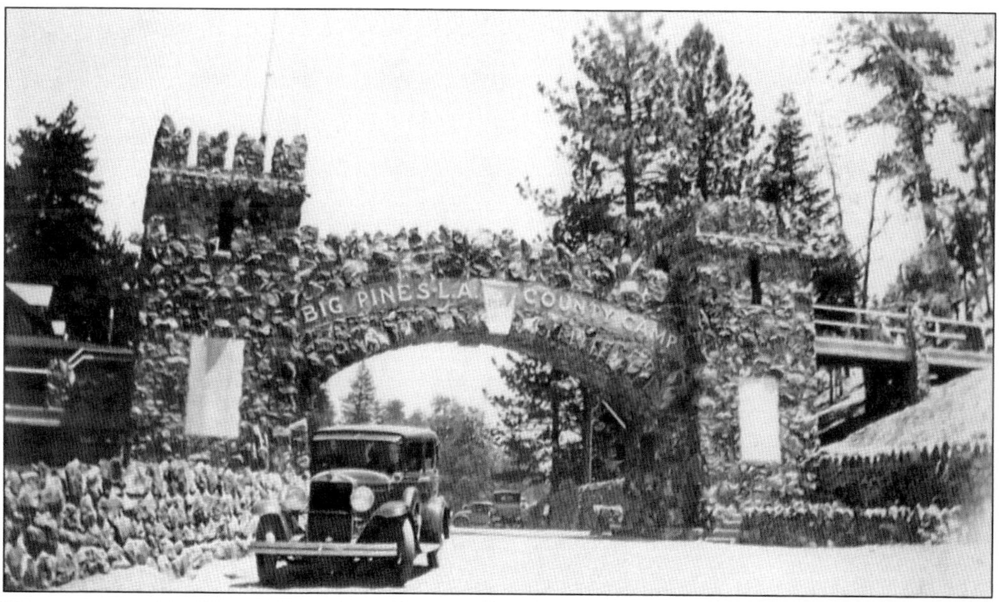

WRIGHTWOOD/BIG PINES. Swarthout Canyon Road joins Lone Pine Canyon Road just after the latter leaves Route 138. Lone Pine travels past the Clyde Ranch and into Wrightwood the back way. This is a favorite drive for adventurous residents of Cajon Pass. Pictured above is Harry Hall's Graham Paige on just such a trip in 1930. The arch was the entry to Los Angeles County's Big Pines recreation area and campground. (RH.)

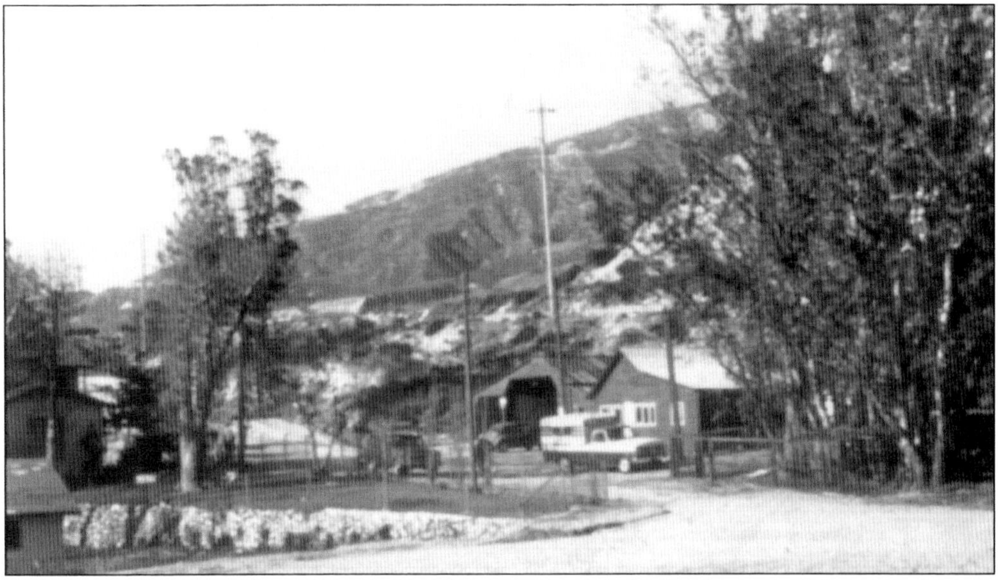

Cozy Dell. Cozy Dell sat on both sides of Route 66, with the residence and farm on the west and the commercial businesses on the east. Children from Riverside enjoyed field trips by train there to picnic under willows and cottonwoods in the 1880s, and local children of the 1930s and 1940s often swam in the Cozy Dell reservoir up on the hill behind the businesses, where the new Route 66 and the I-15 later came through. Philip Hanf sold the 55-acre Cozy Dell to Jacob and Melissa Roesch in 1919. They built a beautiful Spanish-style house north of the old toll gate in 1934 and contributed to local communities by founding Roesch Transportation and by teaching local children even after the freeway bypass of Route 66 killed Cozy Dell's commercial value. The house burned down in 2003. (Both, AHCRFL.)

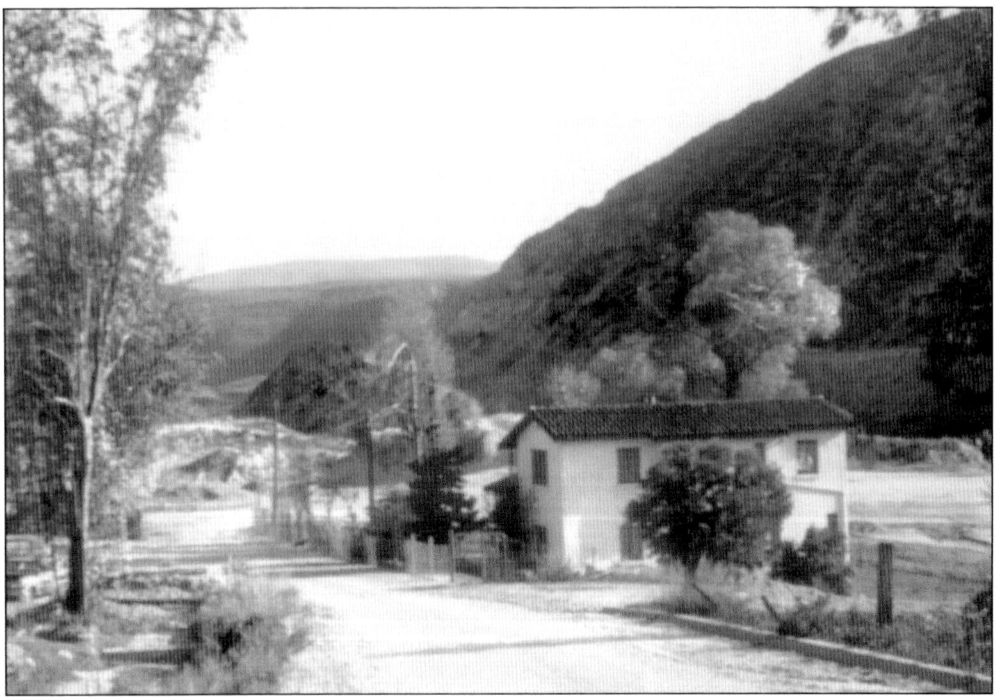

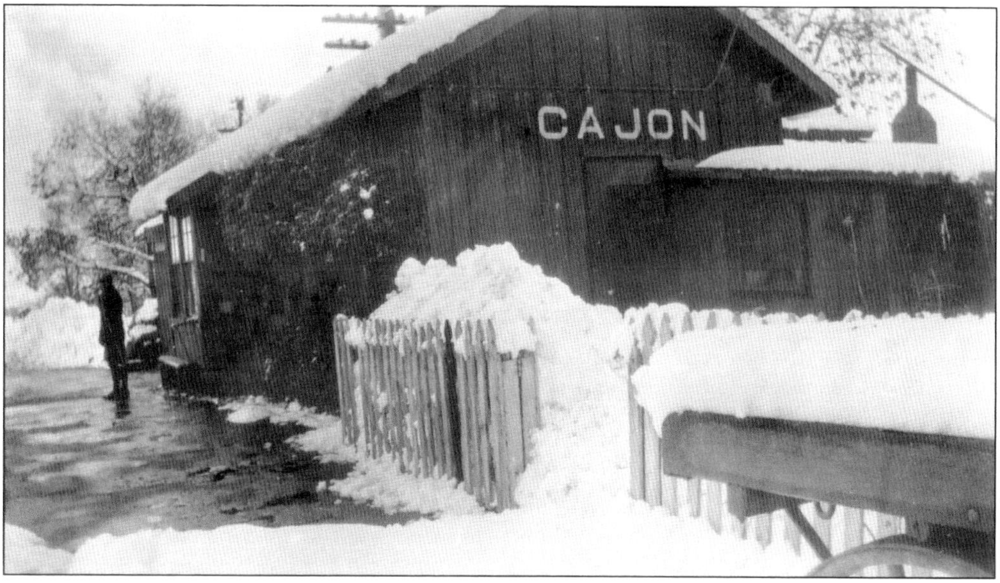

CAJON STATION. The residents at Cajon Station saw the beauty of their home in all seasons, but winter, having purified the landscape with white, was their favorite. However, the snow could cause problems on the railroad tracks, stopping train traffic for lengthy periods. As with most railroad stations, Cajon had the necessary facilities, like water tanks and purification plants, to keep engines running smoothly up and down the Cajon Pass. Below, a supply train has just unloaded, and Edward Ehwegen, telegrapher, helps check the supplies on the platform. The roads forked here, with the Mormon Trail going west and the toll road going east up Crowder Canyon. (Both, RB.)

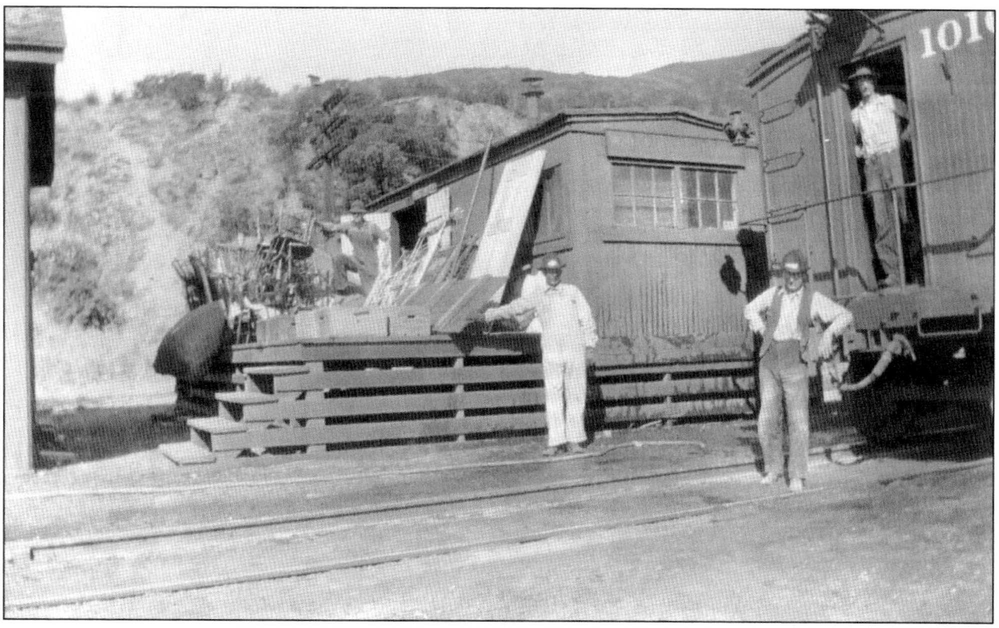

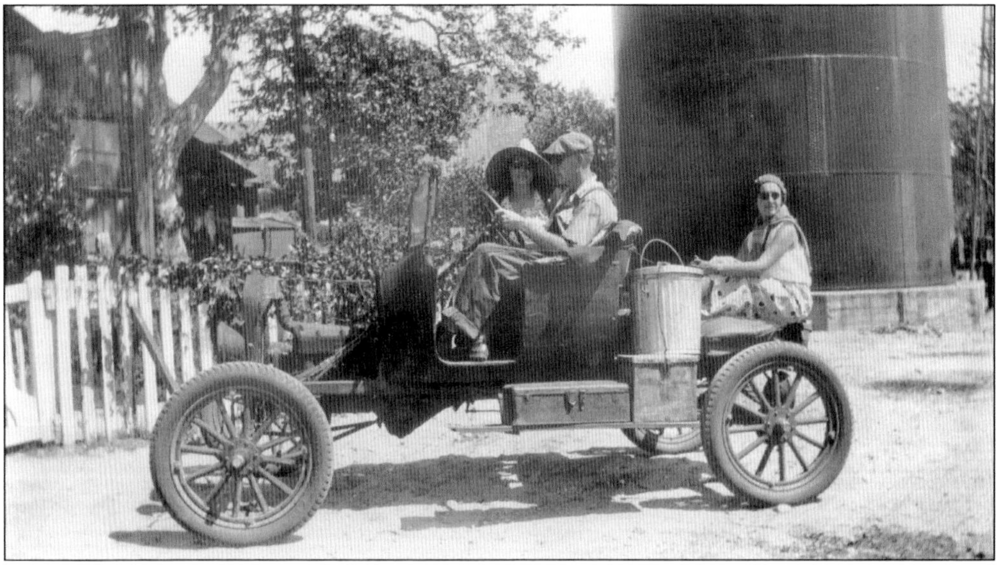

For Fun. In 1931, Ed Ehwegen remodeled this 1909 Ford Model T. He enjoyed giving friends rides around the Cajon railroad station, where he was telegrapher from 1910 to 1937. For more fun, he might even have driven it to the cabin he owned in Wrightwood. (RB.)

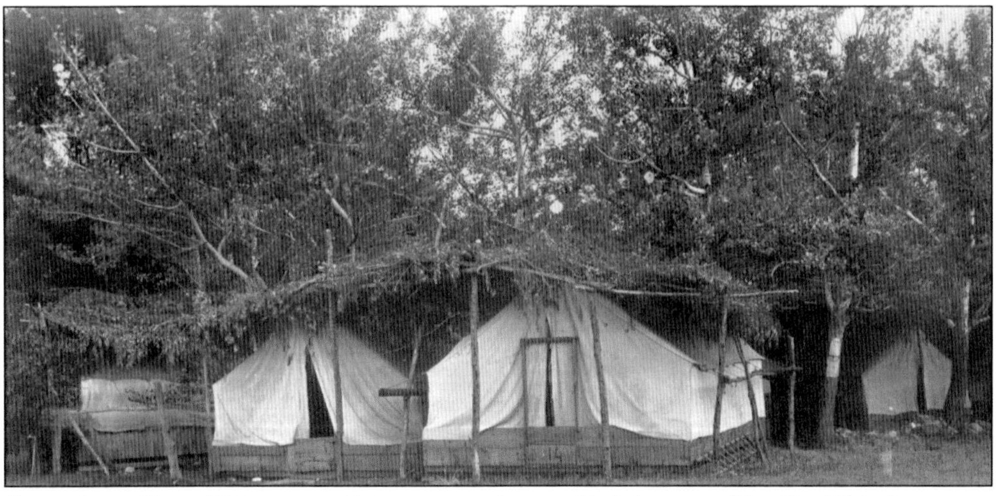

Cajon Army Camp. This camp at Cajon very much resembled the one at Blue Cut. This close-up on a 1901 postcard shows more clearly how the soldiers on assignment in the pass coped with primitive living conditions. The army was stationed in Cajon Pass to protect railroad interests. Armed guards protected Alray tunnels and Devore bridges and points between and beyond. (RB.)

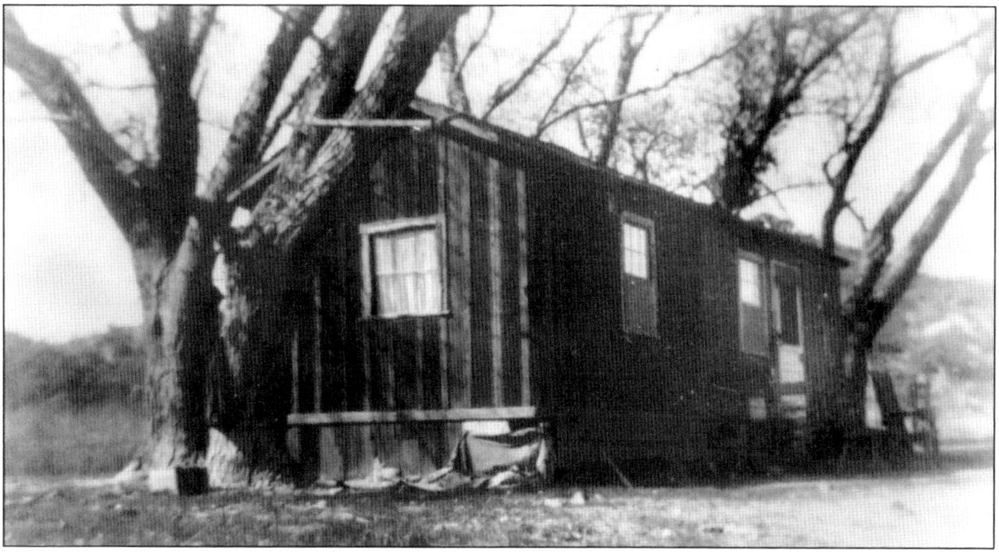

EDSON'S POST OFFICE. Just across the creek and north of the Cajon Railroad Station stood Carlos "Dad" Edson's house, which served the area as a post office for a time. Edson arrived in the Cajon area in 1915 and later became caretaker of Cajon Campground. His daughter lived with him in 1919. (MHS/VVM.)

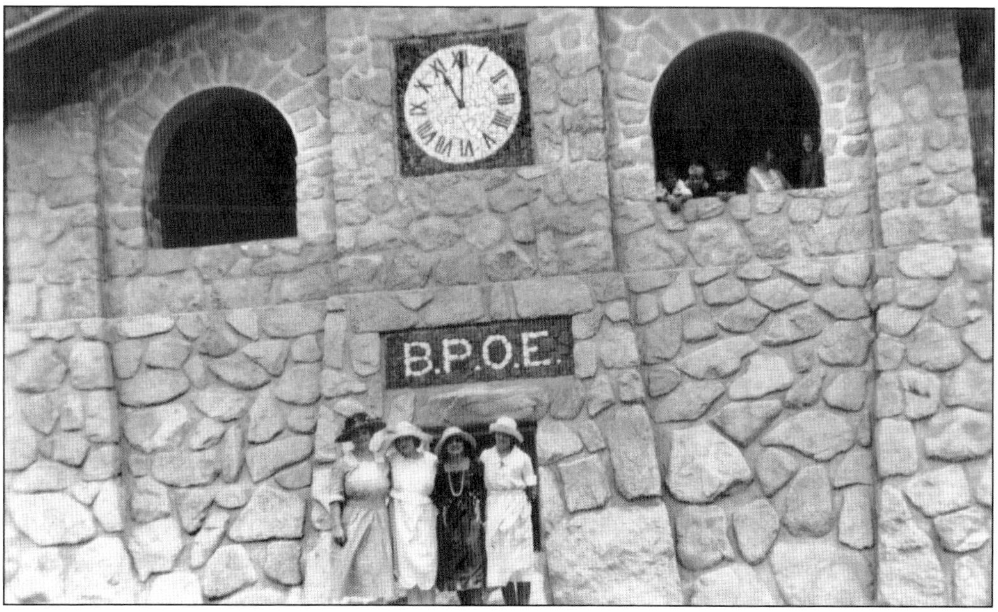

CAJON CAMPGROUND. Jennie Cook Davis's poem "The Overland Trail" inspired William Bristol to build Cajon Campground in 1919 south of the I-15/138 junction. Cajon Campground offered free rest and picnic facilities to travelers on both sides of the Old Trail Highway (Route 66). For a time, the Baileys and Ehwegens picked up their mail at the camp. Camp Cajon was highly appreciated by travelers until the flood of 1938. (RB.)

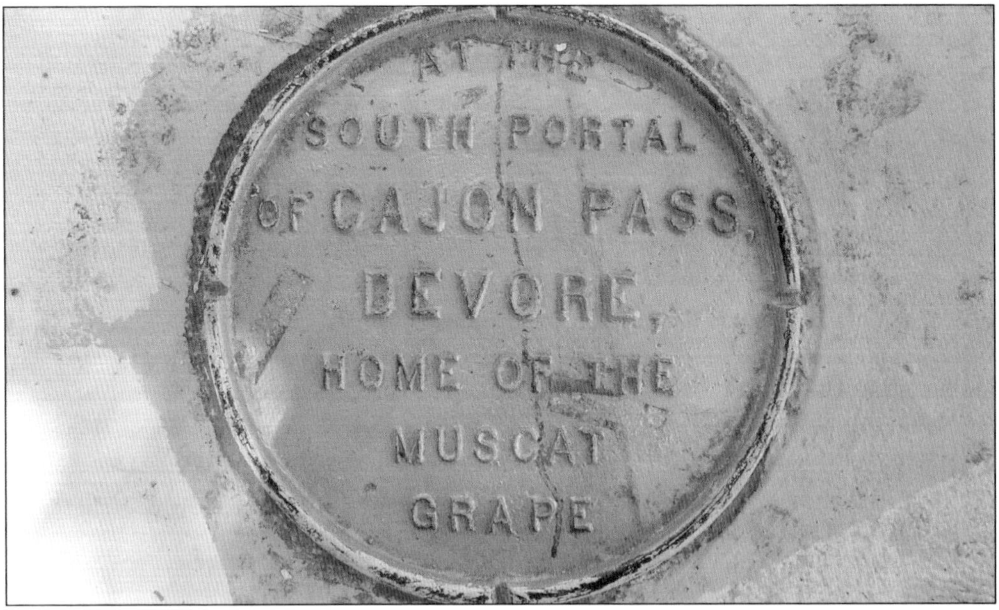

THE TABLES. The Camp Cajon tables were round, heavy concrete structures with matching benches. Each one had a bronze-colored plaque in the center embellished with a message from the sponsoring group. Devore's is shown. The Cajon Pass plaque said, "A welcome and God speed from the residents of Cajon Pass." The tables can be seen at Perris Hill and Lytle Creek Parks in San Bernardino. (AH.)

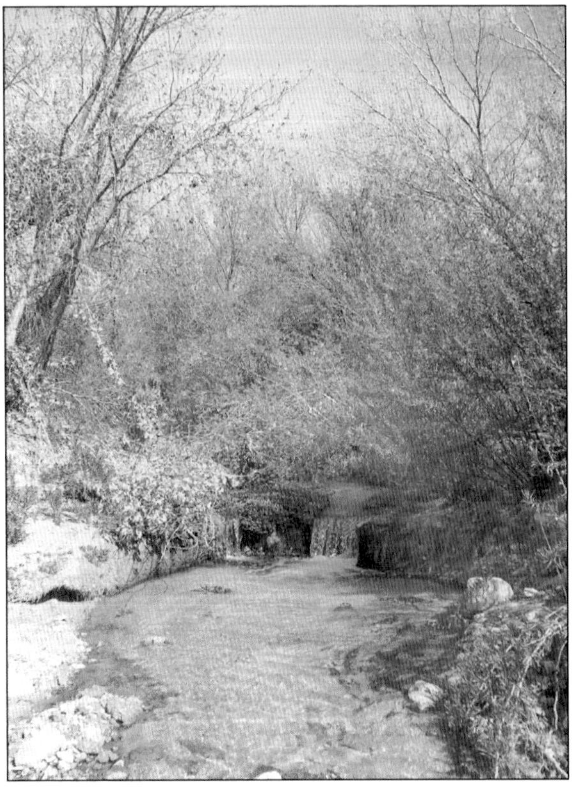

INMAN/SULLIVAN-MAY MUSEUM SITE. In the 1880s, this was Muscupiabit and then Willow Grove, and after the toll road went through, it was Salisbury House. Then it was Cajon, and in 1913, the Stoddard/Waite monument was dedicated near here. From 1940 to 1975, Inmans lived near this part of Cajon Creek. Now the county museum owns this nature center where local students have visited beaver ponds. (AHCAFL.)

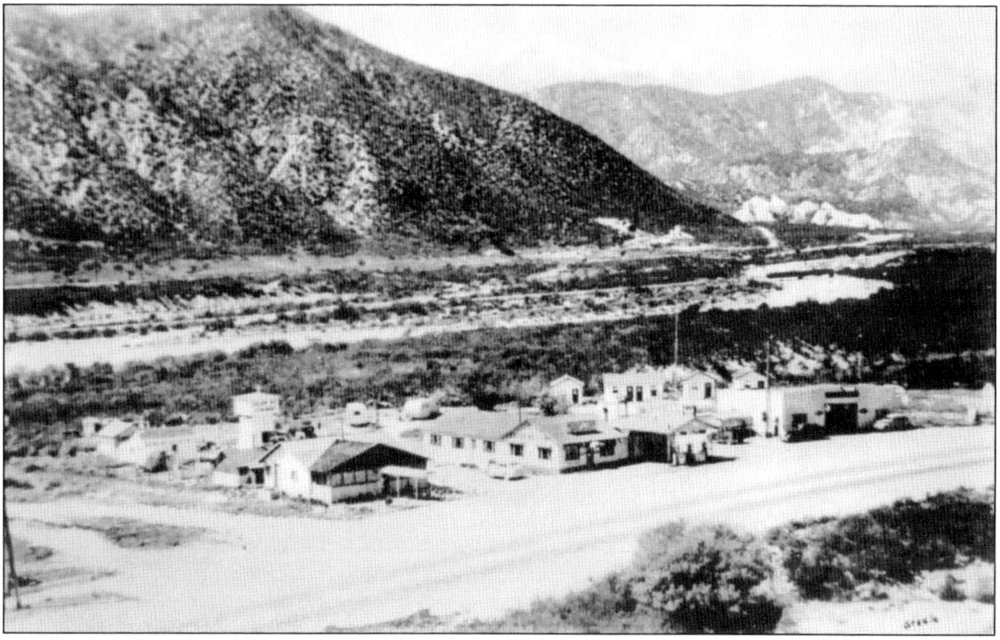

COMMERCIAL ENDEAVOR. The Christiansons obtained permission to build a commercial center along Route 66 near Camp Cajon. The water tower proclaims it Cajon Mountain Camp. Grava can be seen against the far hills, and the Mormon Rocks are visible against the mountains at the right of the photograph. (MHS/VVM.)

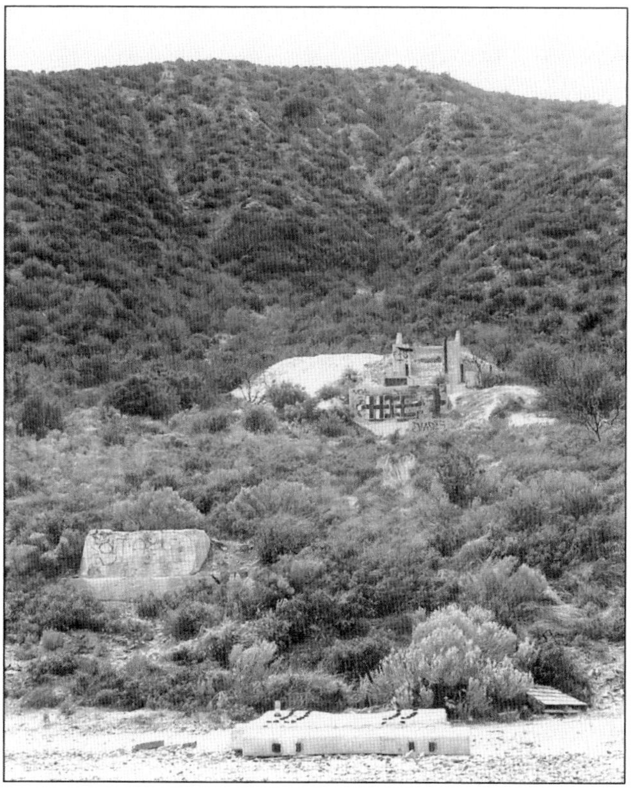

GRAVA. When lime was king of Cajon Pass, Cajon Lime Plant at Grava employed 100 people. Raw materials from Lone Pine Canyon, taken by trackless trolley, were dumped at Grava, which was right beside the railroad. Its remains can be seen just west of I-15 on the hillside south of Highway 138. (AH.)

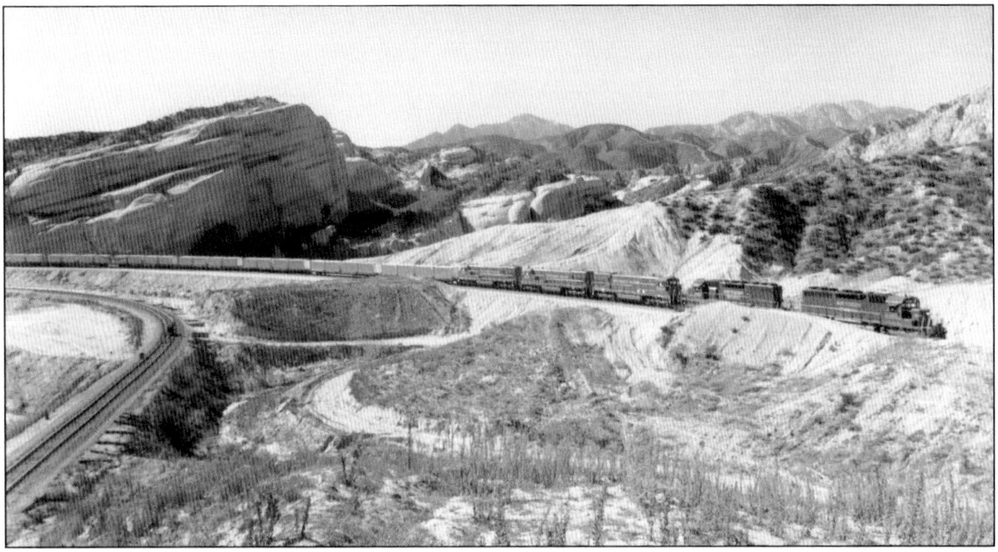

Mormon Rocks. Highway 138 west of I-15 is called West Cajon Valley. It is one of the three branches of Cajon Pass—the route the Mormons took in 1851 and the route cattle drivers chose to avoid the toll gates. The railroad passes by Mormon Rocks, a picturesque sandstone formation in West Cajon Valley. Highway 2 to Wrightwood leaves Route 138 at its summit. (SBHPS.)

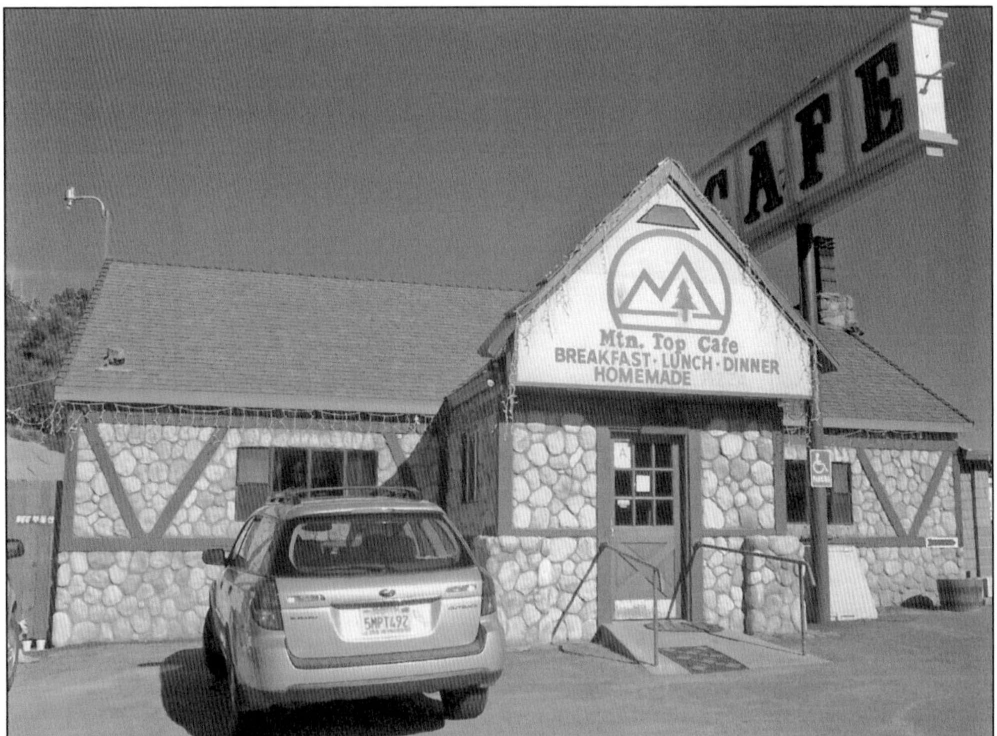

Hilltop Business. Leaving Mormon Rocks behind and continuing west on Highway 138, one reaches the West Cajon Valley Summit at the intersection of Highway 2 into Wrightwood. The summit has been marked for decades by the cozy Mountain Top Café. Passing the Wrightwood turnoff, Highway 138 continues into Pinon Hills and Phelan. (AH.)

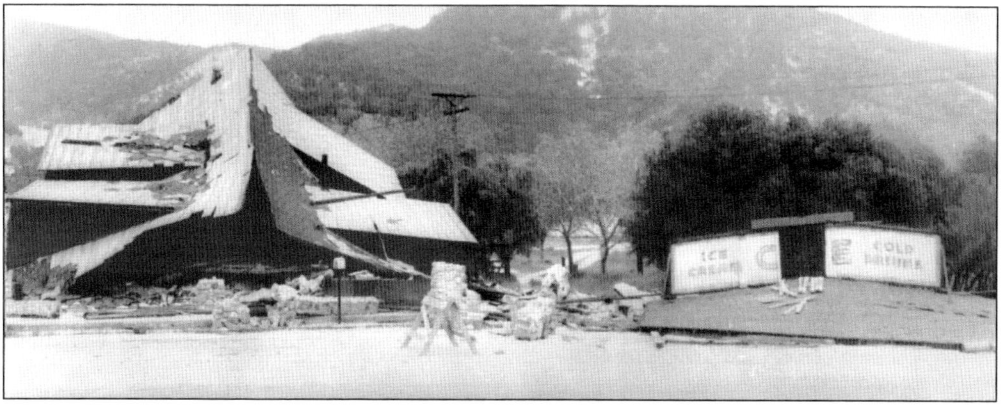

A Highway Wreck. A bus careening out of control down the steep Cajon Pass grade of Route 66 wiped out the popular eatery at Highway 138 on Route 66 in 1945. By 1946, Meeker's was rebuilt and functioning as well as before the accident. The new structure in no way resembled the rock building that was demolished. Tiffany's replaced Meeker's at the I-15/Highway 138 interchange, and now McDonald's has replaced them all. The freeway is about the only human embellishment that exists between Highway 138 and the Cajon Summit. (Both, MHS/VVM.)

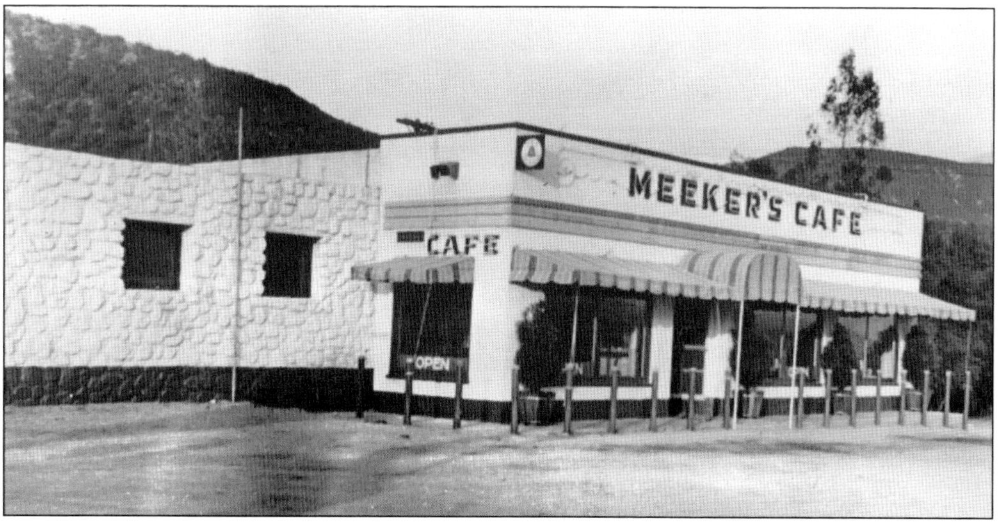

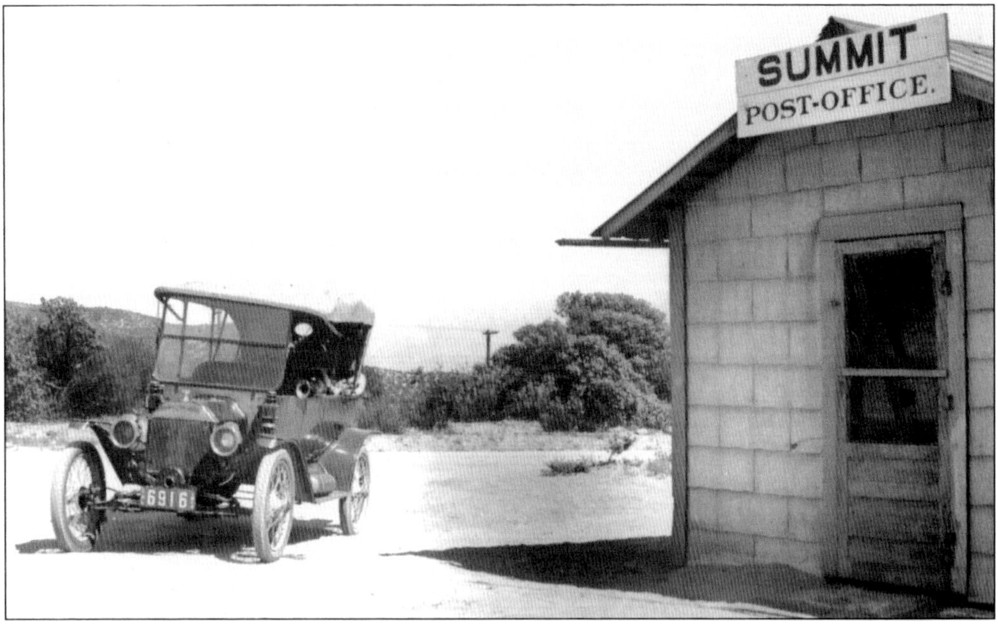

SILVERWOOD LAKE. East out Highway 138 from Summit Valley, which no longer has its quaint post office, lies Silverwood Lake. Now a popular recreational site for fishing, swimming, and boating, Silverwood Lake covers a quaint village called Cedar Springs. The dam is named after the town it destroyed. The dam and lake overlook Las Flores Ranch in Summit Valley. Cedar Springs was begun by Dr. Carl and Ella Hewitt, the health team that served the area from Camp Seeley near Crestline to Hesperia. They built Cedar Springs Health Resort for tuberculosis patients in Sawpit Canyon in 1919. By 1925, Cedar Springs was a cozy Seventh-day Adventist community. It was destroyed in 1966 by construction of Silverwood Lake, which was completed in 1972. (Both, AHCRFL.)

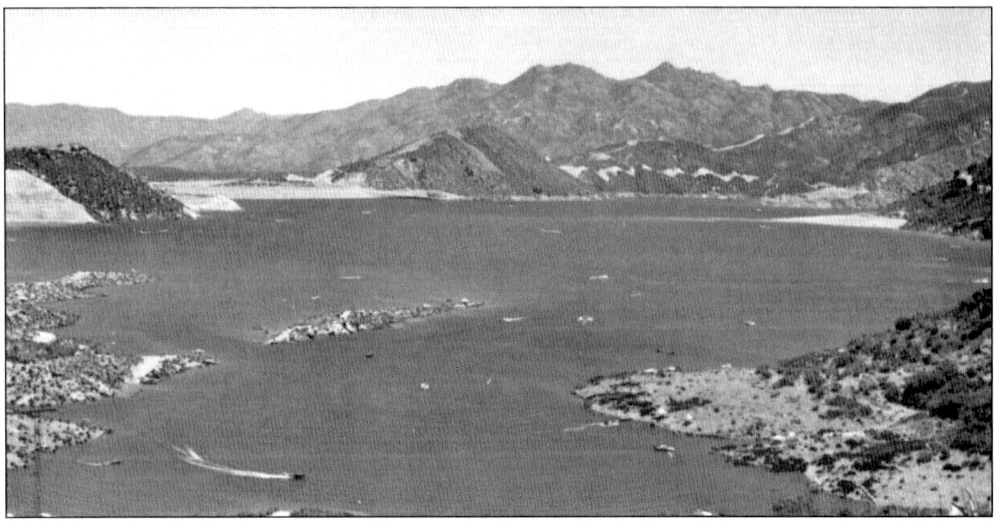

Five

Summit and Points North

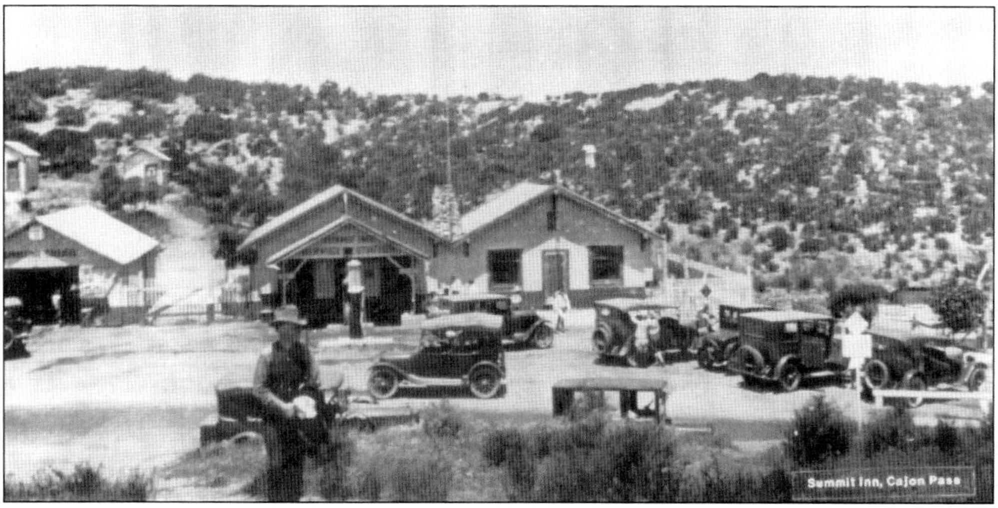

Cajon Summit. The Historic Summit Inn, complete with outhouse, is pictured here on Route 66 in 1929. The current Summit Inn has served travelers since 1952, and Cecil A. Stevens is only its second owner. He closed the motel, but his restaurant still offers ostrich egg omelets, ostrich burgers, and date shakes. A large ostrich farm exists in Oro Grande. A short section of the original two-lane (one each direction) Route 66 runs behind the restaurant. The nearby gas station is not part of the inn, which features a collection of "petroliana," like antique cars and hand-crank gasoline pumps. The old bus depot sign hangs on the wall. Now the ancient water tower south of the inn, to which water was hauled for many years, says Oak Hills. (CS.)

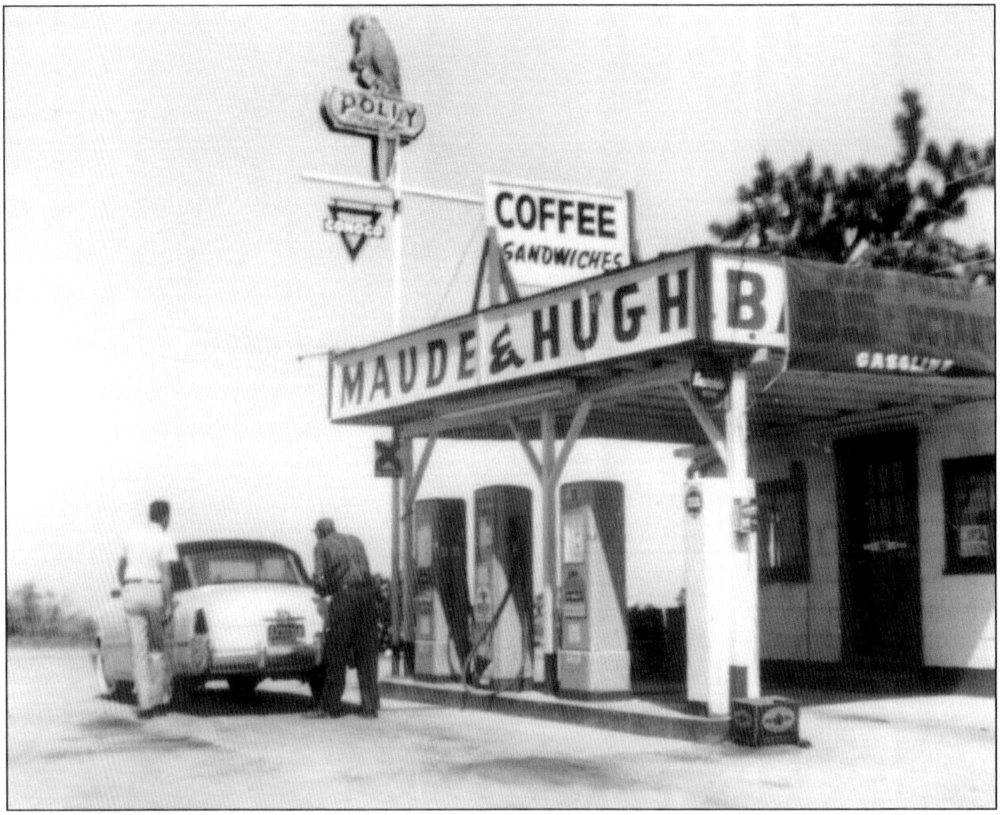

BALDY MESA. The Baldy Mesa area north of the Cajon Summit also boasted numerous commercial accommodations in Route 66 days, including the Outpost, which is still there. Hugh and Maud Hickman moved their Blue Cut business to the junction of Route 66 and Highway 395 on property they bought from Leroy and Della Rolar in 1950 when they heard about plans for a freeway. The Rolars had homesteaded 160 acres in Baldy Mesa by 1913. (TJ.)

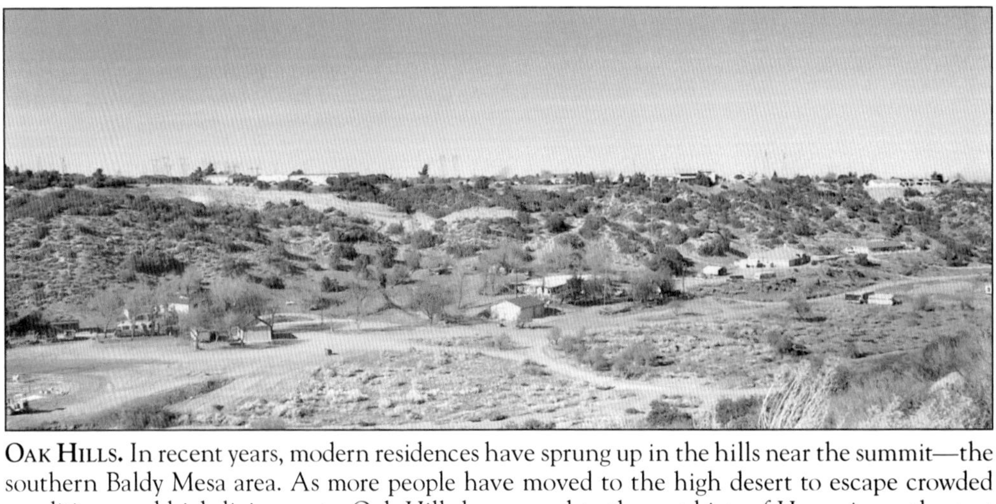

OAK HILLS. In recent years, modern residences have sprung up in the hills near the summit—the southern Baldy Mesa area. As more people have moved to the high desert to escape crowded conditions and high living costs, Oak Hills has spread to the outskirts of Hesperia on the east side of I-15. This planned rural living community appeals to people because of its easy access to the freeway. (AH.)

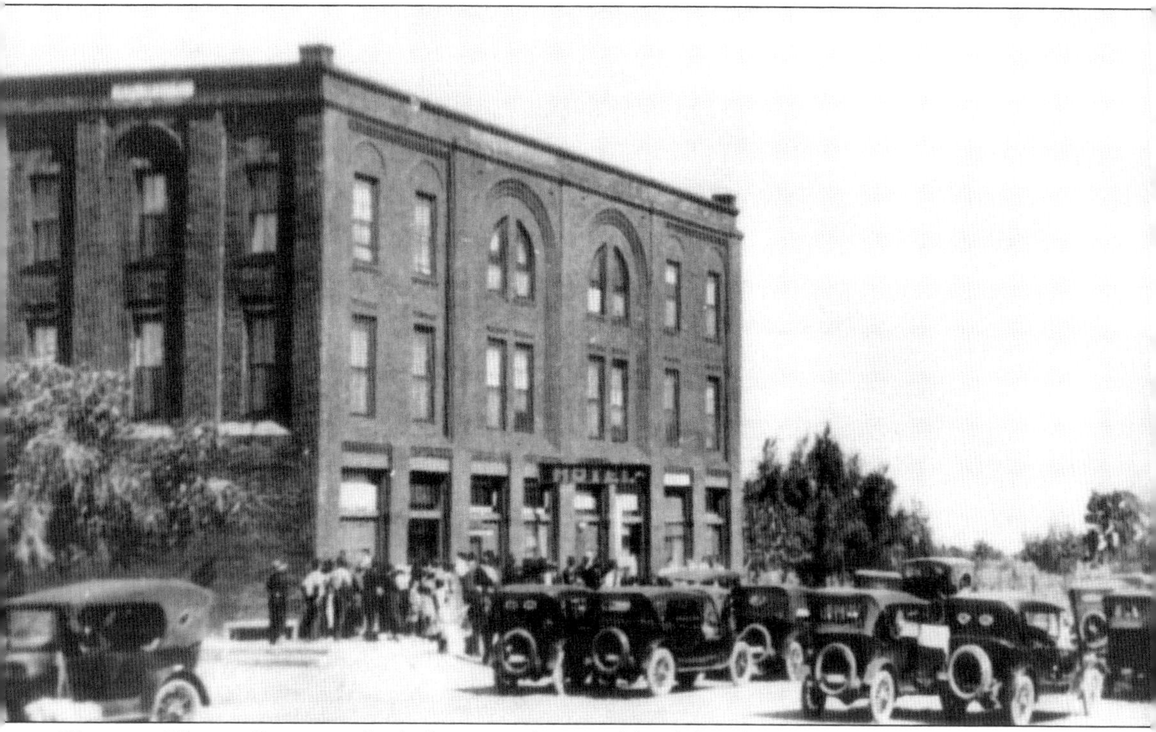

Hesperia Hotel. Promoters built the magnificent red-brick hotel in Hesperia at the same time the railroad was completed through the pass, 1885. It housed prospective investors as well as train passengers whose trips were interrupted, as in 1910. The westbound *California Limited* was held at Hesperia until the pass was cleared of an avalanche and wreck at Summit. Passengers waiting in the lobby were treated to passenger Ignace Jan Paderewski's impromptu piano concert. In 1890, Hesperia was described as a small town on the main line of the ATSF Railway, about 25 miles northeast of the county seat at an elevation of 2,500 feet. According to a county promotional brochure, in Hesperia Valley, north of the San Bernardino Mountains, "the delightful climate is unrivaled for pulmonary, bronchial, and nasal disorders." Settlers as early as 1874 made a living cutting juniper wood to fuel bakery kilns in Los Angeles. That practice later became illegal to protect the junipers. Hesperia was settled on the site of Atongaibit, the Vanyume Indian village, and near the route of the Old Spanish Trail. It boomed as the last stop on westbound Route 66 before treacherous Cajon Pass. (MHS/VVM.)

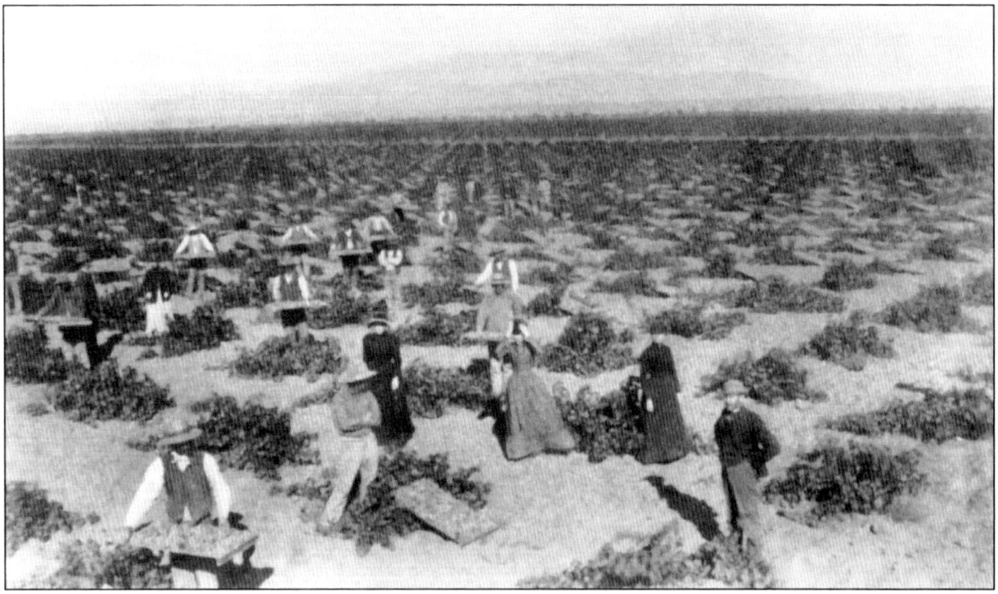

DESERT AGRICULTURE. Farming was also important in early Hesperia. This picture from 1891 depicts laborers drying grapes into raisins in the cooperative desert sun. In Devore, residents dried grapes into raisins on roofs of sheds as well as on the ground. Apple orchards, corn fields, and alfalfa fields also dotted the desert, and cattle roamed widely for graze. (MHS/VVM.)

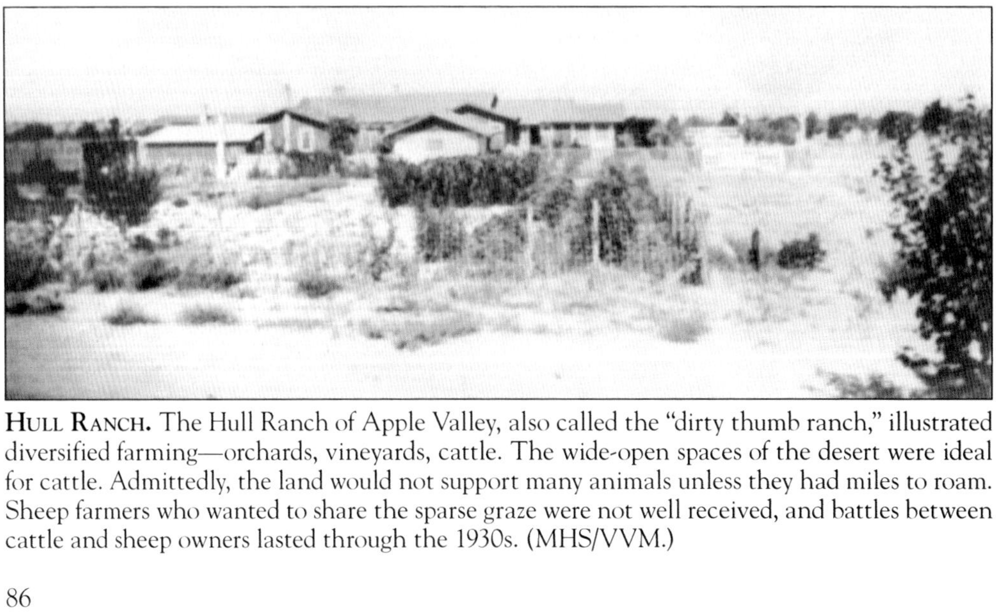

HULL RANCH. The Hull Ranch of Apple Valley, also called the "dirty thumb ranch," illustrated diversified farming—orchards, vineyards, cattle. The wide-open spaces of the desert were ideal for cattle. Admittedly, the land would not support many animals unless they had miles to roam. Sheep farmers who wanted to share the sparse graze were not well received, and battles between cattle and sheep owners lasted through the 1930s. (MHS/VVM.)

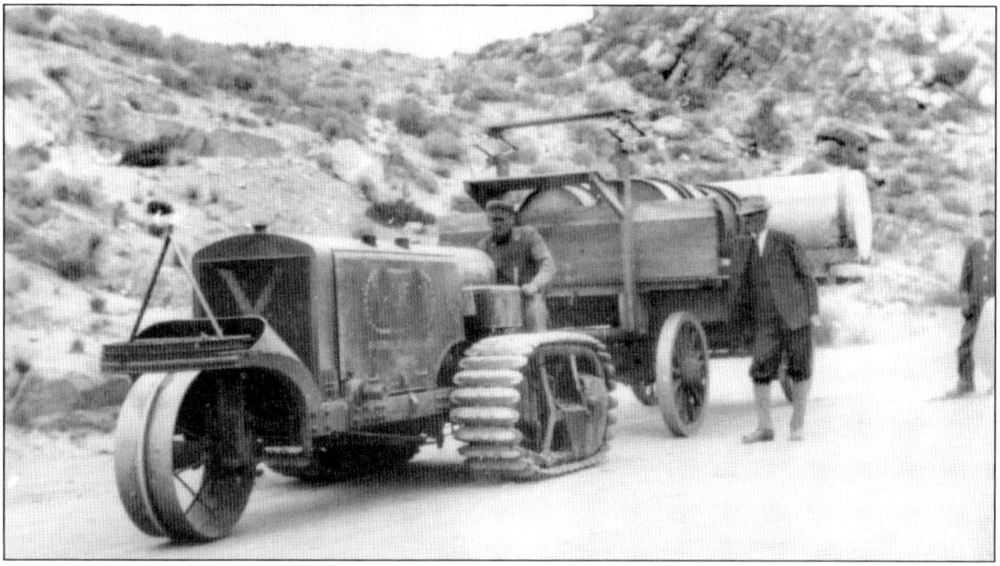

Technology Arrives. A Yuba tractor hauls tops for a Fairbanks Morse water pumping engine at Hull Ranch in 1915. These huge, heavy machines moved slowly. Manufactured in California, like its neighbors Best and Holt that unified to form Caterpillar, this early tractor used tracks instead of wheels, a concept borrowed by the military for World War I tanks. Hart-Parr advertisements popularized the word tractor for traction engines in 1906. (MHS/VVM.)

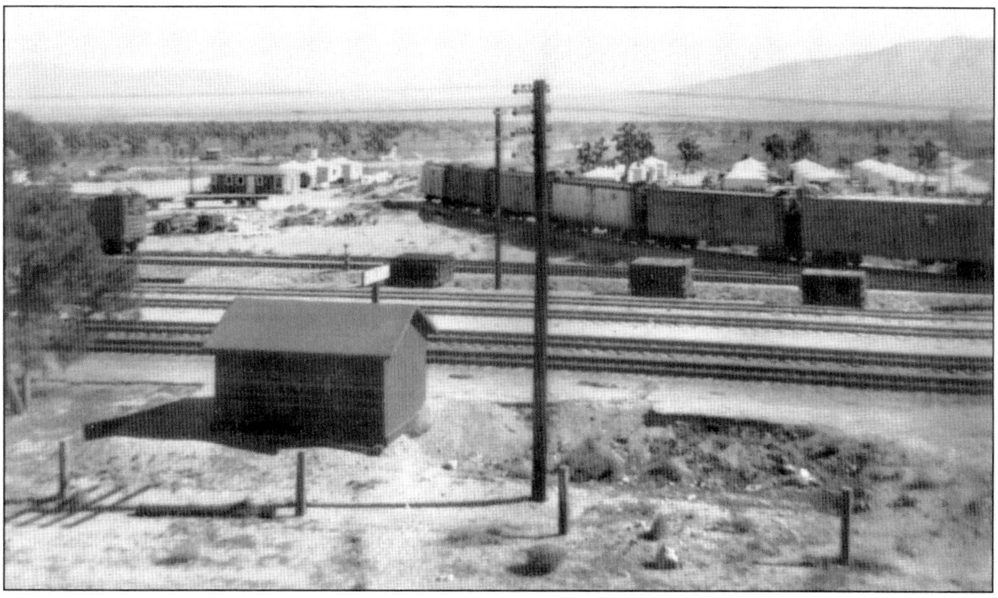

Railroad and Agriculture Meet. In 1949, trains entering the depot area at Hesperia circled around the processing shed for Tatum's potatoes. The Tatum brothers had the largest potato field in Southern California. Hesperia even crowned an annual potato queen. Railroads have been instrumental through the years in transporting food to eager consumers. (RM.)

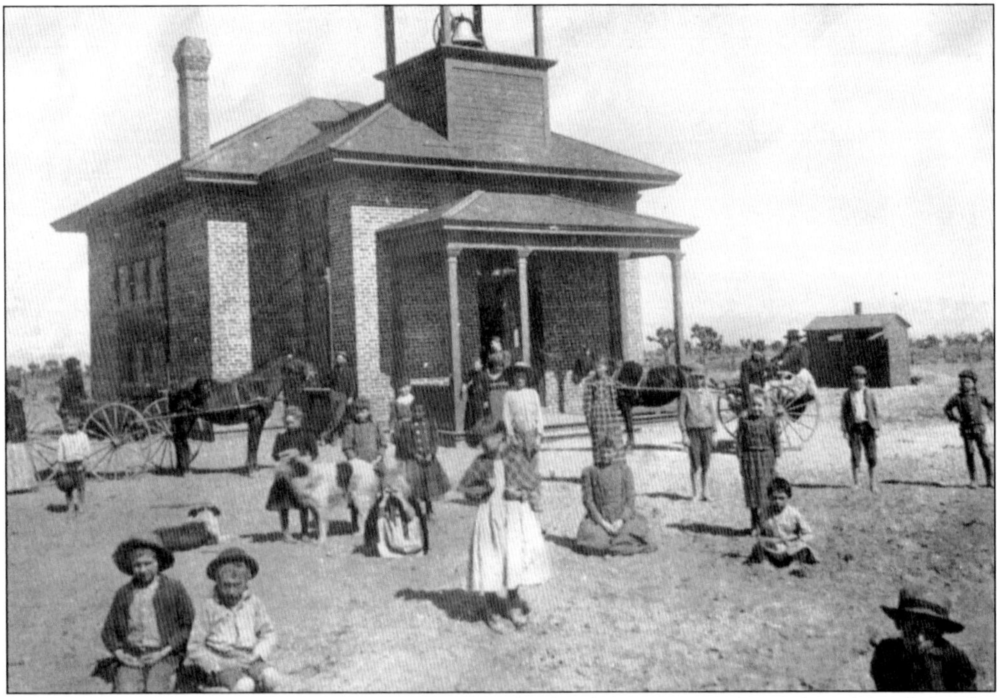

Hesperia School. Hesperia built this substantial school in 1891. Englewood "red fired" bricks, taken by rail to Colton, were transported over the pass by wagon to use with the redwood-framed windows. Children traveled long distances from outlying farms and ranches by horse-drawn wagon if they were lucky. Many of them trudged through the sand and dust. (MHS/VVM.)

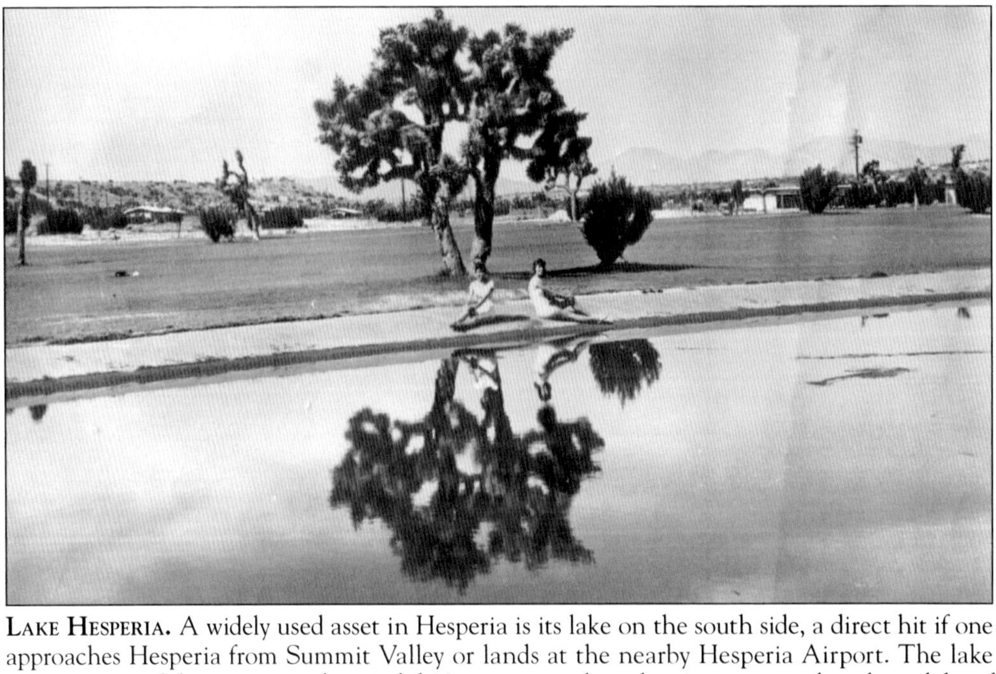

Lake Hesperia. A widely used asset in Hesperia is its lake on the south side, a direct hit if one approaches Hesperia from Summit Valley or lands at the nearby Hesperia Airport. The lake caters more to fishermen now than it did 40 years ago, when the picture was taken, but a lake of several acres is still appreciated in the desert. (MHS/VVM.)

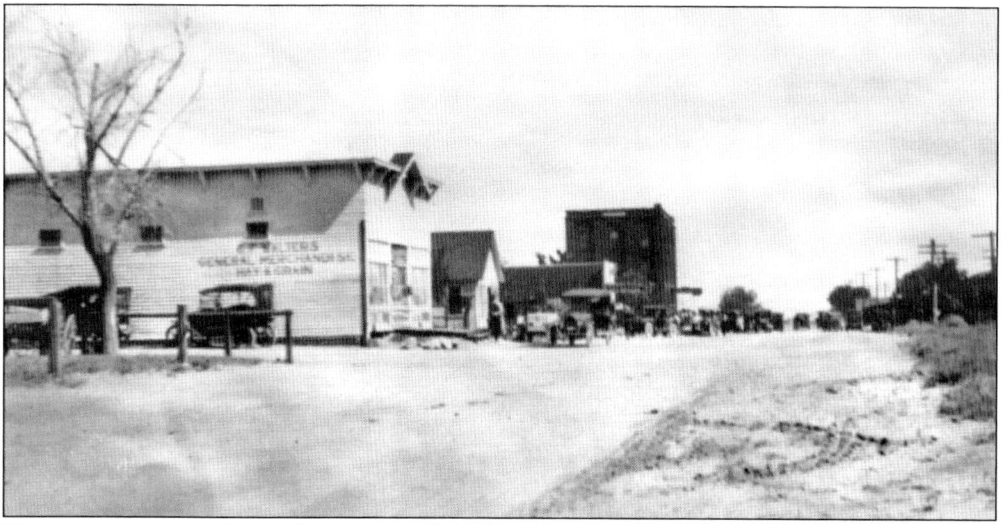

Hesperia of 1917. This early photograph looking north up Hesperia Road from Yucca Street shows C. F. Walters General Merchandise, a hay and grain store. The three-story hotel can be seen in the background. A livery stable stood behind the hotel. South of the photographer's location today, the Main Street overpass dominates the scene. Hesperia was a thriving community until Route 66 was relocated to the west after the 1938 flood. (MHS/VVM.)

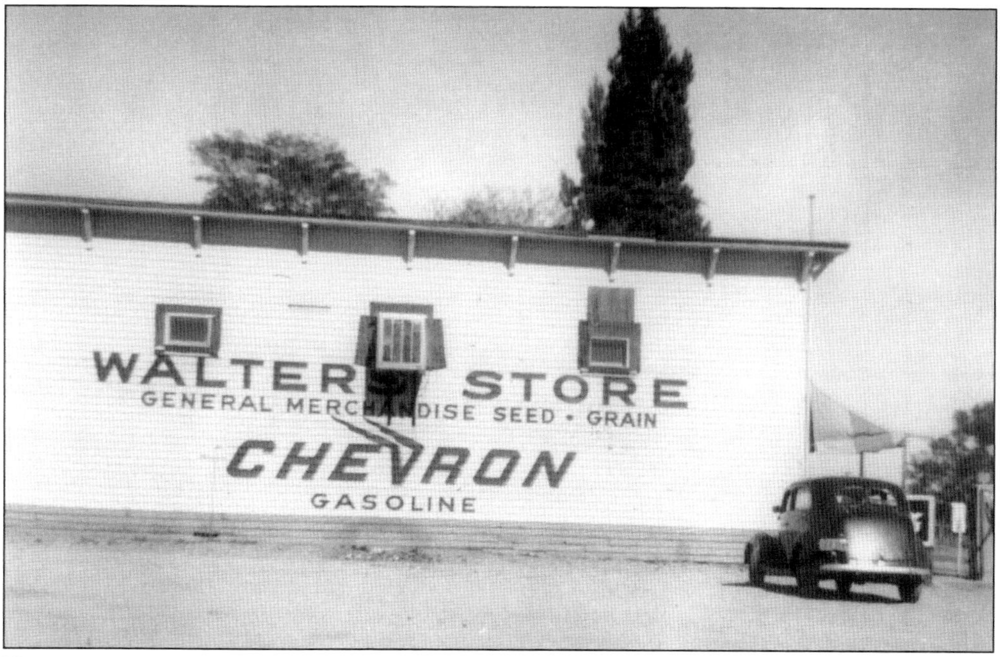

Hesperia of 1949. Walter's store was the only store in Hesperia in 1949. Besides general merchandise, it sold gasoline, seed, and grain. The men who manned the California Division of Forestry building between May and December appreciated having general supplies available to them. (RM.)

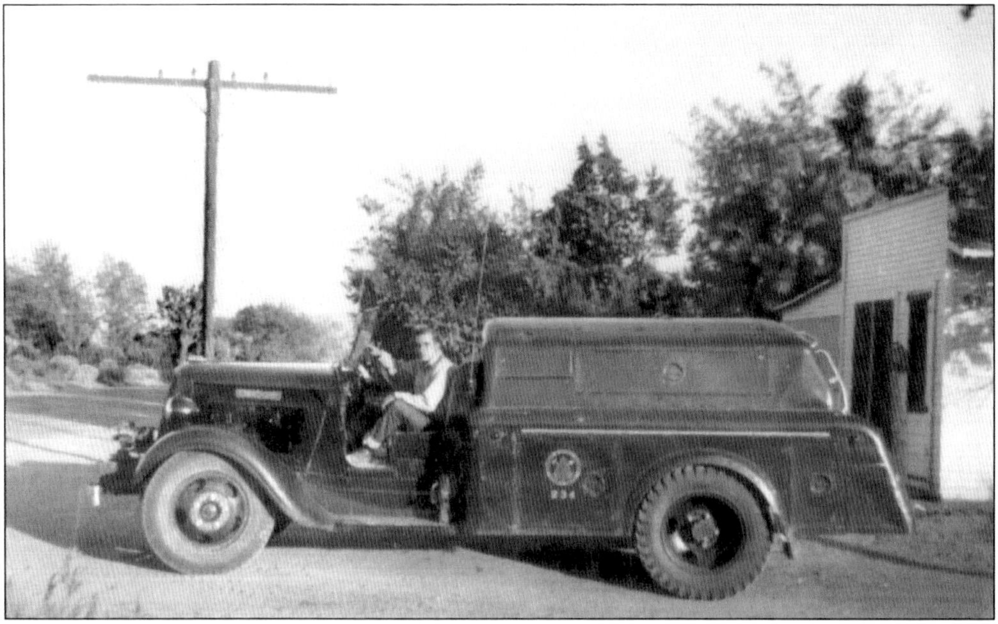

Hesperia's Fire Protection. Bob Mathews, in 1949, sits in one of California Division of Forestry's fire trucks, a late-1930s Dodge. CDF rented this old store building with residence facilities within from May to December each year. It was the first building on Main Street off Route 66. CDF offered fire protection from Oro Grande to Lucerne Valley and provided water for the summit lookout just west of Route 66. (RM.)

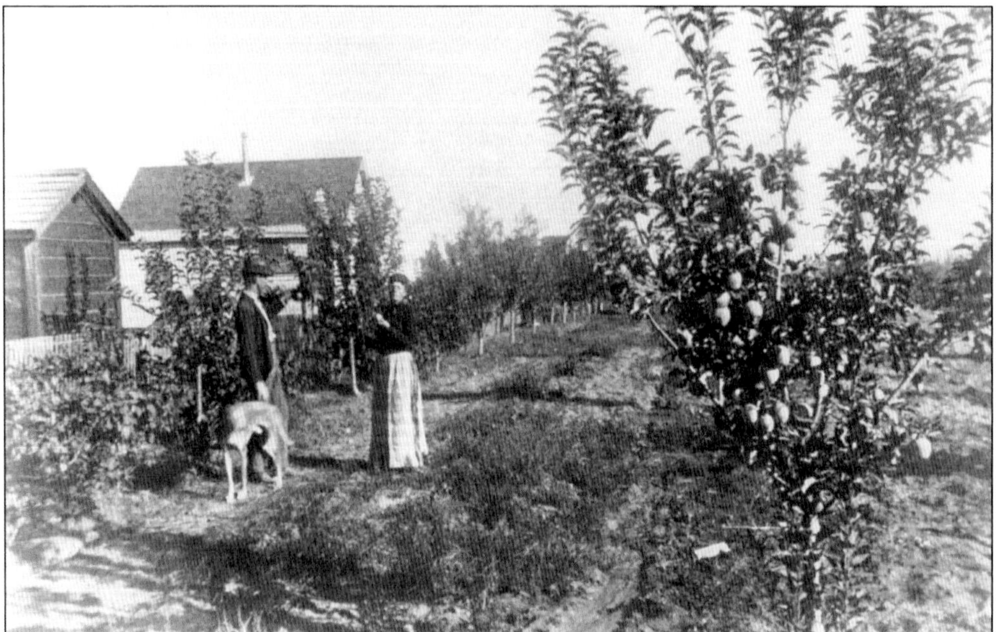

Apple Orchard. As far back as 1891, apple orchards graced the desert. They are no longer seen, having gone the way of most agriculture in modern Southern California. Some peach orchards still survive in the high desert, and Hesperia still has a nursery that provides young peach trees. Desert orchards are susceptible to late freezes. (MHS/VVM.)

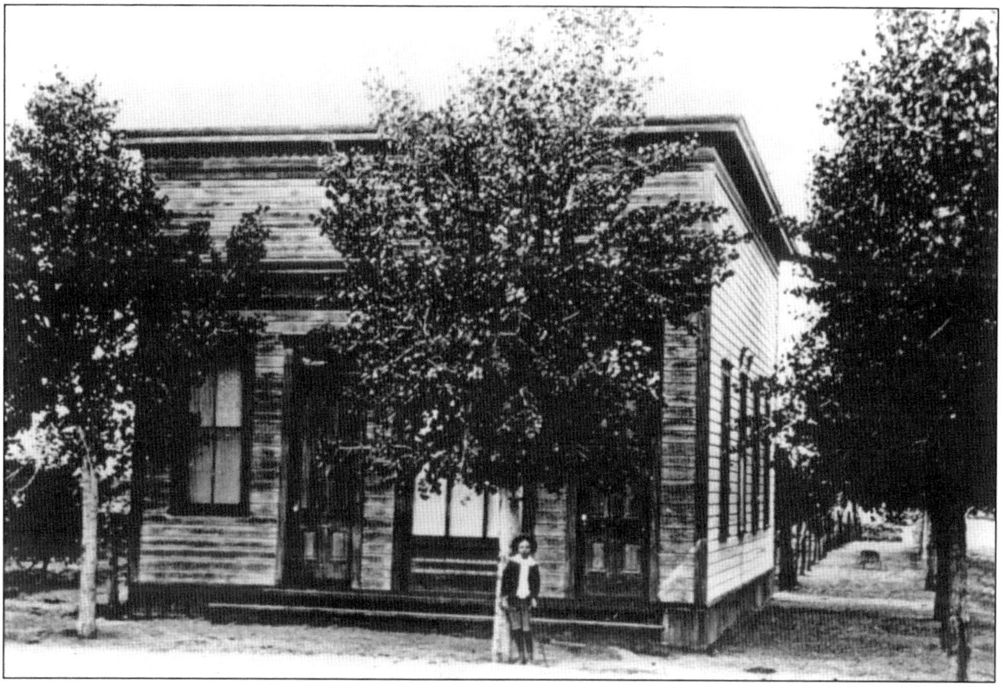

Hesperia Elegance. Two businesses in early Hesperia that added a touch of elegance to the town were Mrs. Arrel's stationery store (above), which also housed the post office, and Mrs. C. B. Shaw's cottage (below), which illustrates the use of extensive porches to protect people from the hot summer sun. Mrs. Arrel was the postmistress. The Shaw cottage was located on Shaw's 180 acres of grapes. (Both, MHS/VVM.)

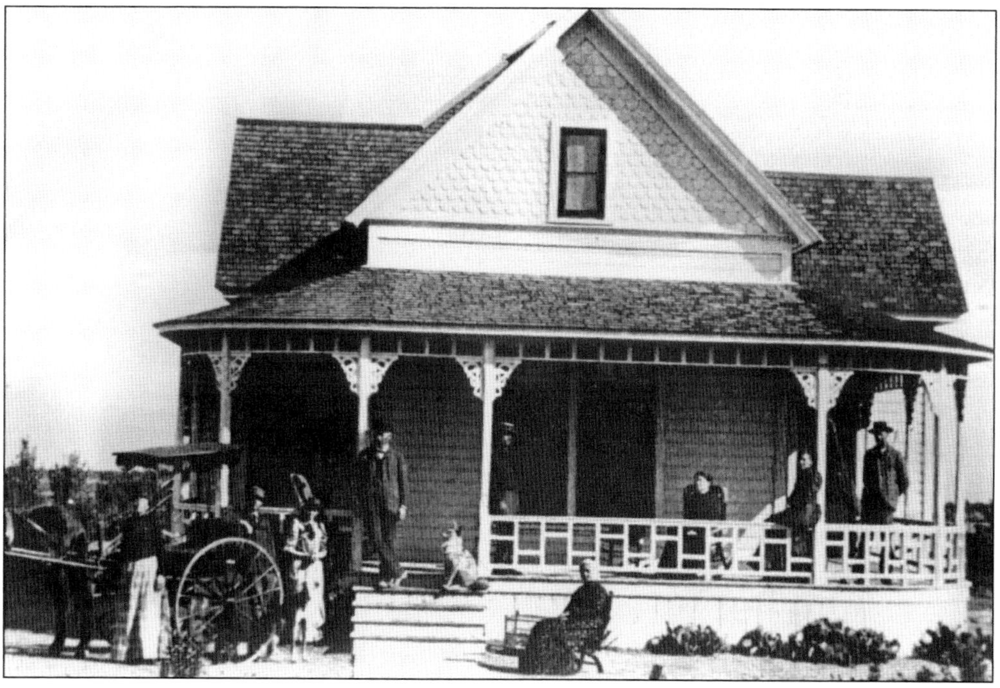

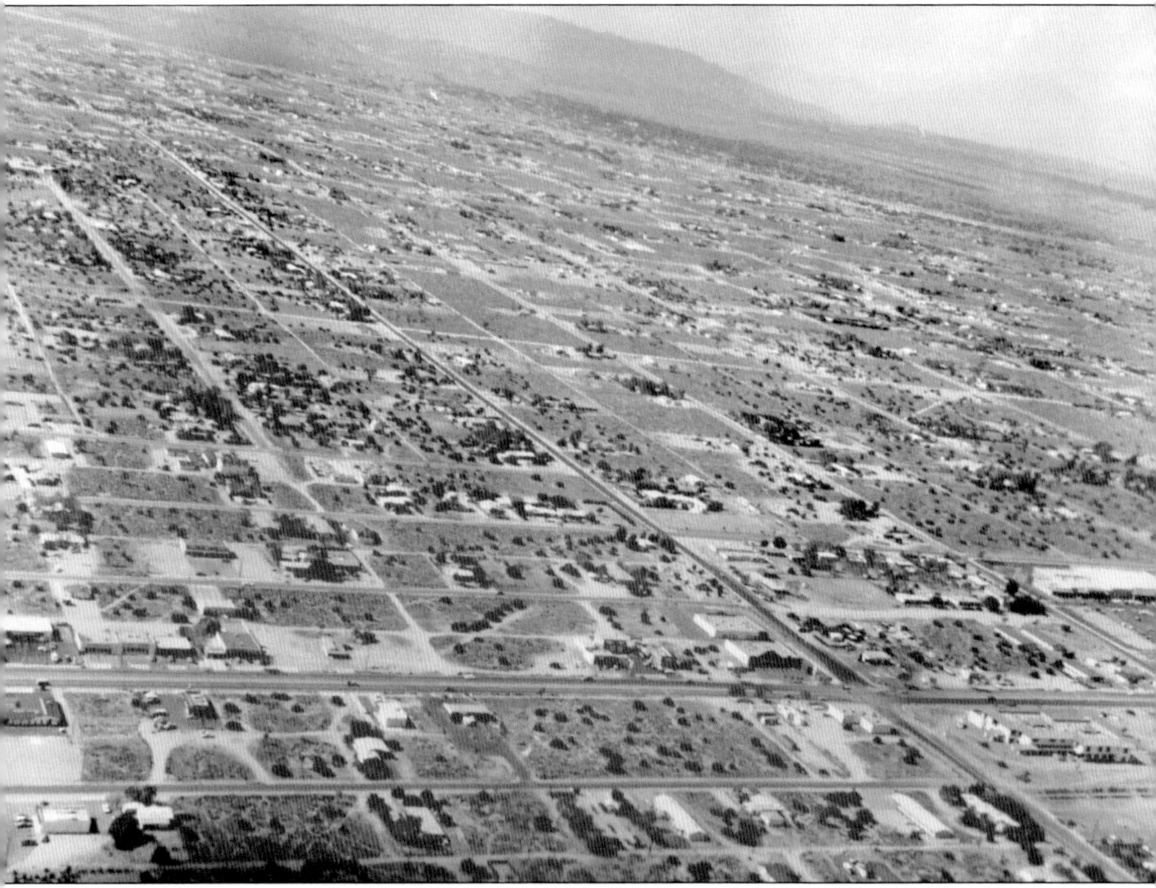

Recent Hesperia. It is easy to see, comparing this aerial photograph with some of the earlier pictures, that Hesperia is no longer a quiet little rural town. Its growth in contemporary times has been phenomenal, and out in the desert, there seems to always be plenty of room to stretch and grow, especially for a city whose water was rated number one in the nation. Hesperia's population in 2000 was 62,582, and it is estimated to be over 80,000 less than a decade later. Hesperia's elevation is from 3,200 to 4,000 feet above sea level. The Mojave River flows north on Hesperia's east side, and the California Aqueduct divides the city on the west side before it goes underground to Silverwood Lake. The city sits on silty sand and volcanic rock. Mormons settled there in 1854, and the railroad contributed much to its layout in 1891. (MHS/VVM.)

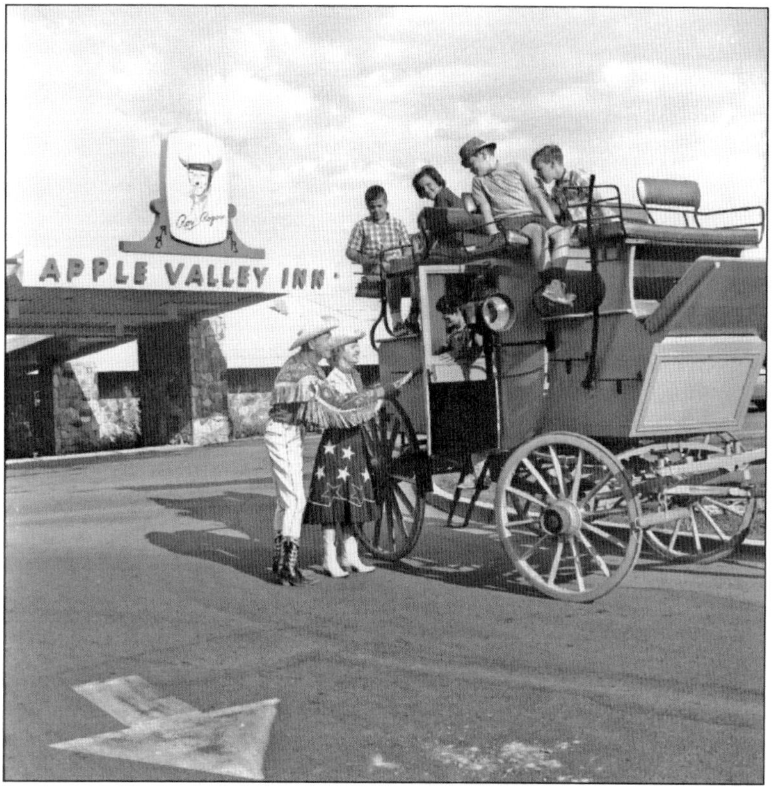

Apple Valley. Off the beaten track of railroad and highway, Apple Valley is northeast of Hesperia and east of Victorville. Roy Rogers and Dale Evans (pictured at right) put Apple Valley on the map with their museum (now in Branson, Missouri) and Apple Valley Inn. That and several other dude ranches like Yucca Loma and Murray's Ranch pulled stars and dignitaries of all kinds into Apple Valley. (MHS/VVM.)

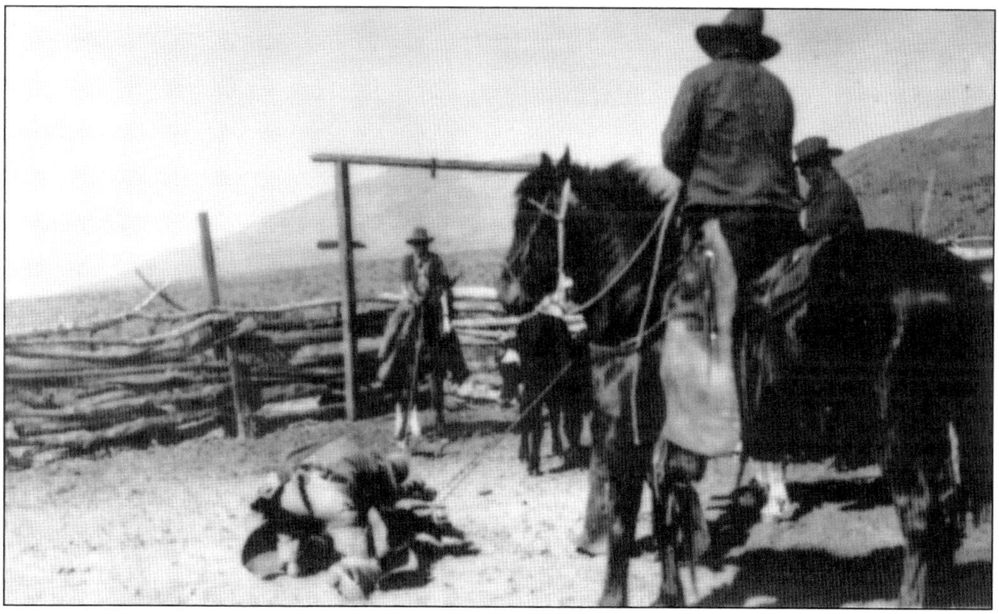

Real Ranching. The Hitchcock and McGinnis Ranches in Apple Valley in 1933 stretched all the way to Deep Creek, where headquarters were located. Roy Rogers and other actors like Tom Mix and William S. Hart thrilled people with their desert-filmed, Hollywood-style ranching activities, but the ranch cowboys did the real thing. In this picture, they are branding calves to be moved to the hills. (MHS/VVM.)

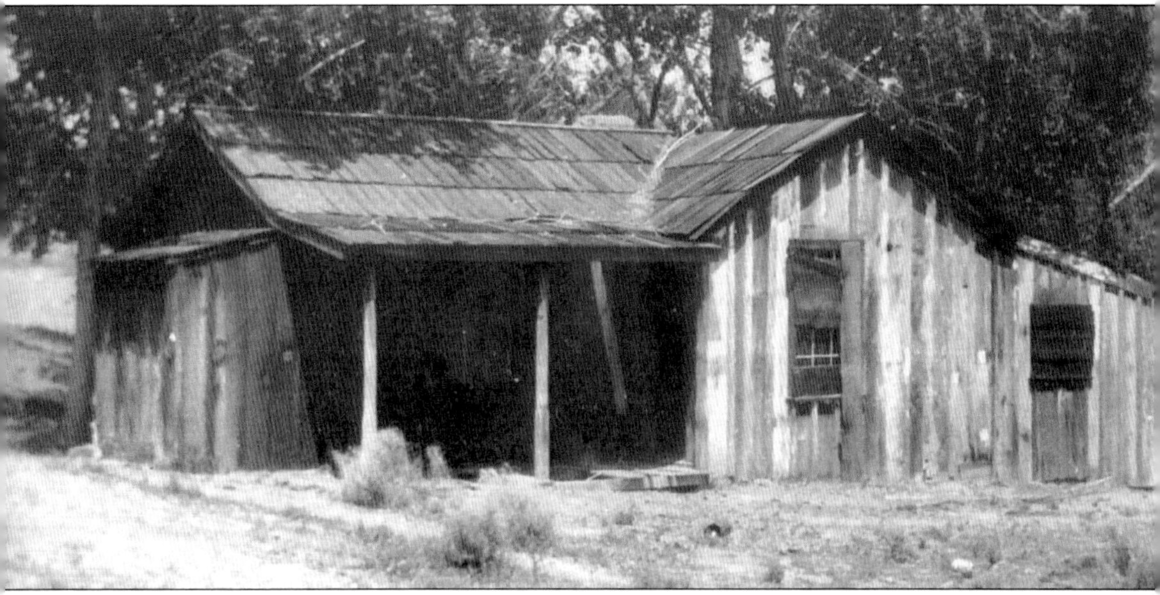

VICTOR VALLEY'S FIRST SETTLER. Aaron Lane settled at the lower crossing of the Mojave River by 1858 for his health. He opened a travelers' station, offering food, lodging, and groceries to travelers. He even served Lt. Edward F. Beale, head of the government's camel caravan, in 1860. Alfalfa had only been in the United States for seven years when Lane started raising that "green gold." The Arabic word *alfacfacah* means the best fodder or feed. In Australia, it is called Lucerne. Lane also raised barley and corn, and he partnered with James Fears of Cajon Pass on the Monarch claim in the Ord Mountain Mining District. The lower crossing of the Mojave is north of Victorville near Oro Grande (Coarse Gold), but it was called Lane's Crossing for years. Back then, the Mojave River was bordered by lush vegetation that attracted game as large as deer and antelope. (MHS/VVM.)

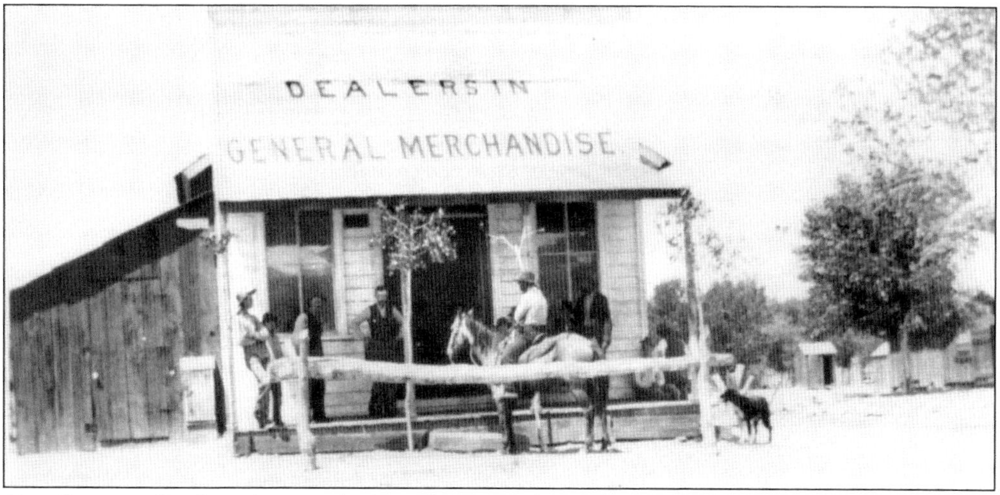

ORO GRANDE. Back in those early days, Oro Grande was bigger than Victor. The two towns are only a few miles apart. Pictured is George W. Varney's store in 1889. The name of the store is covered with canvas, as Varney had just purchased it and had not yet painted on his name. The donor of the photograph is a relative of the store owner. (RM.)

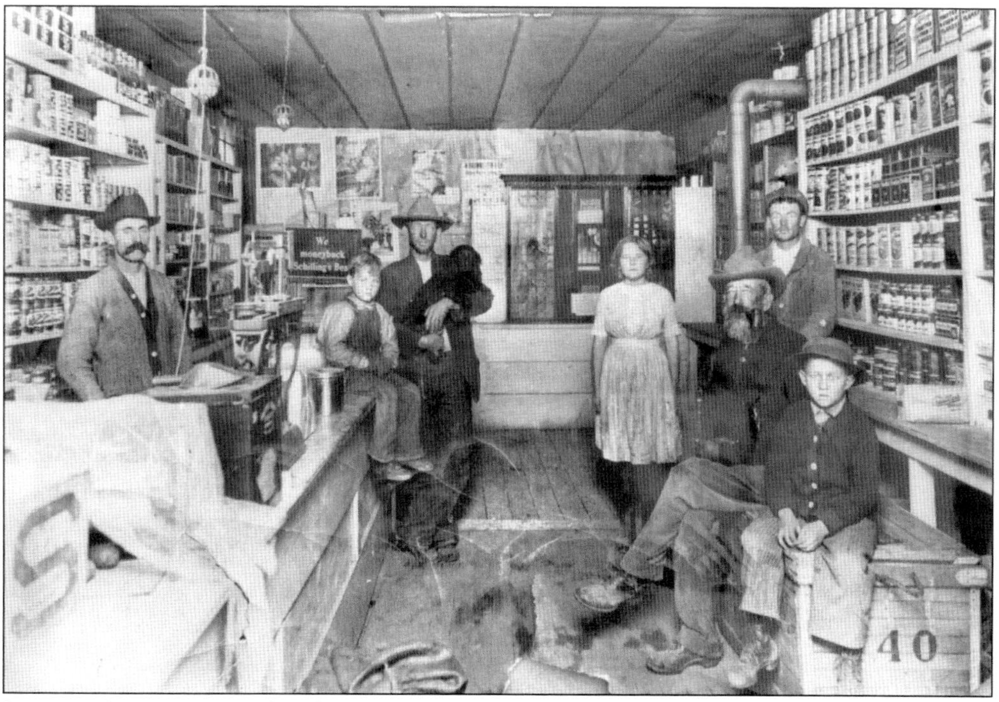

INSIDE A STORE. Pictured is the inside of an Oro Grande store and post office. It is compact and cozy, but almost anything a consumer of the late 1800s might want is there. In addition, the store was a gathering place where local residents could meet and catch up on the news and gossip. (SBHPS.)

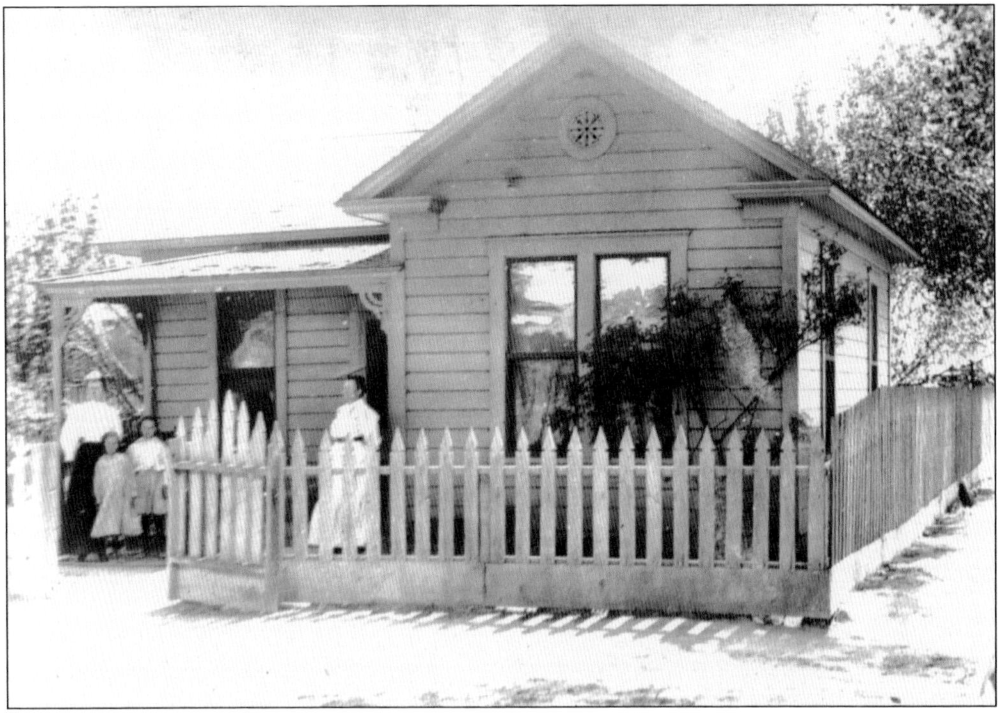

Turner Ranch and Home. In the 1880s, the Turner family bought Aaron Lane's holdings and developed them into a very successful farming venture. They also started businesses in Victorville: a store and a hotel. The Turner House hotel was built on the corner of Seventh and D Streets in 1893 and was famous for good meals and clean beds. It was moved around the corner onto Seventh Street when the Stewart Hotel was built in 1910. A Turner residence, pictured above, was also in Victorville. Below is one of the fine structures on the Turner Ranch. For a time, at least three generations lived in various houses on the ranch. Even when individuals worked in Victorville instead of on the farm, they often lived on the farm. (Both, MHS/VVM.)

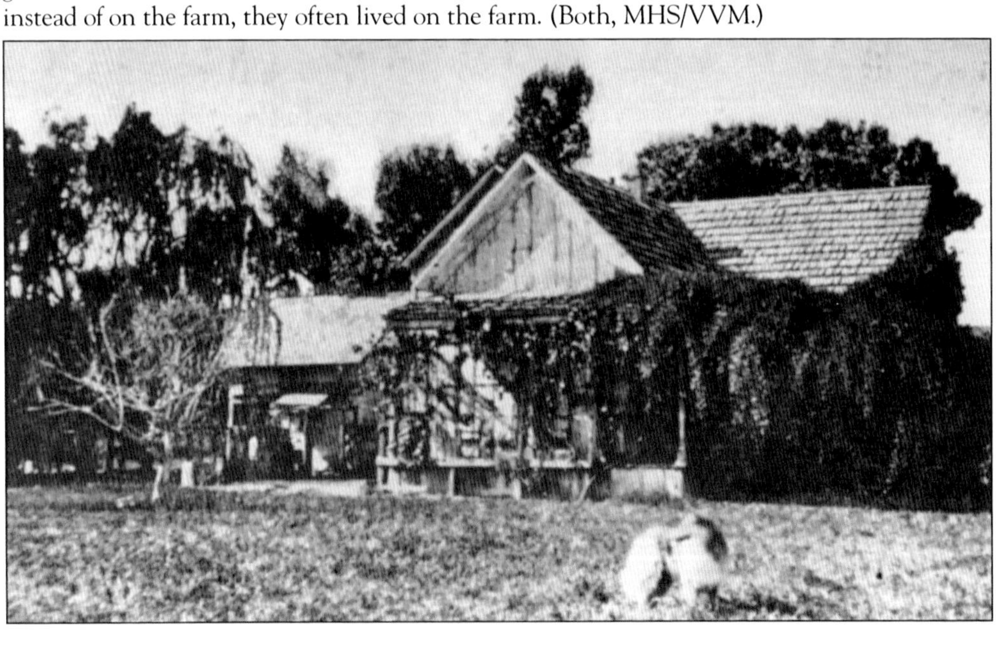

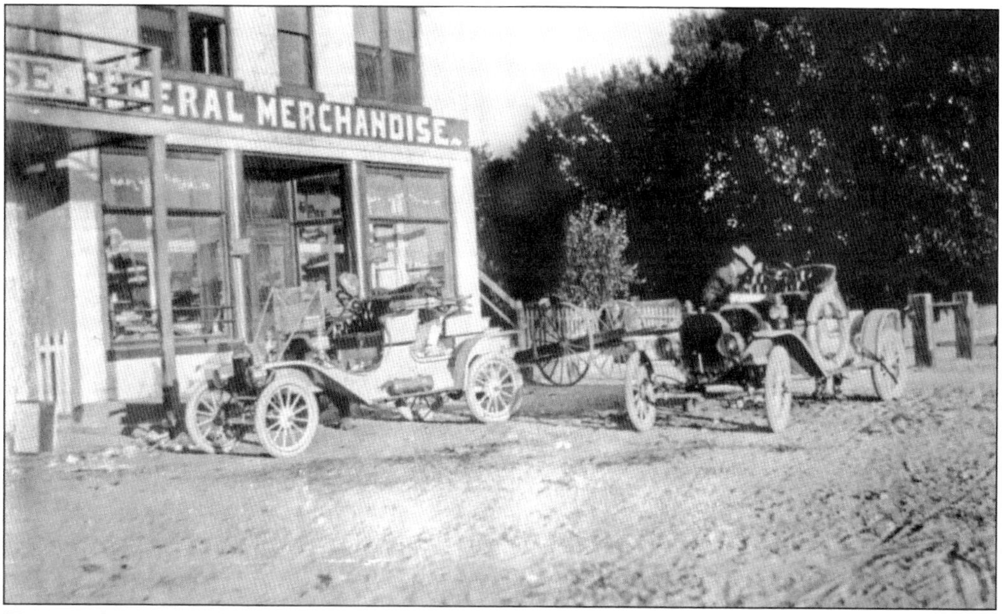

Turner Stores. Robert and Susan Turner bought vacant land in Victor, a block bounded by present Seventh, D, Sixth, and C Streets. Above is Turner's General Merchandise Store, built by Robert and Susan's son John C. on D Street. John also built one of the first concrete buildings in California using railroad rail for reinforcement. He served as postmaster, justice of the peace, and a member of the County Board of Supervisors, whose district was larger than some eastern states. He worked on the construction of South West Portland Cement Company in 1917, and Turner freight wagons using 10 or 12 horses hauled cement to Big Bear for the dam. Below is Turner's wagon headed for a satellite store in Big Bear in 1903. The second wagon contained feed and equipment for the horses. The trip took a week. (Above, MHS/VVM; below, AHCRFL.)

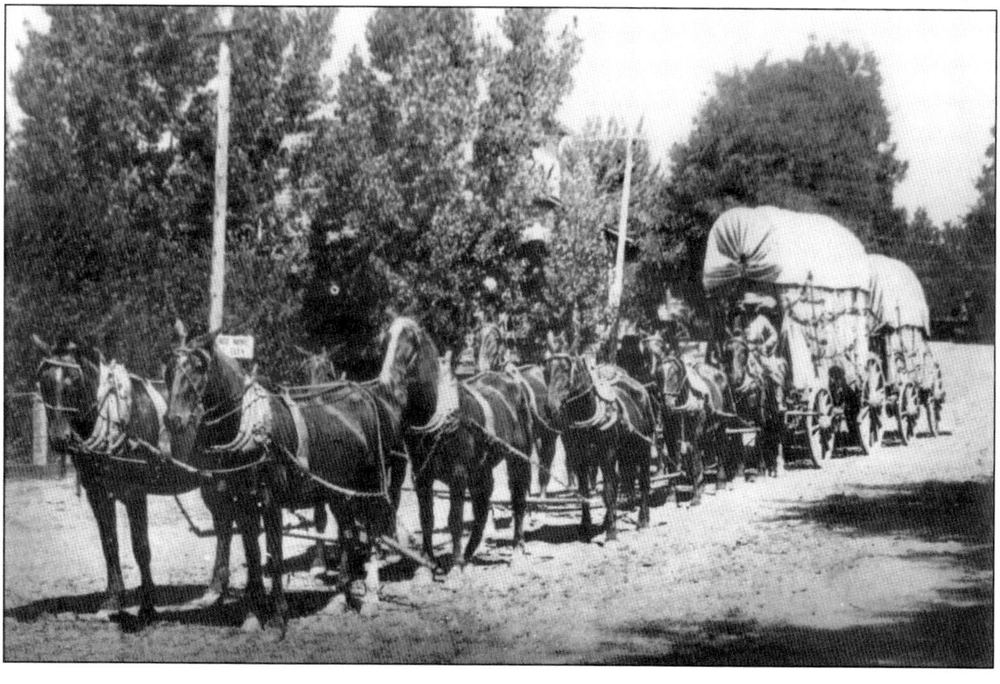

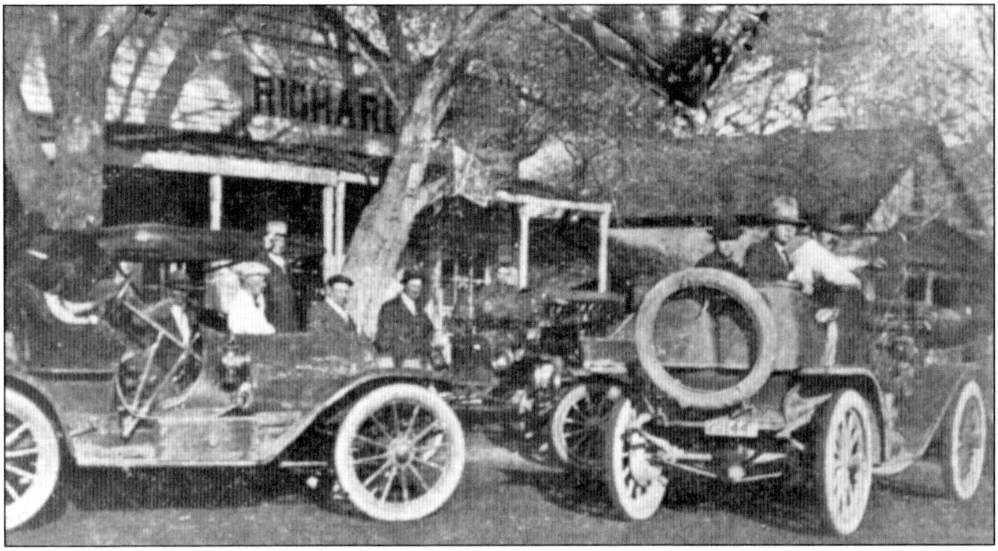

Richardson's Store. The Turners were not the only ones who ran businesses in early Victorville. Above, patrons of Richardson's Mercantile gather after doing business. Richardson's Store was across the railroad track from Turner's with the Mojave River on the other side of the store. Richardson's ranch was a little past Turner's, and it also earned a modern street name. (MHS/VVM.)

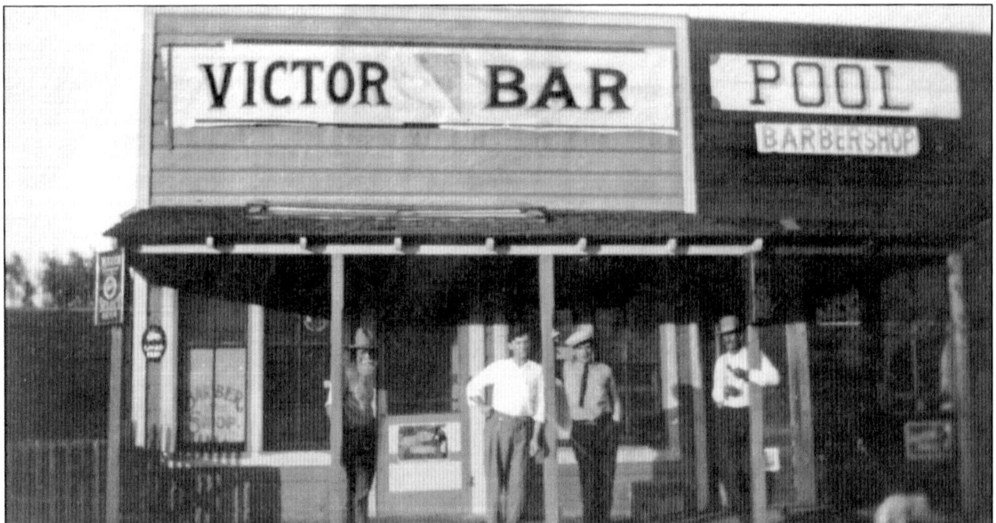

Victor Bar. Victor was the name of the town until the post office requested a name change between 1899 and 1901. At that time, Nettie Bemis Turner was postmistress, and she reported much confusion between the names of Victor, California, and Victor, Colorado. The building above contained the bar, pool hall, and barbershop. After the name change, Victorville Pool Hall took over. This 1916 picture may have been a reenactment. (MHS/VVM.)

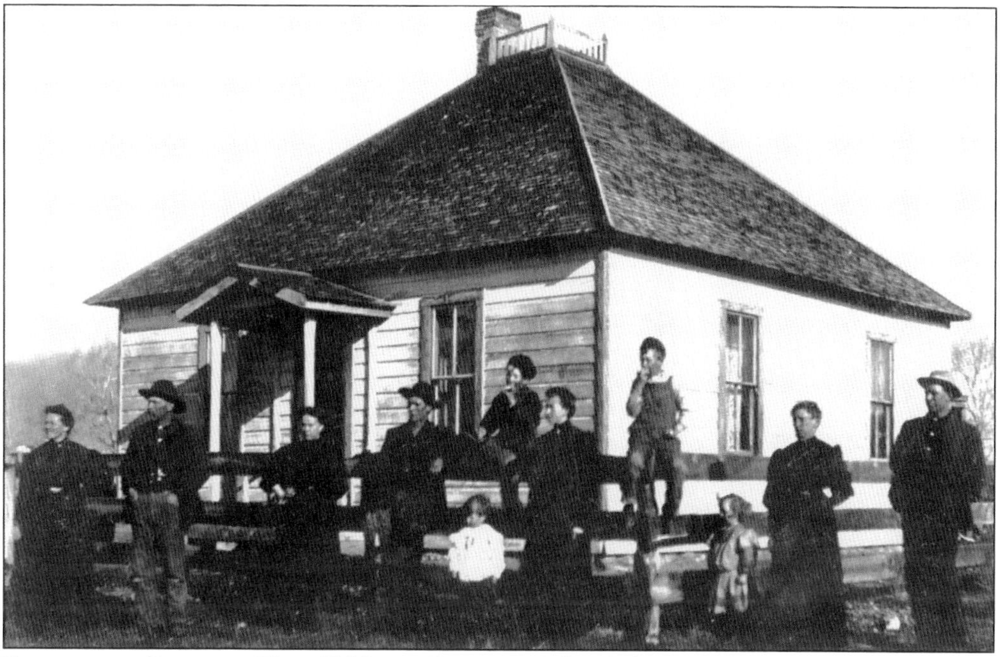

Elementary Schools. The old Victor Grammar School also served as a community center. This photograph was taken before 1890. The first Victorville School opened around the dawn into the 20th century, not too many years after the name changed. In 1914, attendance doubled when the Portland Cement Plant opened. The school had to be expanded, and a second teacher was hired. (MHS/VVM.)

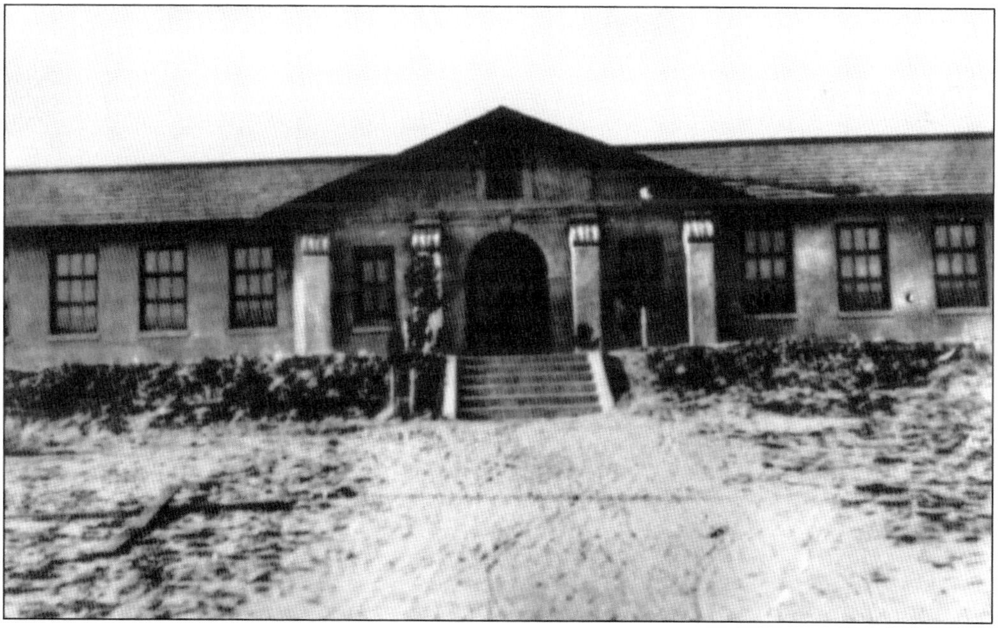

High School. Victorville Union High School had an early start. It was a proud structure in 1917 and has continued that grand tradition. When the new high school was constructed, this building became the junior high school. Before 1917, youth seeking a high school education often lived with relatives or family friends who lived where a high school was available. (MHS/VVM.)

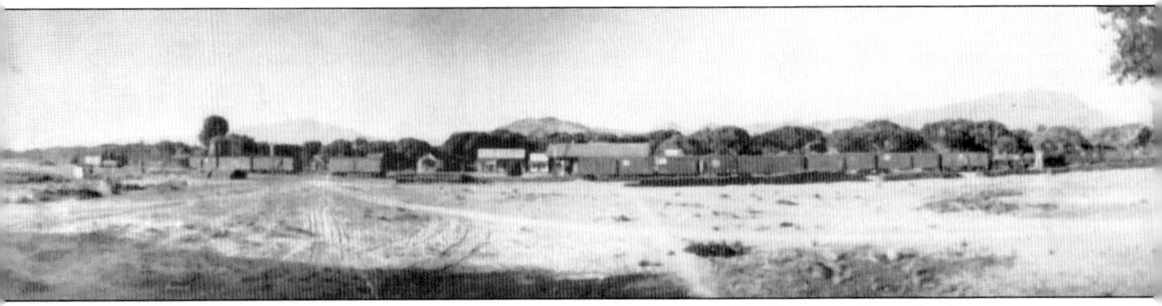

Victorville Panorama. This 1902 panorama of the Victorville depot and nearby businesses was taken from the roof of the Turner House (hotel). At that time, urban growth was minimal. In 1890, Victor, located 40 miles northeast of the county seat by California Southern Railway, was said to be near "the Mojave River, which supplies a fine supply of good water, [it has] charming scenery," according to a county promotional brochure. The population in 1890 was about 300, and the town had a post office with two daily mails, telegraph and express offices, a church, a school, two general merchandise stores, and a blacksmith shop. "The town is famous for fine marble and granite quarries." (MHS/VVM.)

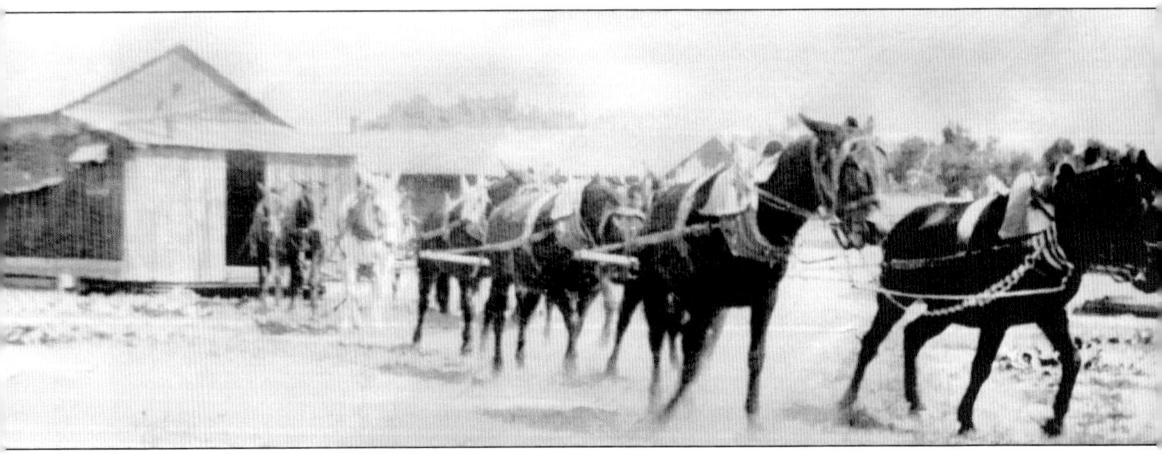

Mobile Buildings. Moving buildings was popular in older times. As the picture above shows, this was accomplished by horse or mule teams in the early high desert days. (MHS/VVM.)

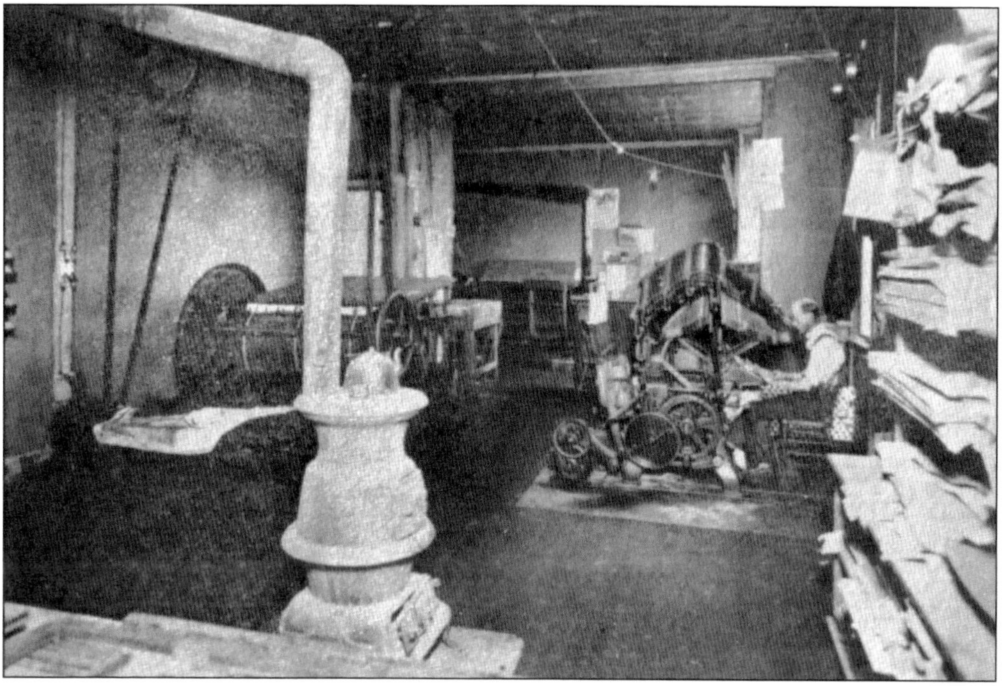

The Newspaper. Pictured is Cliff Moon, editor of the *Victor Valley News Herald*, in 1923. The Moons bought the paper from Walker Jones in 1917 and ran it for 29 years. Allen Fletcher was the editor in 1915. The paper was started in 1913 by A. Murphy, who sold it to Arthur Hull, who gave it the name *Herald*. Printing posters, leaflets, and flyers supplemented the newspaper's income. (MHS/VVM.)

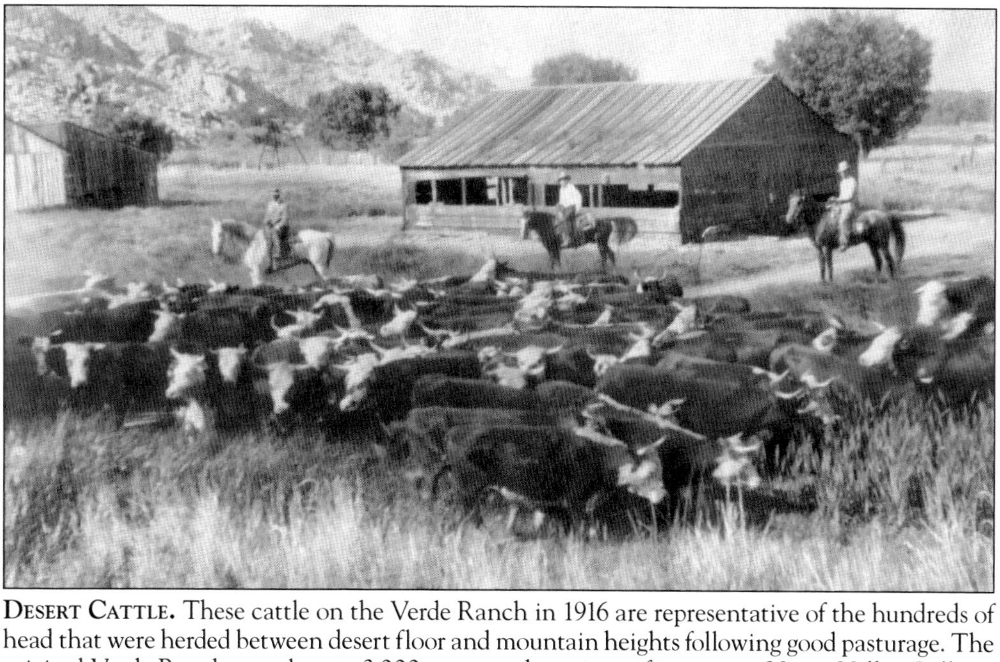

Desert Cattle. These cattle on the Verde Ranch in 1916 are representative of the hundreds of head that were herded between desert floor and mountain heights following good pasturage. The original Verde Ranch was close to 3,000 acres, and portions of it now are Victor Valley College, Spring Valley Lake, and Mojave Narrows Regional Park. (MHS/VVM.)

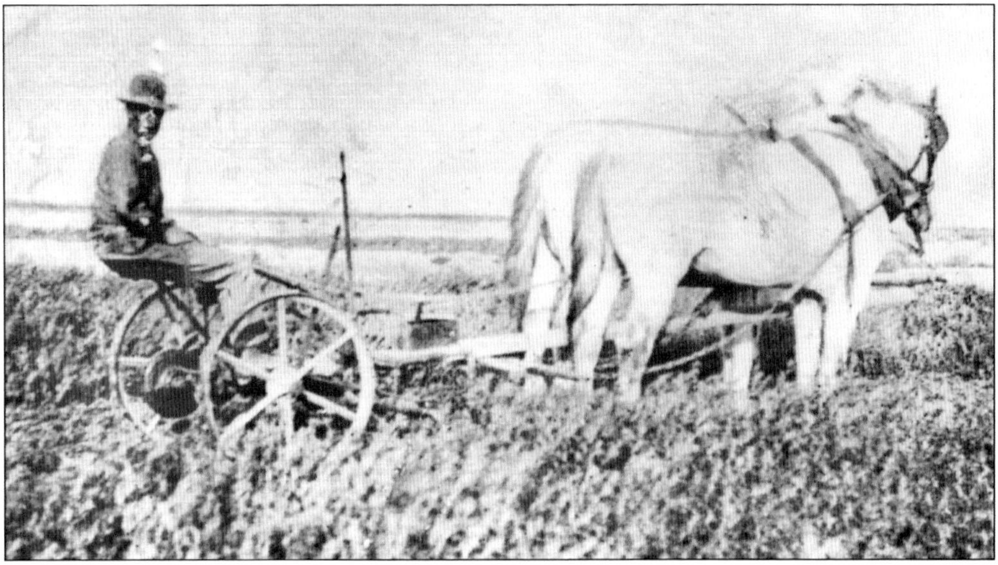

VERDE RANCH. In about 1870, John Brown Jr. bought land near Victorville, where his brothers, James and Joseph, developed a ranch. In 1901, they sold it to John A. Cole, who had also owned ranches in Devore, Glen Helen, and Summit Valley. Cole named it Verde ("Green") Ranch. In the early 1900s, above, plowing and reaping were done by horse team. Below, in the 1940s, horses were still being used for haying. Cole sold to a Mr. Grier, who sold to Kemper and Litte Belle Campbell in 1924, and it was renamed the Kemper Campbell Ranch. Their partner, A. W. Sorenson, took the southern part and sold it to Al Kalin of Kalin Ranch. Another large desert ranch was Jess Ranch, one of the largest turkey farms in the state. Jess Ranch is now a senior community and shopping center. (Both, MHS/VVM.)

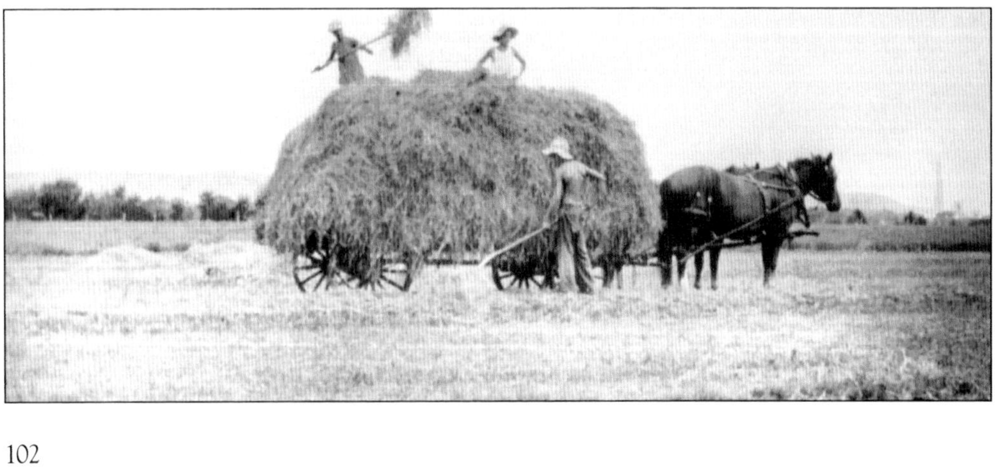

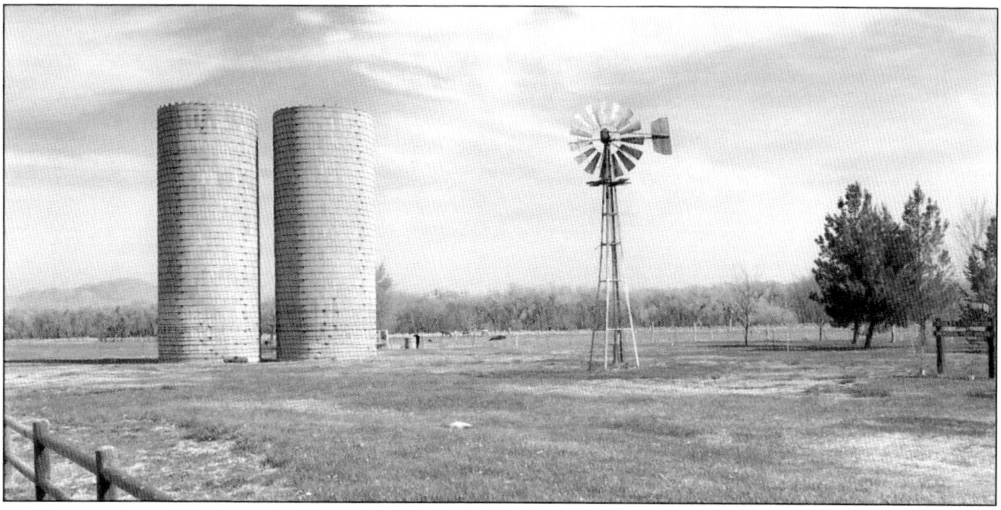

Mojave Narrows Regional Park. The windmill and silos attest to the working background of the park when it was Kemper Campbell or North Verde Ranch. The camels, perhaps to remind people they did trek through Mojave Desert, and alpacas are new additions. The park also offers riparian habitats, wetlands, picnicking, camping, playgrounds, Pelican Lake, riding trails, hay rides, and boating on Horseshoe Lake. Mojave Narrows Park also hosts the annual Huck Finn Jubilee country and bluegrass festival on Father's Day weekend. (Both, AH.)

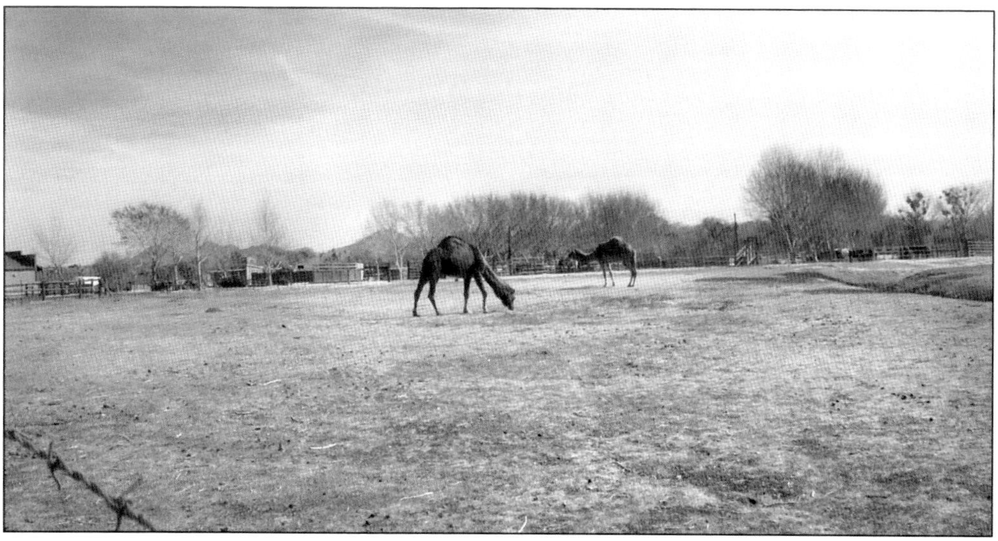

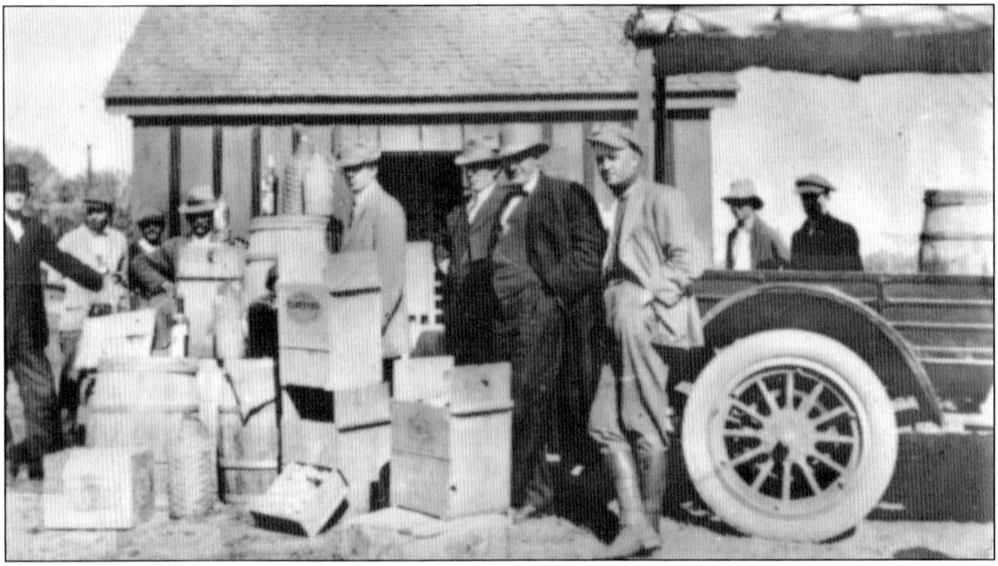

VICTORVILLE LAW. Constable Edward Dulch and the sheriff's men ponder what to do with confiscated bootleg liquor. Bootlegging was also popular in Cajon Pass, where older residents remember seeing stills blowing up. But many families only survived because of income from bootleg. Below is the first Victorville Sheriff's Office. The sheriffs shared their building at different times with the constable, military police, highway patrol, Red Cross, justice court, county welfare, a marriage parlor, brand inspector, notary public, dynamite permits, and other county agencies. County sheriffs are the contracted police for all the communities mentioned in this book. (Both, MHS/VVM.)

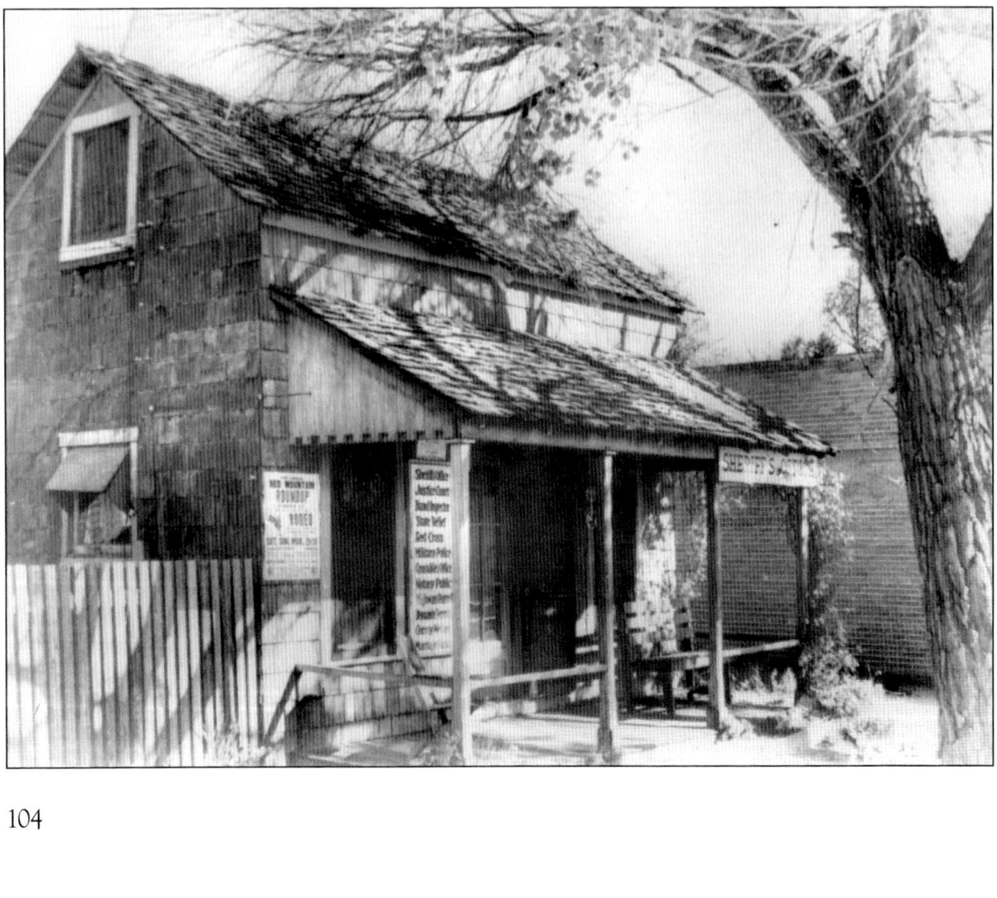

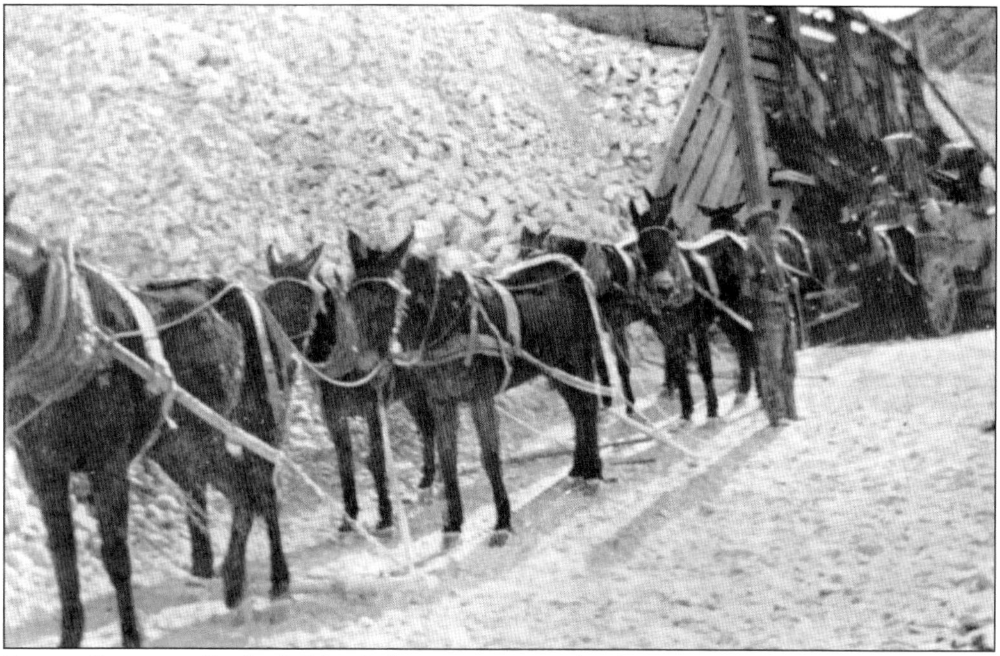

Desert Quarries. Rock of all kinds for many purposes has been mined from desert quarries and mine shafts. In this instance, the mule team hauls lime rock to be used in processing sugar beets raised in Chino Valley. The rock slides down the chutes into the wagons. In 1900, such quarries shipped 250 tons of rock each day. (MHS/VVM.)

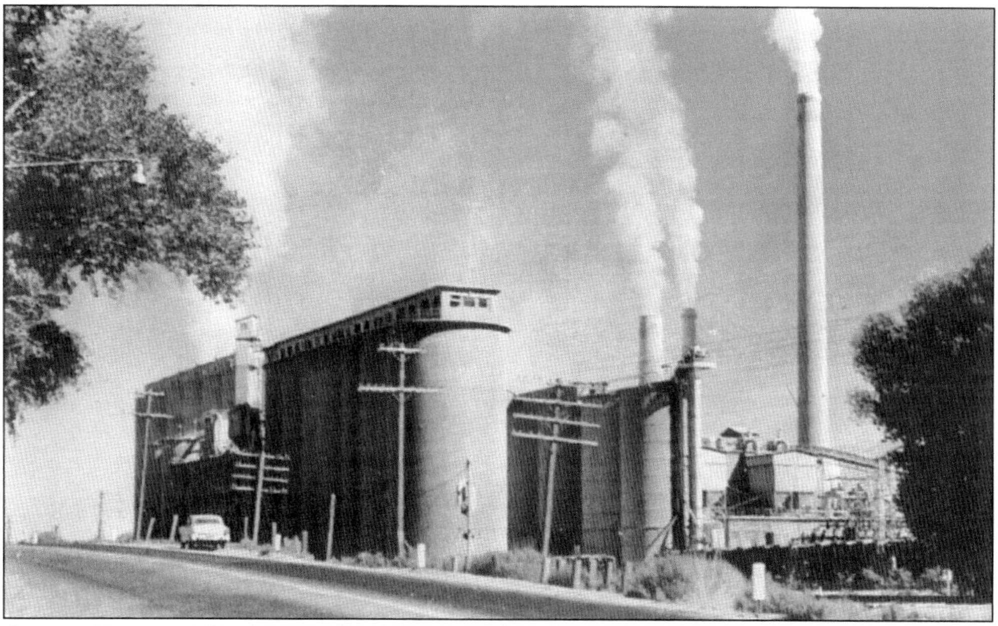

Cement Plants. The first Portland Cement plant located in Victorville in 1914, and one of the Victorville cement plants was the first to use computers in cement production. Lime kilns were no longer needed once cement production occurred locally. Portland cement is a lime/clay mixture that is heated and pulverized. In 1922, the plant produced 12,500 barrels a day, had 125 employees, and kept a $20,000 monthly payroll. (MHS/VVM.)

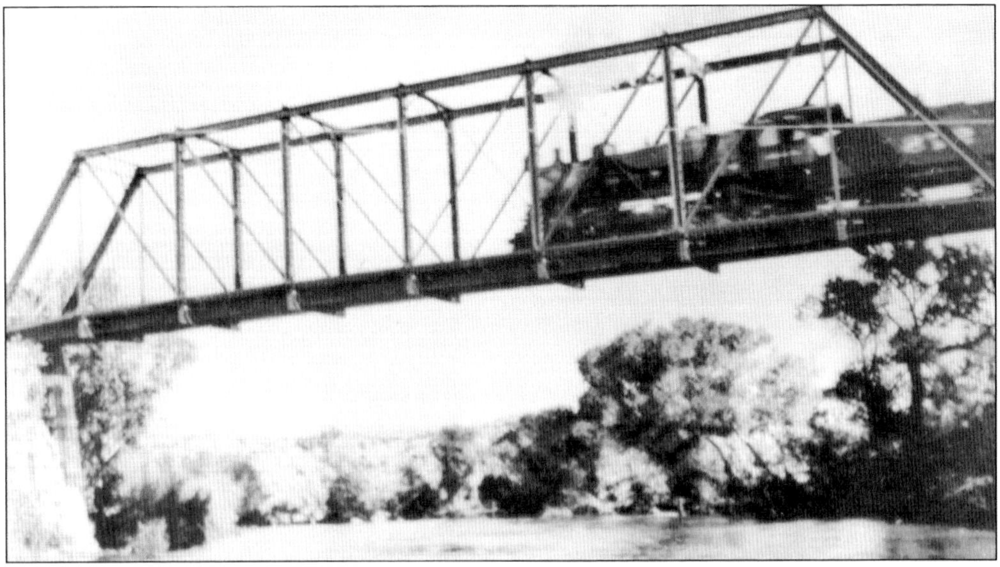

Crossing the Mojave River. Whether the river is on the surface or subterranean, crossing can pose a problem. Only two safe crossings were used by early pioneers. Quicksand was a deadly hazard along much of the river. The railroad bridge over the lower narrows was built in 1916. The postcard below shows the old "rainbow" bridge, the second attempt to build a road over the Mojave River, as well as the new bridge that completes Highway 18 to Apple Valley at the upper narrows. The "rainbow" bridge replaced the first bridge, which collapsed. (Both, MHS/VVM.)

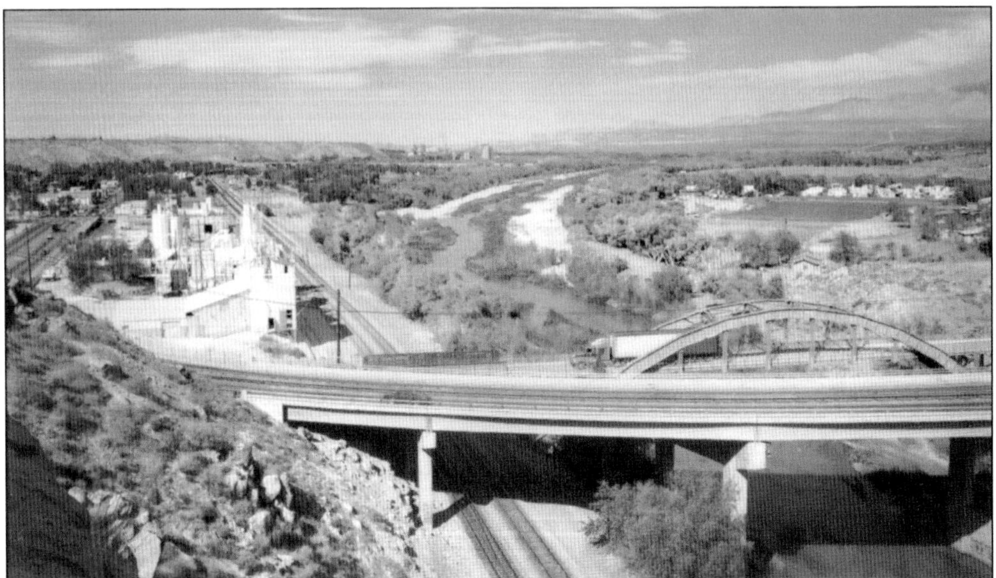

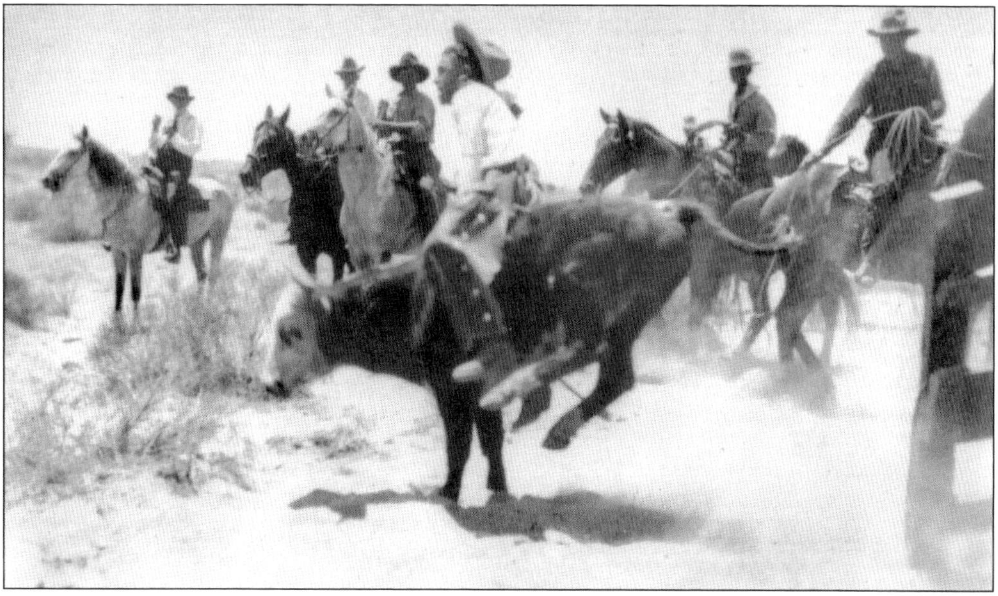

HORSE ACTIVITIES POPULAR. From the 1920s through the 1950s, both in the high desert and Cajon Pass, rodeos and gymkhanas abounded. Several horse groups thrived in the desert, and Devore Rough Riders drew members from all over the San Bernardino Valley. The picture is of a Victorville rodeo in the 1920s. Both Devore and Victorville still host rodeos, and equestrian activities abound throughout Cajon Pass. (MHS/VVM.)

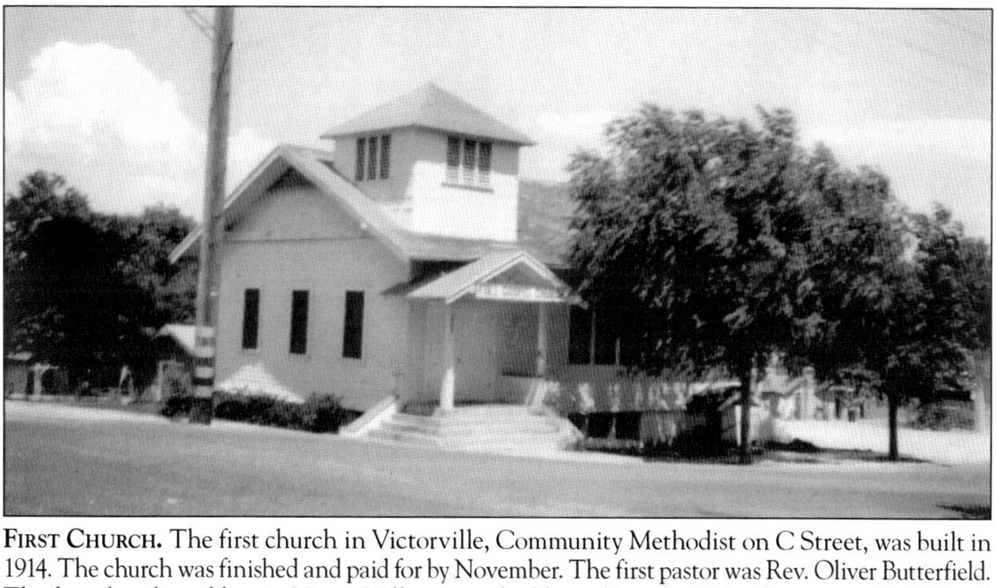

FIRST CHURCH. The first church in Victorville, Community Methodist on C Street, was built in 1914. The church was finished and paid for by November. The first pastor was Rev. Oliver Butterfield. The first church wedding in Victor Valley was a double wedding in 1915, when sisters Harriet and Laurestine Dinsmoor married Ralph Webb and Allen Fletcher, respectively. This church became Methodist Episcopal, then Full Gospel, and finally Assembly of God. (MHS/VVM.)

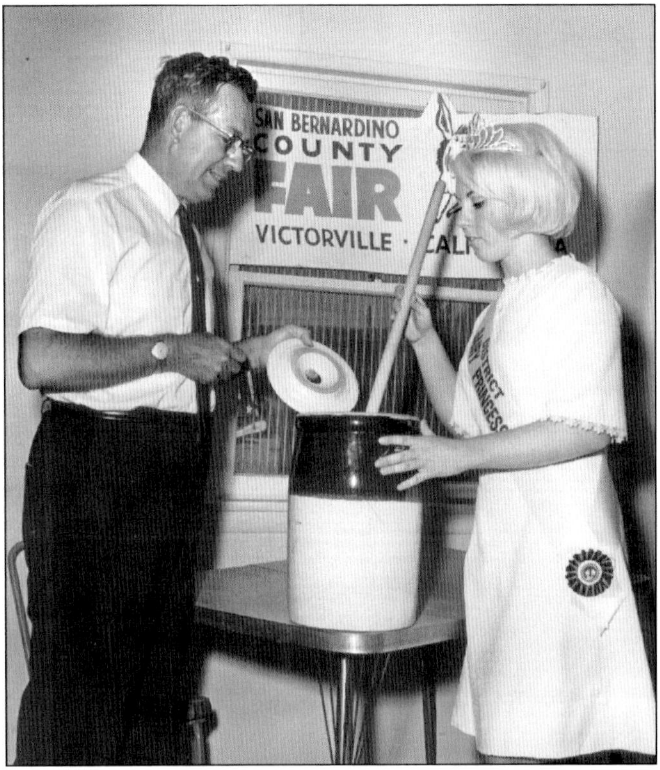

San Bernardino County Fair. Victorville has been home to the San Bernardino County Fair since Clifford Moon held the first one in the Goodrich Garage building before 1920 and officially recorded the name. Since the fairgrounds are right downtown along Route 66, the new slogan for the fair is "Get Your Kicks." San Bernardino County Fair has hosted all kinds of 4-H and Future Farmers of America events through the years, as well as "open division" (adult) livestock competitions, rodeos, gem shows, and music attractions. The queens and princesses of the fair, one pictured from the 1960s, assist with all kinds of activities, yes, even churning butter. (Both, MHS/VVM.)

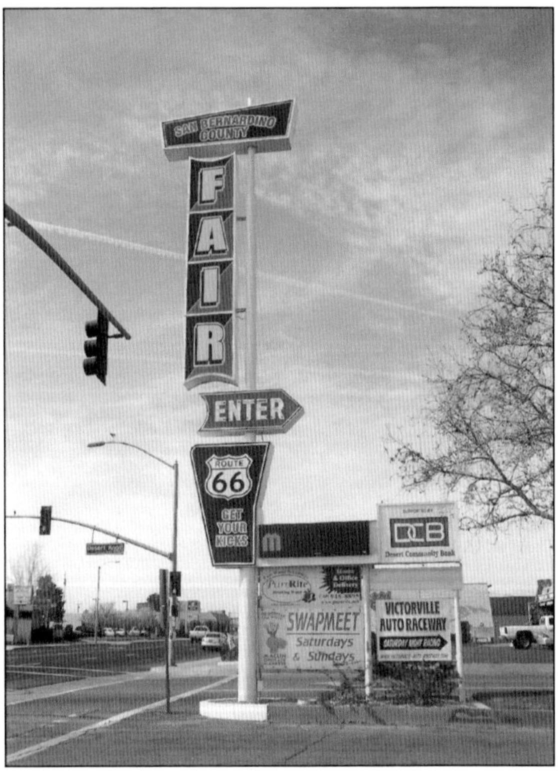

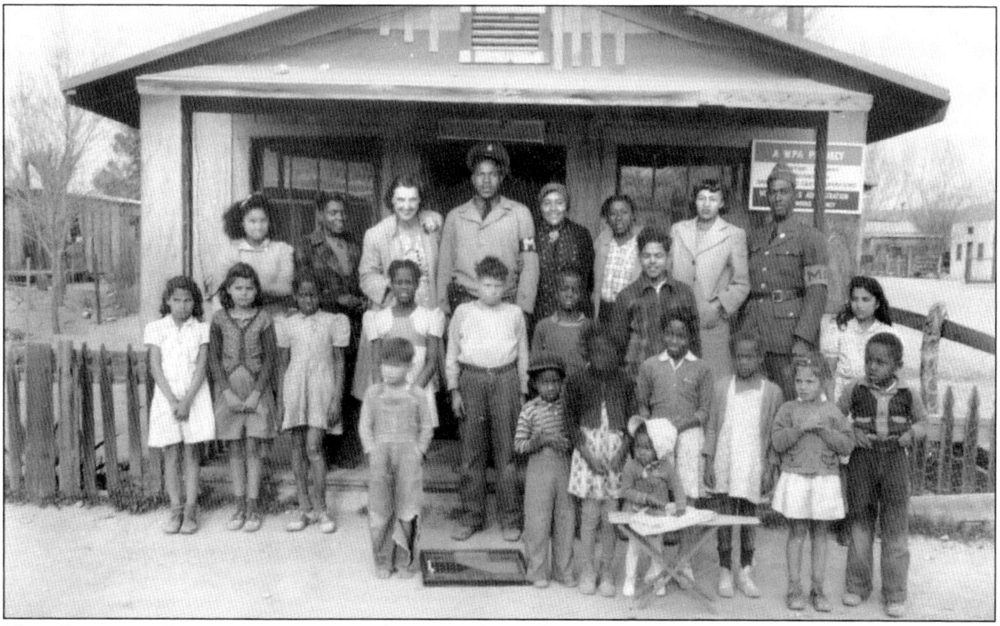

The Colored Club. Murray's Ranch in Apple Valley catered to people of color, but there was not much they could do in Victorville. A rather large number of blacks lived near Sidewinder Mine, and others contributed to communities throughout the high desert. The picture, from 1943, shows that the club was a WPA project. It was also called the Washington Club, and this occasion was the celebration of Washington's birthday. (AHCAFL.)

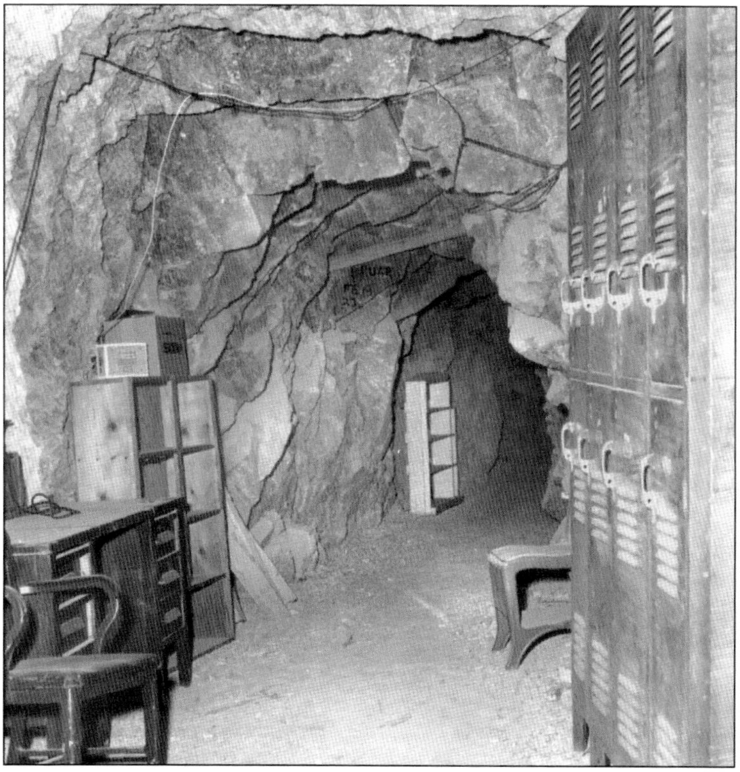

Mine to Bomb Shelter. The Sidewinder Mine was big and productive of gold and silver in its time. The stamping mill for this far-flung mine was in Victorville. In the 1960s, when citizens of the United States were frightened of atomic attack and bomb shelters became chic, the Sidewinder Mine was converted into a bomb shelter for use by desert dwellers. (MHS/VVM.)

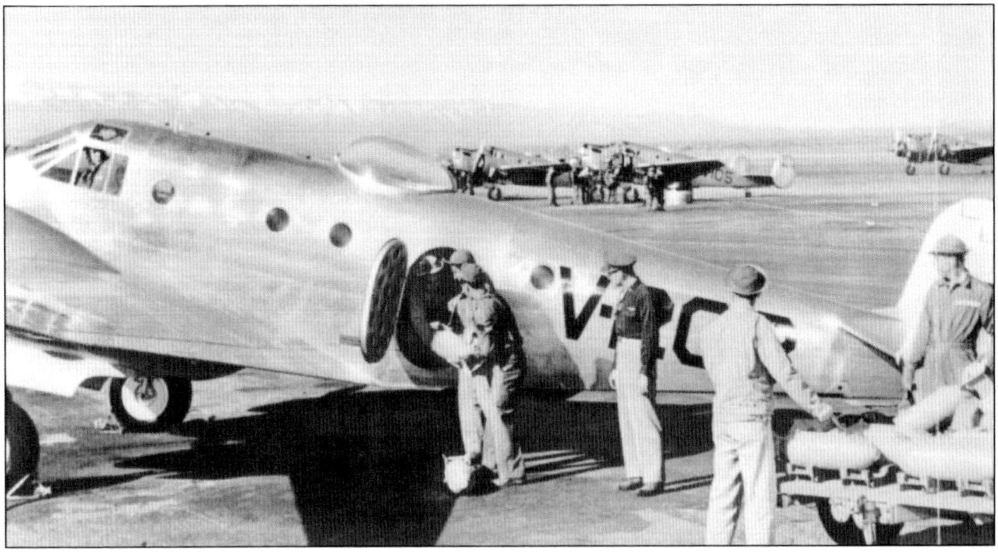

Air Base. During World War II, the Victorville Army Flying School met at the new Victorville Army Airfield, which later became George Air Force Base. The base was closed during the cutbacks of the 1980s, but the facility is still being used for less demanding flying than fighter pilot training. With George AFB in Victorville, Norton AFB in San Bernardino, and March Field in Riverside, military convoys often held up traffic on the highways. But citizens felt protected. Air beacons in Cajon Pass helped planes navigate between mountain peaks, and airplane spotting towers existed at Glen Helen and Clyde Ranch. (Both, MHS/VVM.)

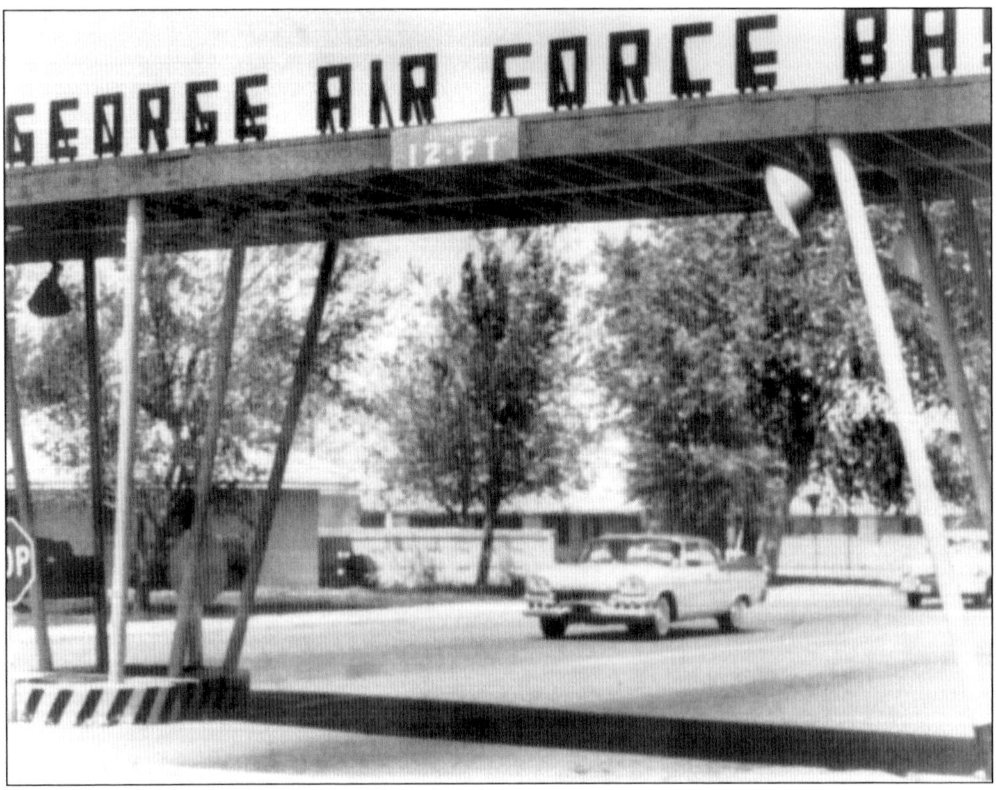

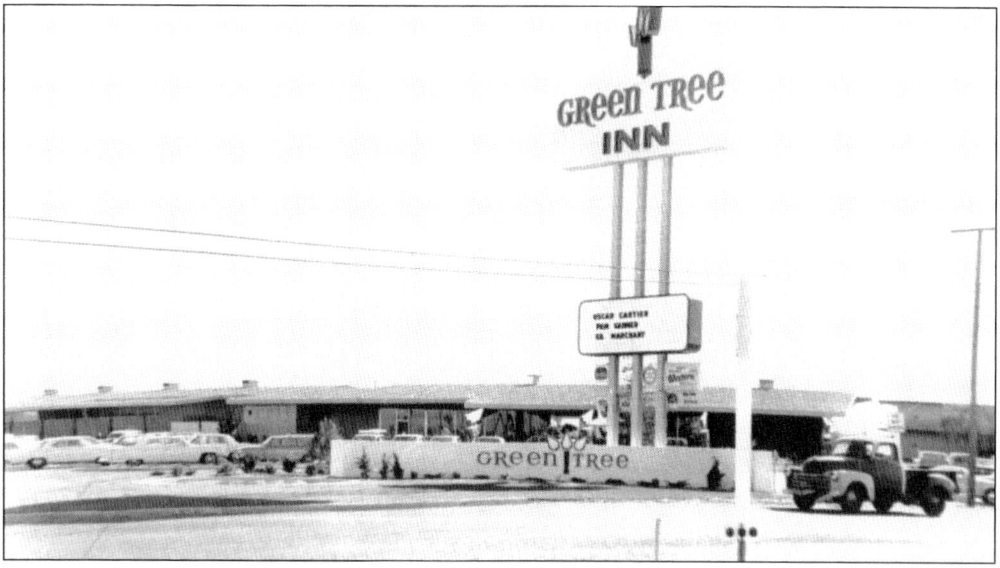

STYLE ADDED. When the Tatums built the Green Tree Inn and golf country club in Victorville in the 1960s, Victorville could compete for a time with Apple Valley for visiting dignitaries. Victorville also boasted the Sage Hens Guest Ranch and C-Bar-G Dude Ranch. Today Green Tree Boulevard runs along the north side of the Quality Inn, Green Tree, and signals on the road stop traffic for crossing golf carts. (MHS/VVM.)

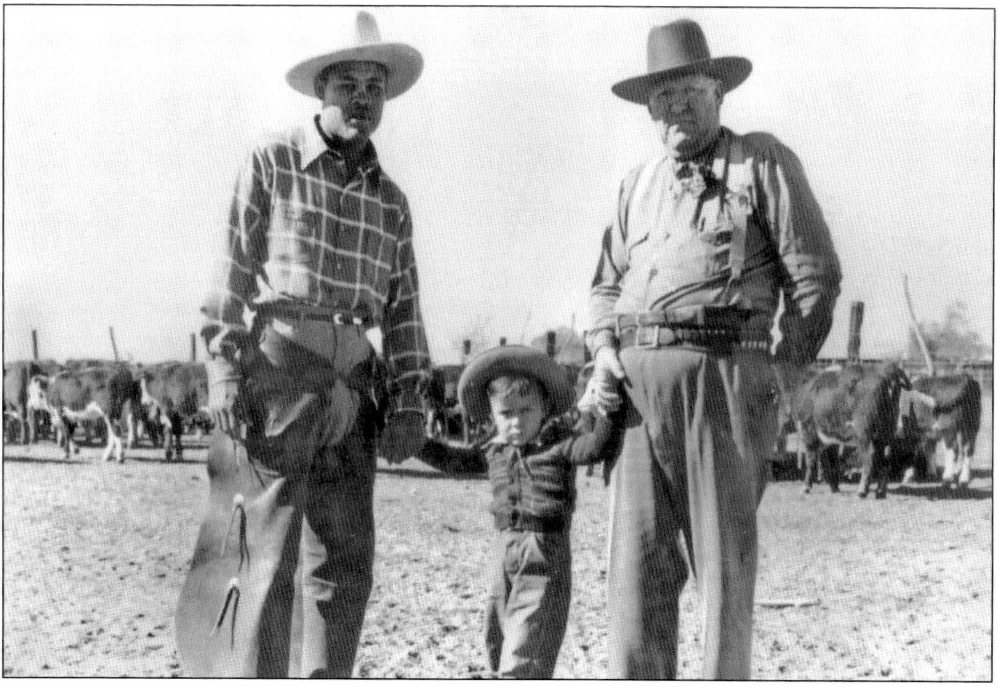

PROTECTION FELT. In 1941, Jackie Brown (center) posed with his father, Victorville's chief deputy sheriff Jack Brown (right), and heavyweight champion Joe Louis (left) at C-Bar-G Dude Ranch. Jackie never felt so safe as when he was flanked by those two. Sheriff Brown taught Joe Louis how to shoot. Jackie Brown grew up to be "Big" Jack Brown, president and CEO of Stater Brothers Markets, 10 of which grace the high desert. (JB.)

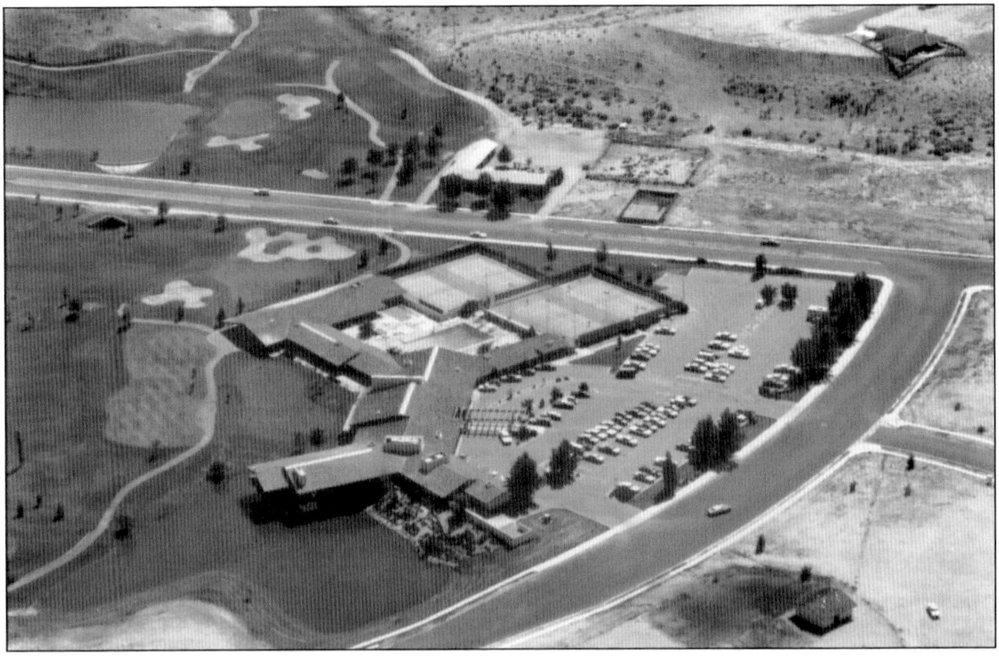

Spring Valley Lake. Out by the Mojave Narrows Regional Park, not far from Victor Valley College, Spring Valley Lake developed in the 1970s. It became a planned community with the country club as its hub. It features all lake activities, and lakeside homes each have a dock. Spring Valley Lake is on land formerly part of the Kalin Ranch. (MHS/VVM.)

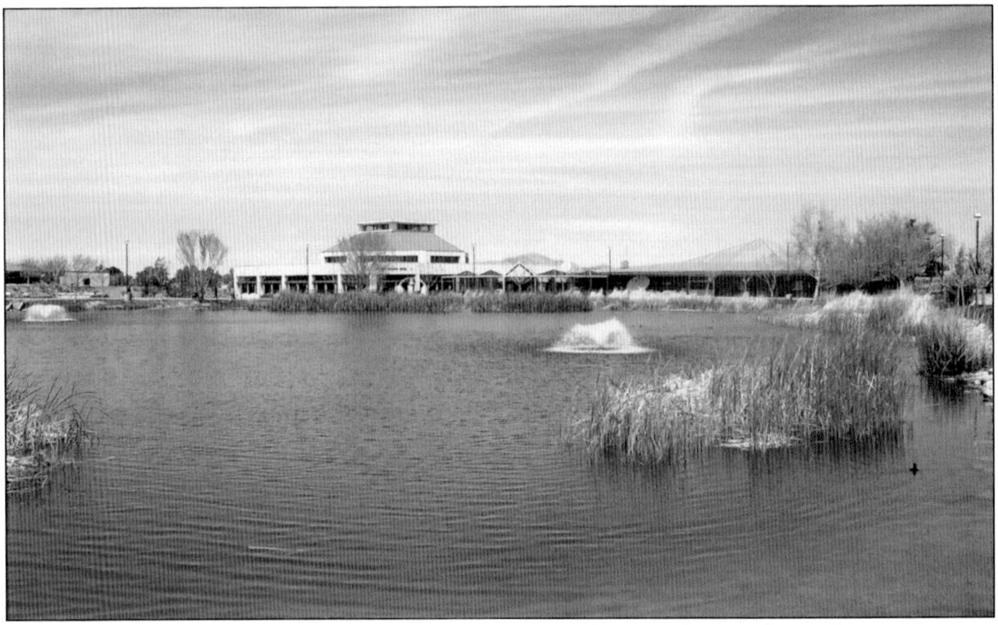

Another Desert Oasis. Started in 1961 with 500 students and 15 staff members meeting at Victor Valley High School, Victor Valley College now has over 11,000 students and 600 staff. The college campus, located on 253 acres of the Verde/Kalin Ranch near the Upper Mojave Narrows, opened in 1965. It serves the entire huge high desert, although another junior college is opening in Hesperia. (AH.)

Six

Dealing with Dangers and Disasters

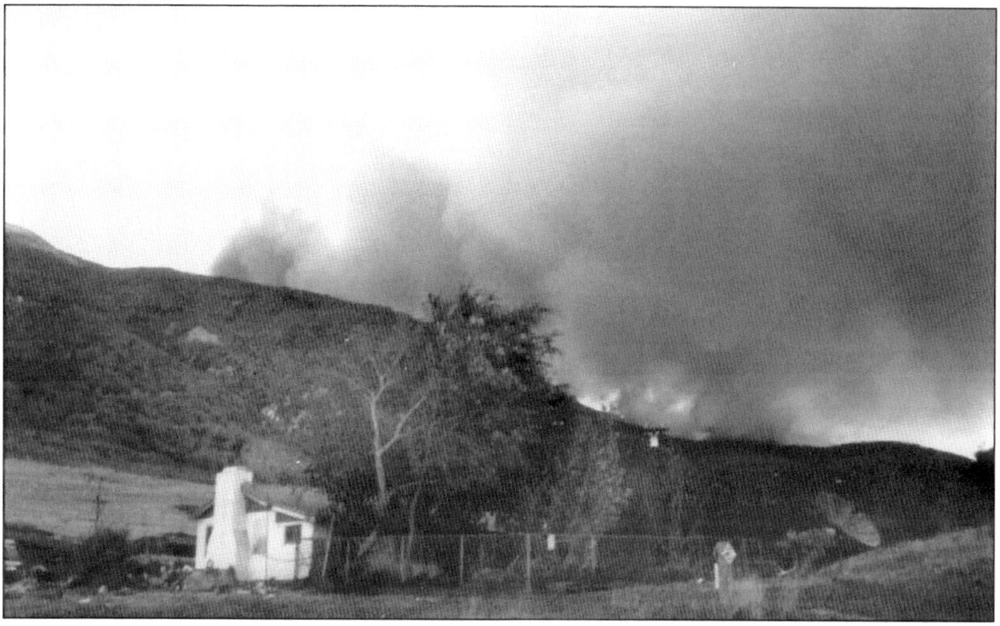

Wildfires. The most dangerous, devastating, and frightening threat to life in Cajon Pass is the wildfire. There have been many. So much loss has been suffered from wildfires that a whole book would be required just to chronicle fire episodes. The usual chain of events is that drought dries out Cajon Pass; the Santa Ana winds kick in and suck every last ounce of moisture from oily, brittle chaparral brush; a fire starts, often along the railroad (less often with diesel than steam locomotive) or freeway from a car fire or carelessly tossed cigarette that denudes the dehydrated soil of all foliage; heavy rain intended to make up for the drought falls, but the naked soil cannot absorb so much; the runoff creates a flood; and residents of the pass suffer multiple problems. It is not a place for the fainthearted. Another threat that could be worse than a fire is an earthquake along the San Andreas Fault that cuts through Cajon Pass. (AH.)

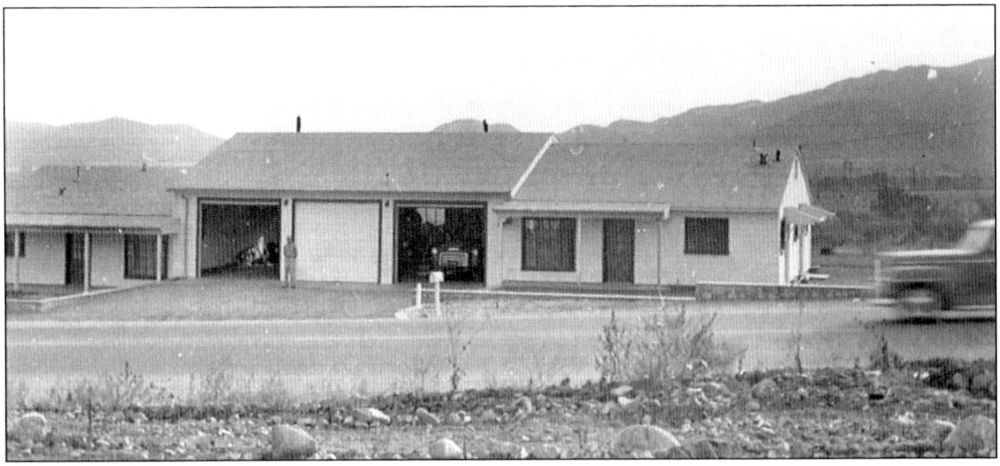

LOOKOUTS AND WILDFIRES. Most pass residents are prepared for a quick evacuation. U.S. Forest Service, California Division of Forestry, and, since 2000, San Bernardino County Fire Departments all have facilities in Cajon Pass. Pictured is the CDF Devore station built in 1951 with ranger Charles Ulrey. Family living quarters were in the south end. Early fire-spotting aircraft followed train tracks through the pass. Railroads, U.S. Forest Service, and local residents unified to build the first lookout in Cajon Pass on Verbryck's Keenbrook land in 1914. The platform, on a wooden tower, was connected to the nearest forestry station by a single-line telephone. When Santa Ana winds blew that down, the Cajon Mountain lookout, much like the pictured 1935 Santa Margarita lookout, was built. A cab over the platform on a 30-foot tower allowed lookout personnel to live and work there. The first Cajon Pass firebreaks were built in 1908. (Above, CDFM; below, CNF.)

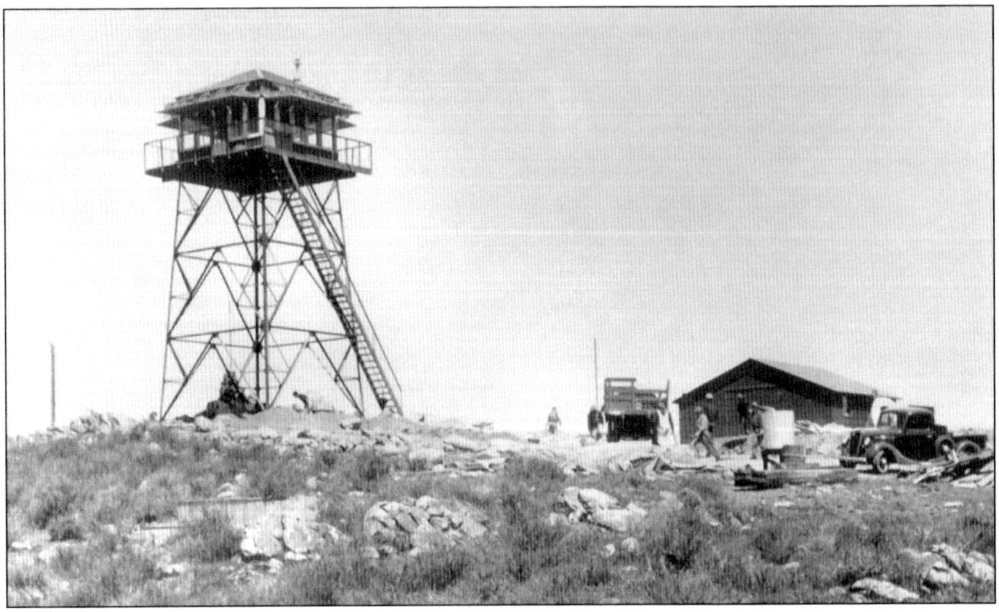

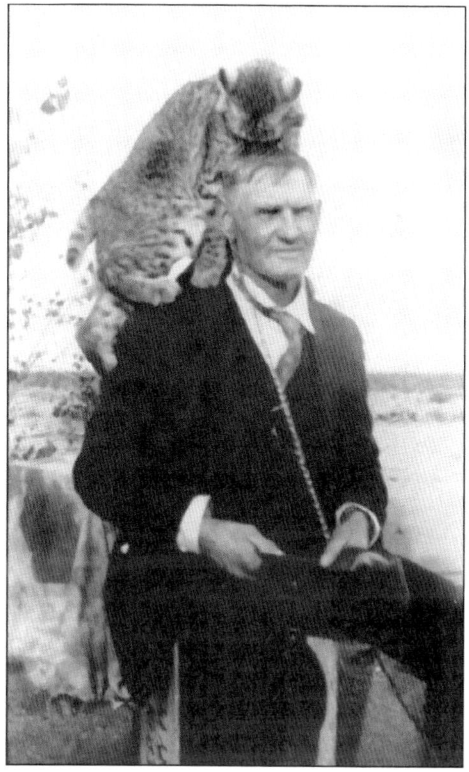

Wildlife. While part of the charm of living in the pass or high desert comes from interaction with local wildlife, the critters become threats at times. Interaction as close as the one shown with the bobcat and the high desert dweller is not recommended. California passed a no-cougar-hunting ordinance in 1976, and by 1994, mountain lions had become so plentiful they were hazardous to domesticated herds and pets—and even people. Whether residents have depredation permits or not, they are allowed to protect their property. Cougars are at the top of the food chain and have no natural enemies except man. Rattlesnakes, on the other hand, have to watch out for king snakes. The picture below shows a king eating a rattler. On the north side of the summit, the Mojave green, a rattler, is the deadliest snake in the United States. (Both, RH.)

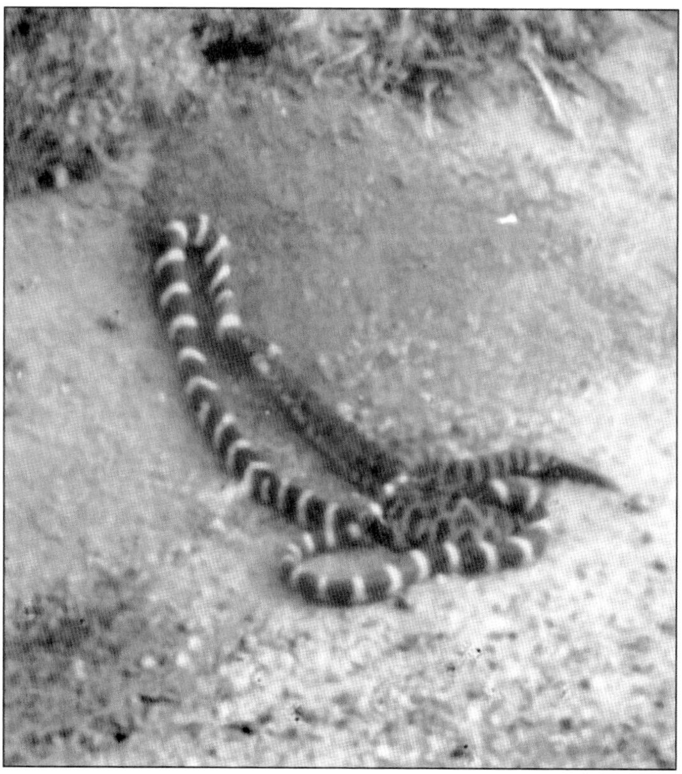

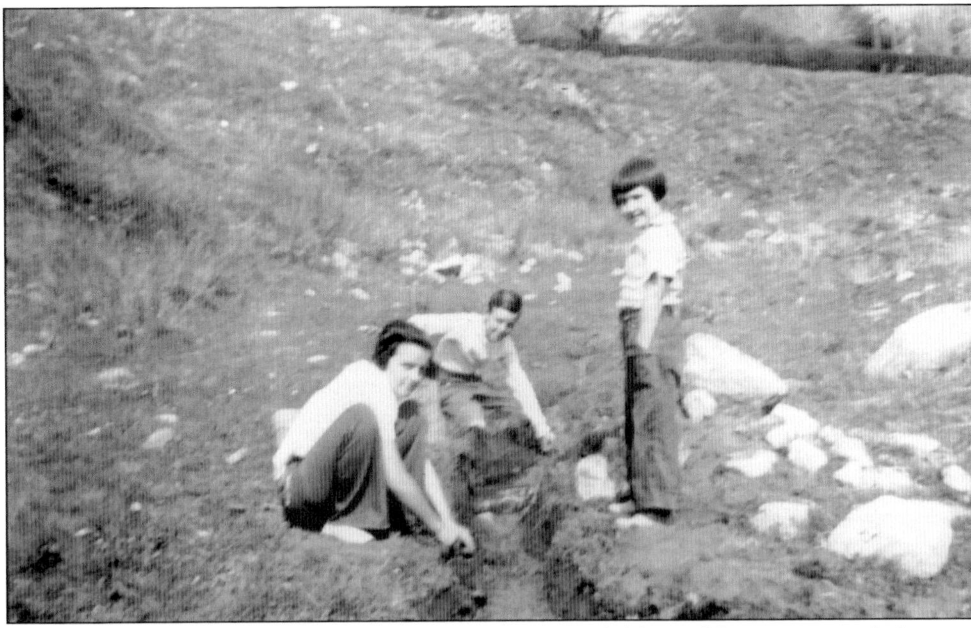

Idyllic Life. From their births until 1937, the Lamson children of Devore enjoyed playing on their spacious lawn and dabbling in their burbling creek. They also enjoyed exploring the sunken garden and "fishing" in the sunken pond in the Devore Park across the street. (GLM.)

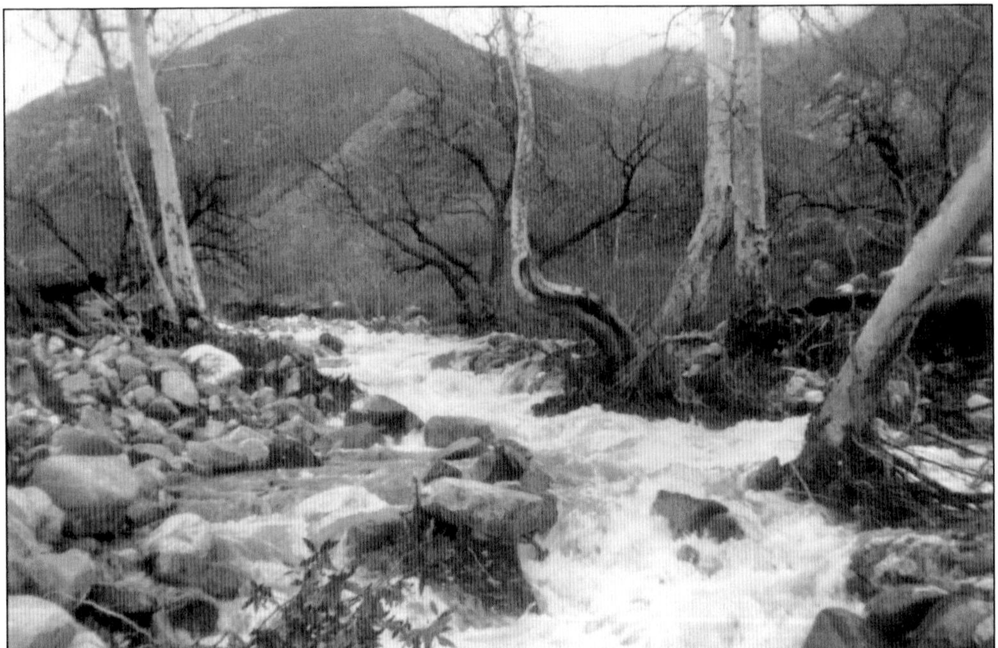

The Flood of 1938. On March 2, torrents flowed down Kimbark Canyon in Devore sweeping away the lawn and park and turning the burbling creek into a raging river. The flood swept huge sycamore trees down from the canyons above. The appearance of the trees suggests a pre-flood fire. Floods are so unpredictable that preparing for them is difficult at best. (GLM.)

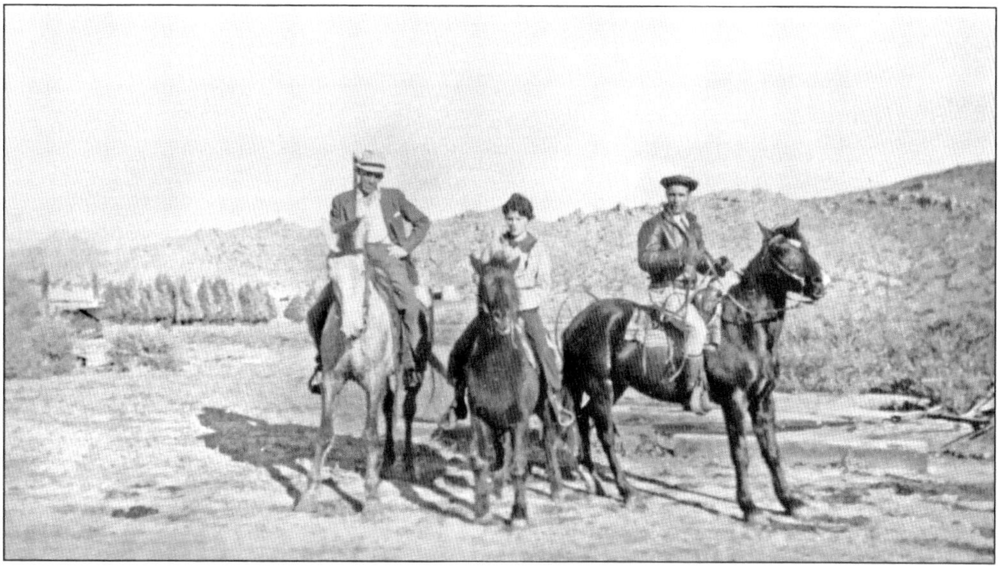

The Mojave River in 1937. This photograph from 1937 shows three horsemen using the Mojave River as their equestrian trail. It was pretty smooth riding and gave plenty of room for racing or whatever the riders wanted to do. (MHS/VVM.)

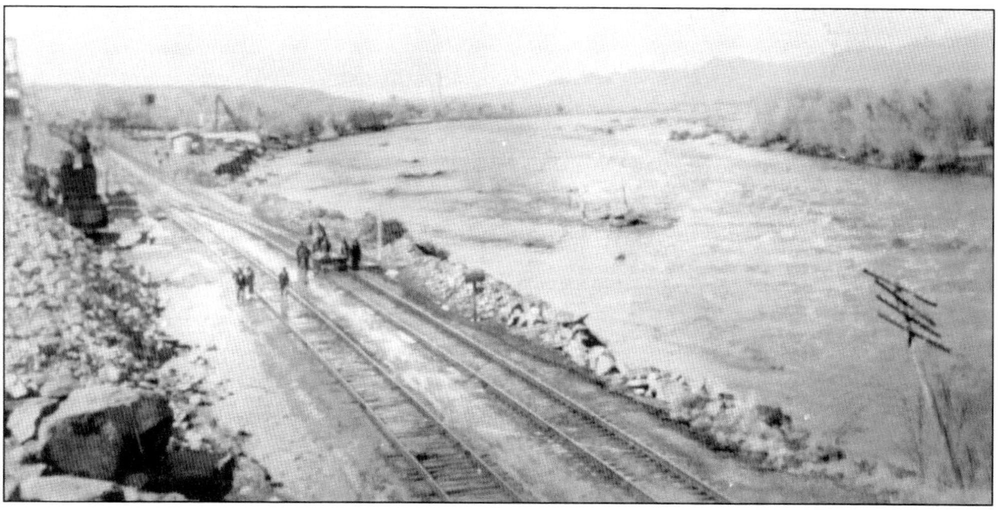

The Mojave River in 1938. Horses did not belong in the Mojave River bed in March 1938. The greatest flood on record was in January 1862, when over 175,000 cubic feet of water per second flowed in both the Santa Ana and Mojave Rivers. The 1891 and 1938 floods yielded about 100,000 cubic feet per second, but with more improvements like railroads and homes in flooded areas, financial damage was greater. (MHS/VVM.)

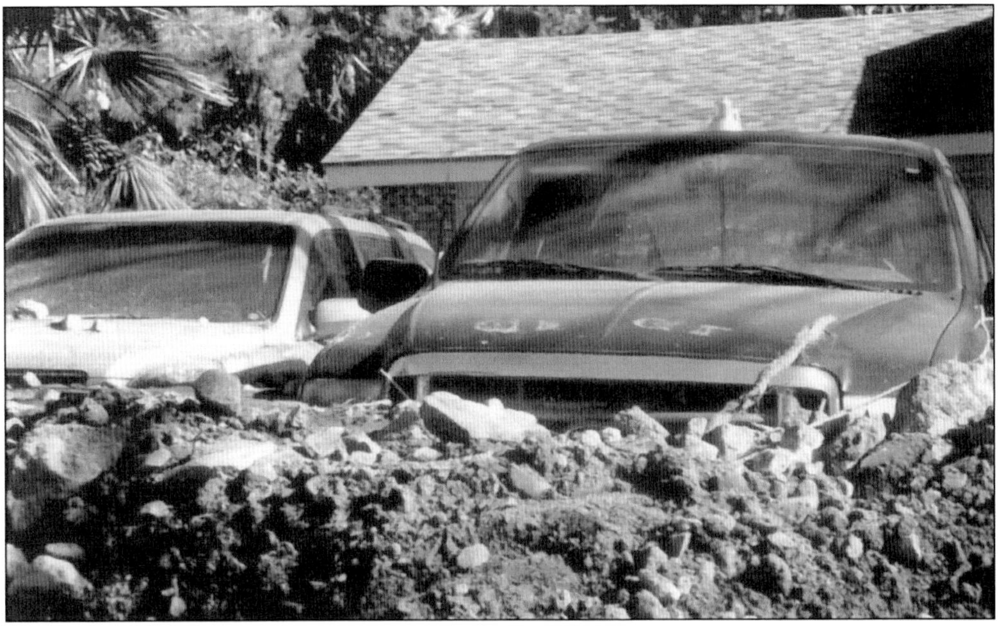

Flood of 2003. Residents on Greenwood Avenue in Devore awoke to the sound of a freight train roaring down the street outside. What they saw was even more terrifying—water, mud, and boulders crashing through fences, block walls, and even houses. Swimming pools filled, and cars were buried. A home video has been used by government emergency agencies to illustrate to residents of other areas what mud flows can do. (PM.)

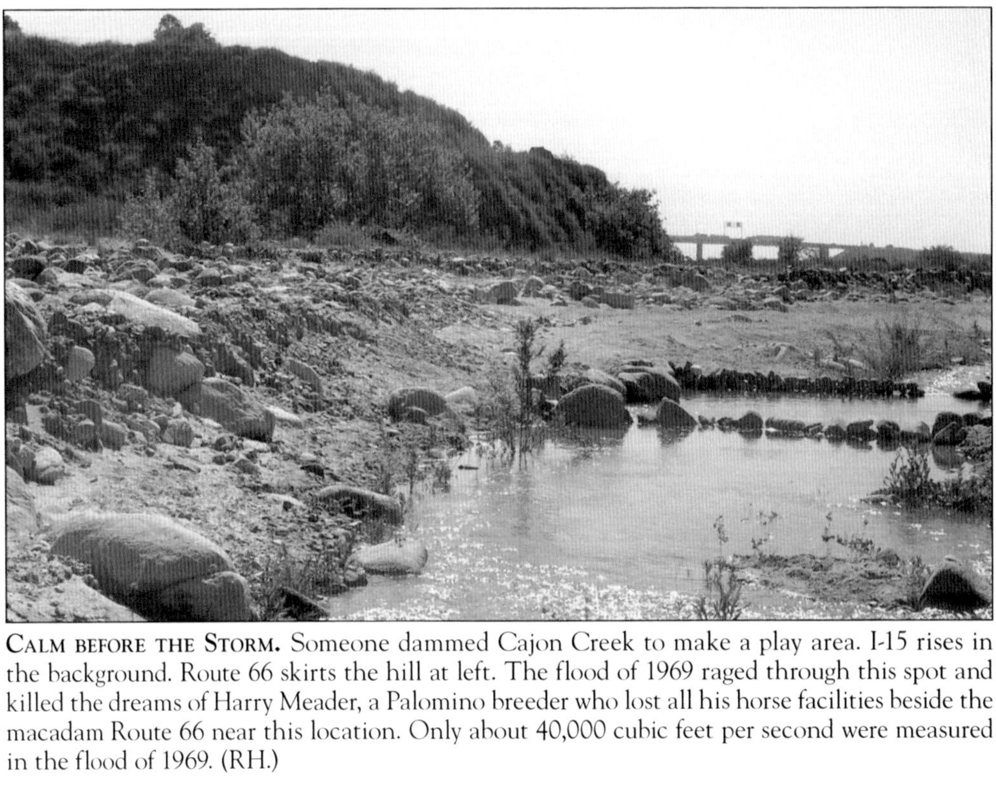

Calm before the Storm. Someone dammed Cajon Creek to make a play area. I-15 rises in the background. Route 66 skirts the hill at left. The flood of 1969 raged through this spot and killed the dreams of Harry Meader, a Palomino breeder who lost all his horse facilities beside the macadam Route 66 near this location. Only about 40,000 cubic feet per second were measured in the flood of 1969. (RH.)

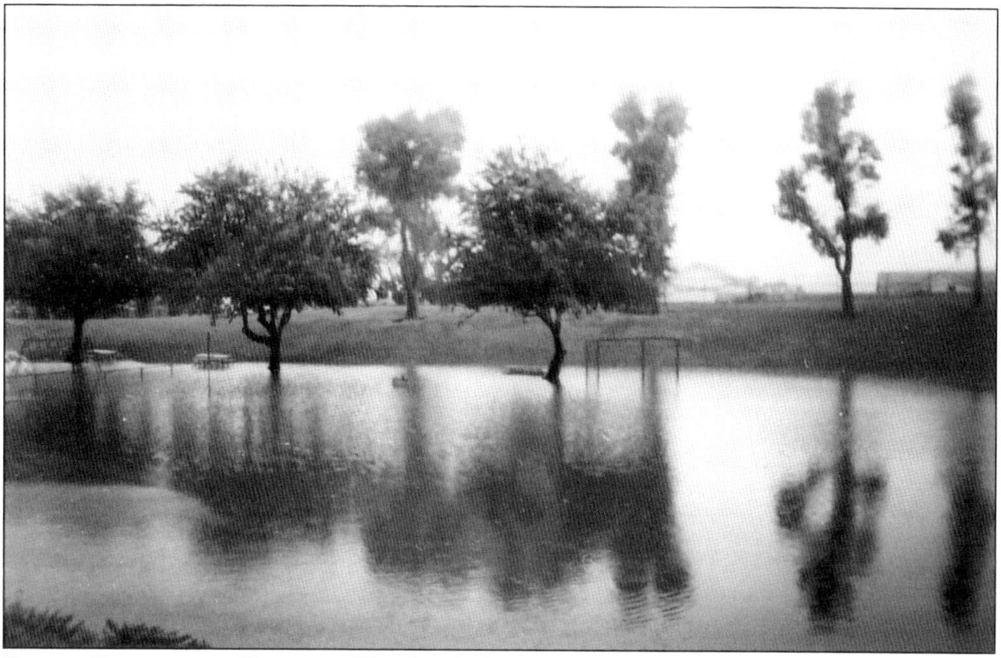

School Playground Flooded. The flood of 2003 rendered the Kimbark School playground in Devore useless. Water submerged the bottom half of the monkey bars, and other playground equipment was covered. So many of the school buses could not reach the school that a few days off were enjoyed by many. A teacher at the school took the photograph. (AH.)

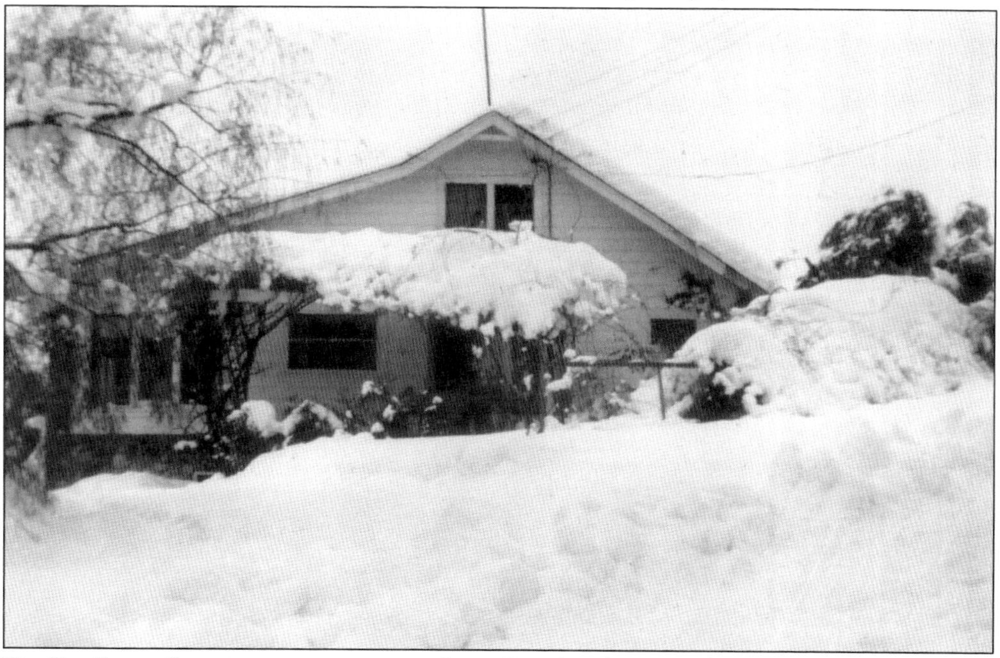

The Big Snow. Snow is not uncommon in Cajon Pass, but the snow of January 1949 left memories. Over 28 inches fell in Devore, and much more than that hit the higher elevations. Most people were snowed in for over a week. Neighbors slogged through drifts to check on one another, and mail was delivered by a neighbor on horseback who met the mailman on Route 66. (GLM.)

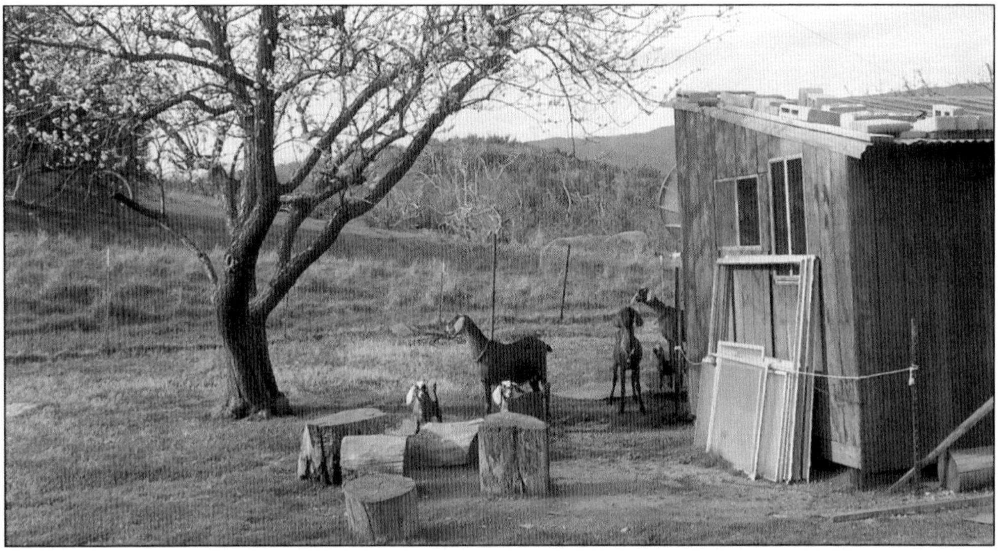

Behold the Barn. Concrete blocks on metal roofs are not glamorous but beat reroofing after every wind. Santa Ana winds, born on the Mojave Desert, tear through Cajon Pass, damaging buildings. The Santa Anas are not typical Chinook or Foehn winds since they form in dry instead of damp conditions. The desert does not experience Santa Anas, but high deserts suffer winds when the pass is foggy or rainy. (AH.)

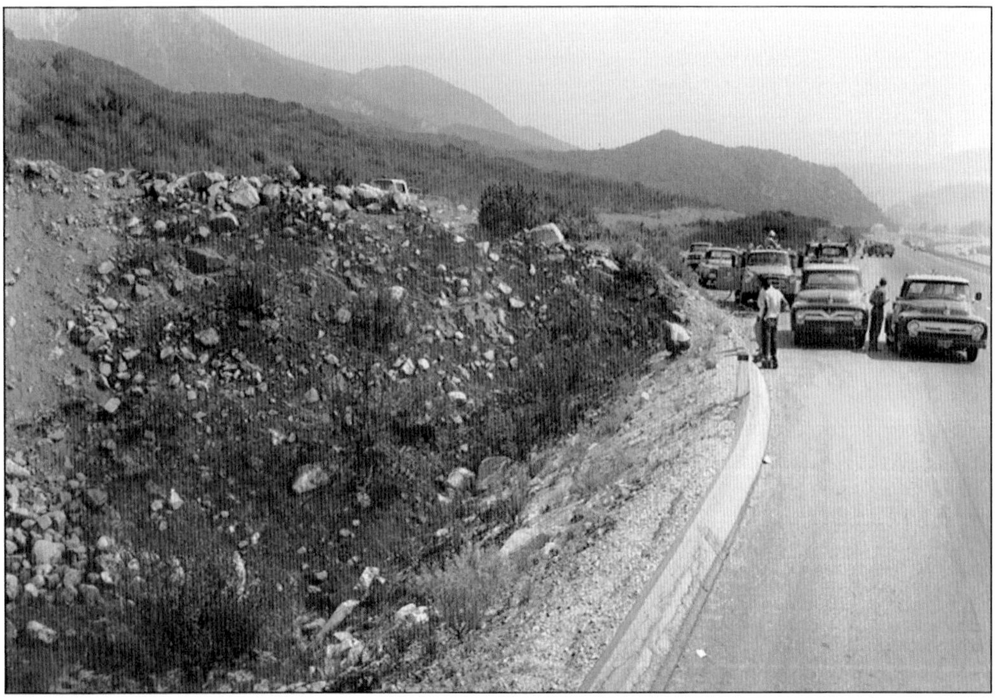

Cajon Pass Shut-Downs. The picture shows a Route 66 closure in 1960 by CDF and U.S. Forest Service because of fire. Pass closures also occur in heavy snows, after mud slides, multiple-vehicle pile-ups, and when a train derailment or big-rig overturn releases noxious gasses from their cargo. When I-15 closes, motorists can sit on the roadway for hours. Alternative routes are rare and inconvenient. (CDFM.)

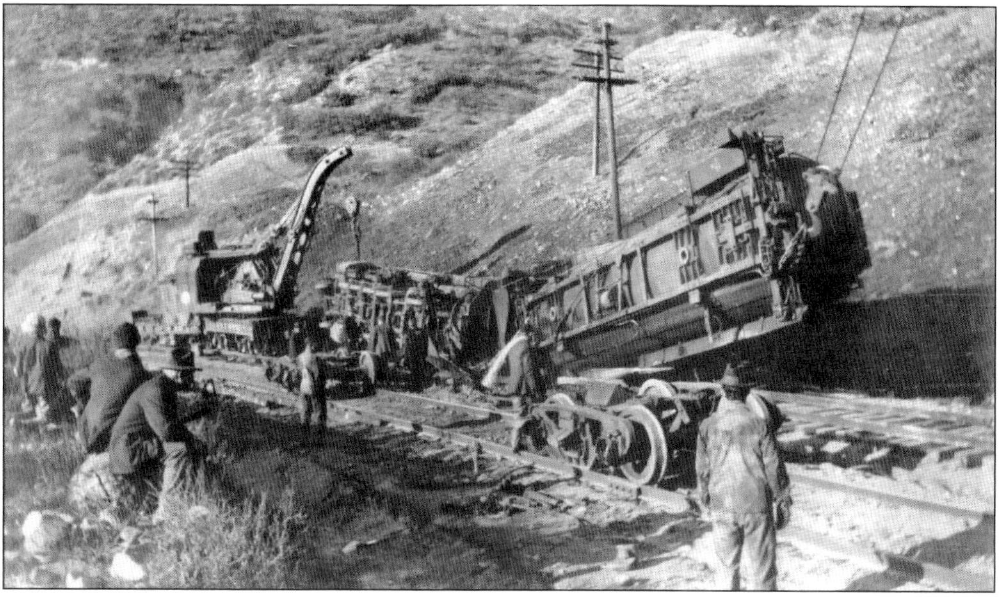

Derailment. It does not take a whole lot to derail a train, and when the tracks run through unstable land that washes, slips, and slides, derailments occur more often than those who have to repair them would like. These photographs were taken in the Keenbrook/Cajon area in the first third of the 20th century. Railroad crews still patrol and inspect the tracks through the pass constantly during inclement weather. Engine No. 952, built in 1904 by Baldwin, was rebuilt in 1918 in San Bernardino and finally scrapped in 1950. (Both, RB.)

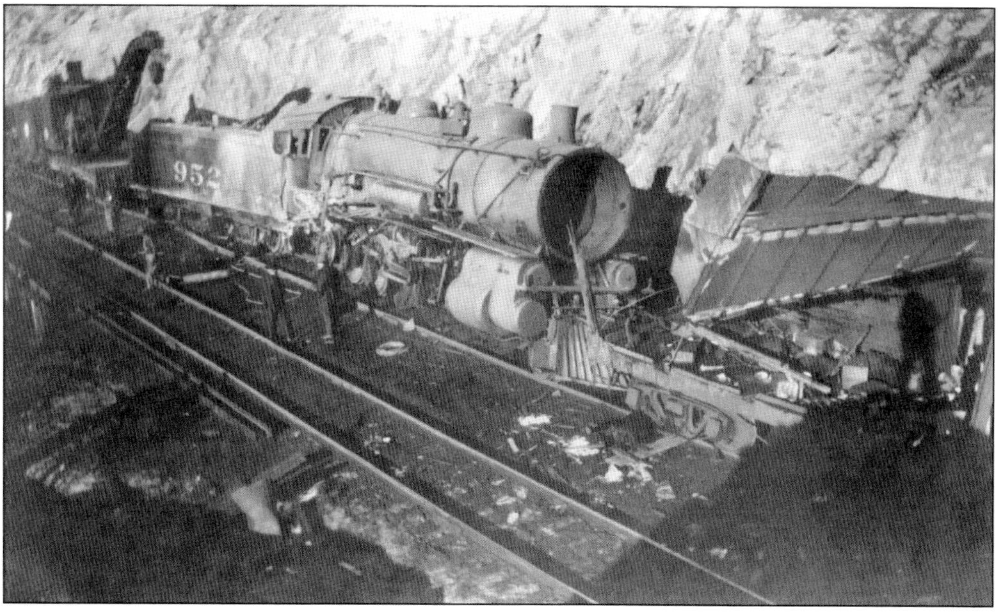

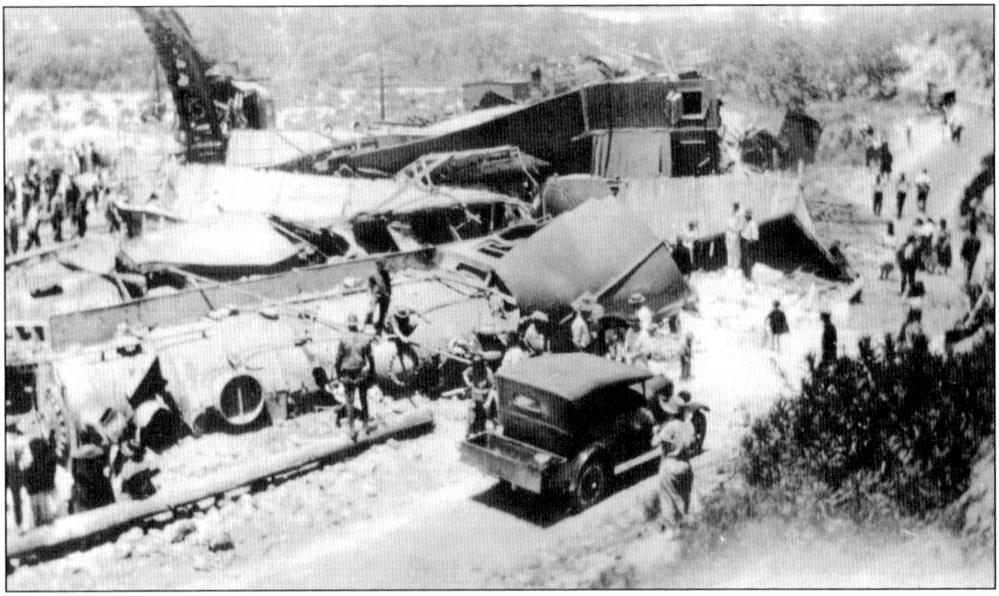

Wrecks. Train wrecks do not seem to be as common in Cajon Pass as they once were, but every so often, a train on the tracks, like the trucks on the interstate highway, gathers too much speed to stop or slow down on the steep inclines before they hit the next curve, and disasters like these are the result. If the cargo is toxic, residents are evacuated and motorists are delayed or detoured. (Above, MHS/VVM; below, RB.)

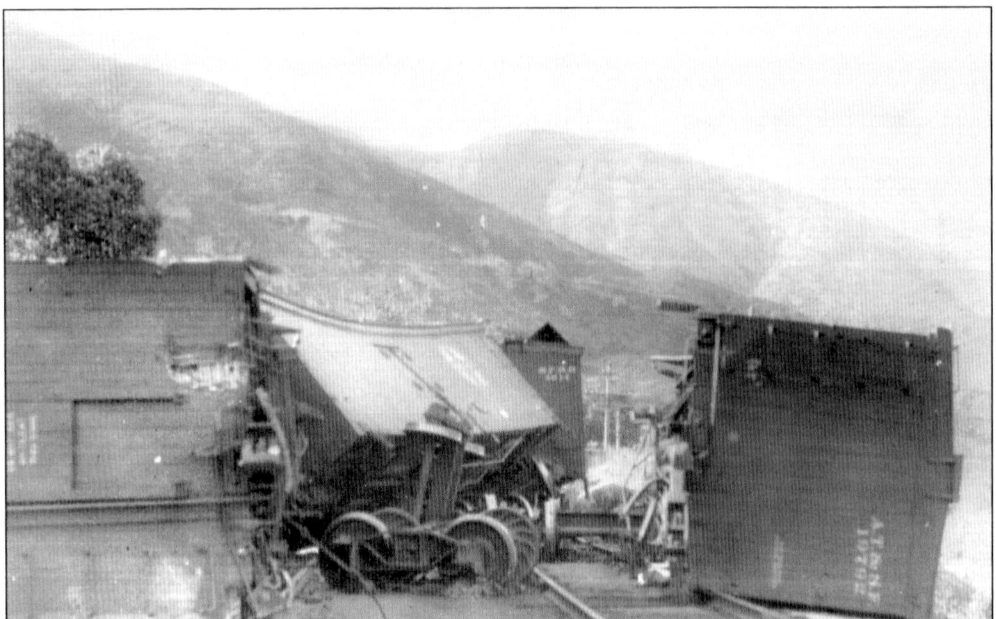

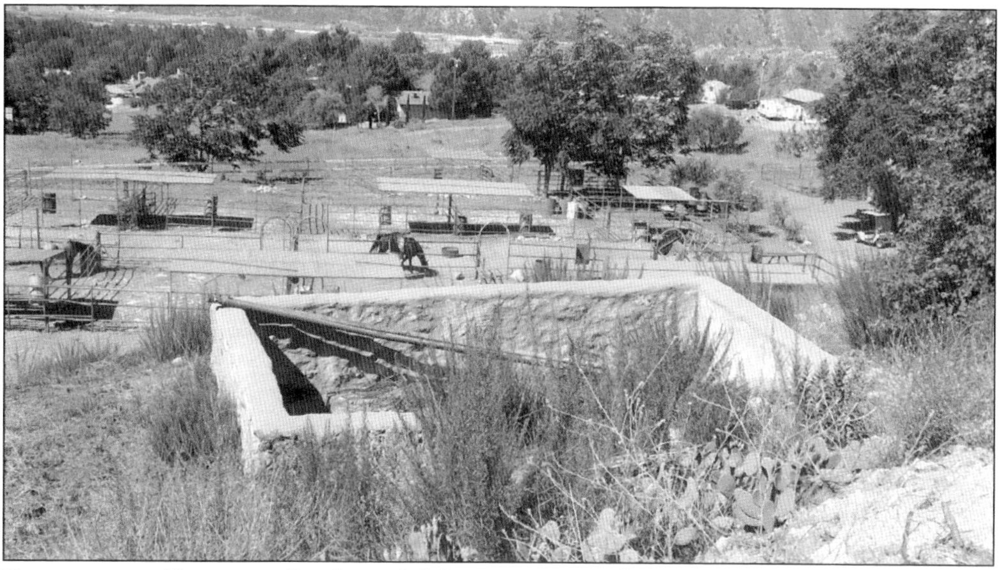

Dealing with Drought. Southern California is semi-arid to arid. Residents have to learn to cope with drought conditions. Many individuals store water in reservoirs, tanks, or various smaller containers. Communities like Devore used to use open reservoirs, even knowing that youth swam in them and deer sometimes drowned while seeking water. Modern health requirements dictate that tanks such as those in the second photograph replace open reservoirs for community water storage. Mark Slobom of Devore Water Company explains to the author how it all works. Automatic chlorination stations dispense their chemical throughout the water system. (Both, RH.)

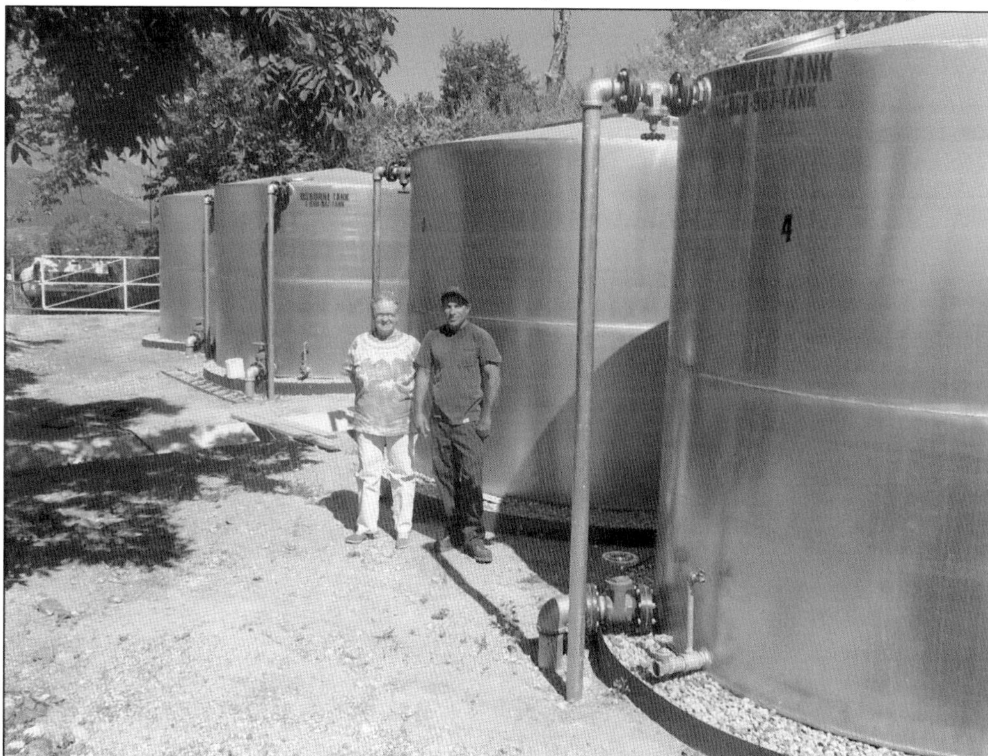

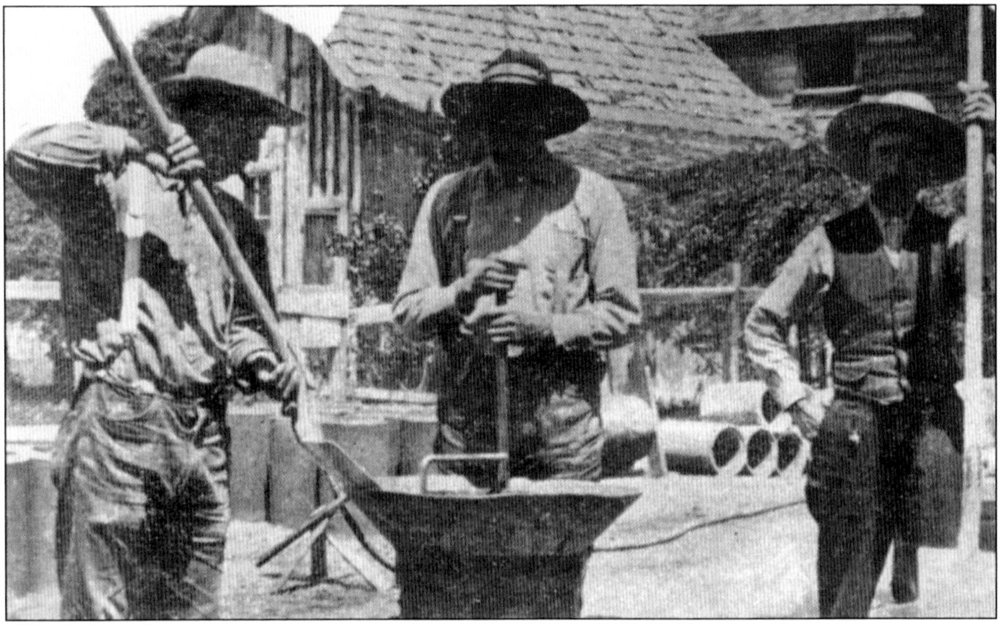

Before the Aqueduct. A hundred years ago on the Turner Ranch, Niles Turner instructed Alex Nicholson and Eddie Dempsey in the manufacture of cement pipe. This was used to deliver water from the wells or tanks to houses and barns and to crops that required irrigation. (MHS/VVM.)

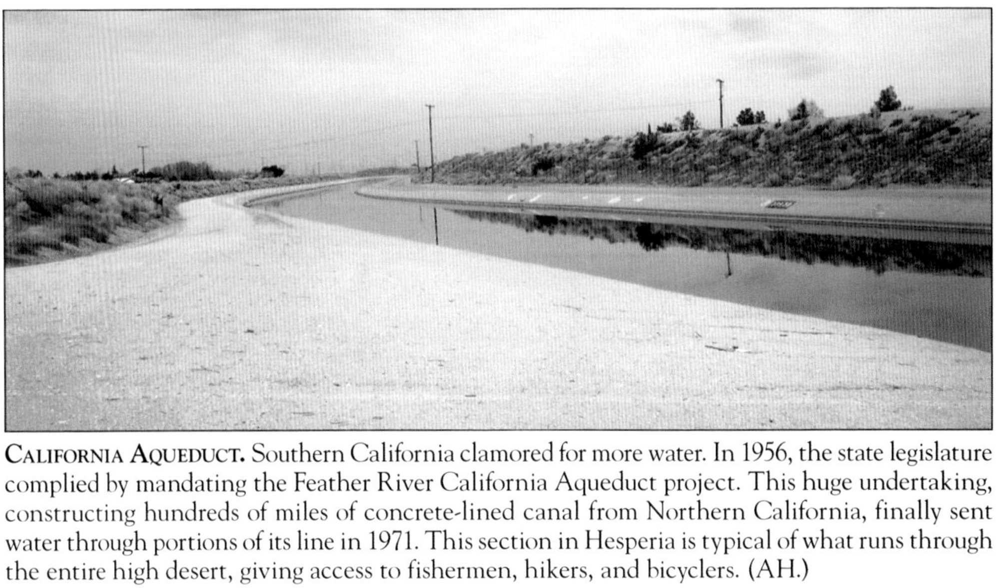

California Aqueduct. Southern California clamored for more water. In 1956, the state legislature complied by mandating the Feather River California Aqueduct project. This huge undertaking, constructing hundreds of miles of concrete-lined canal from Northern California, finally sent water through portions of its line in 1971. This section in Hesperia is typical of what runs through the entire high desert, giving access to fishermen, hikers, and bicyclers. (AH.)

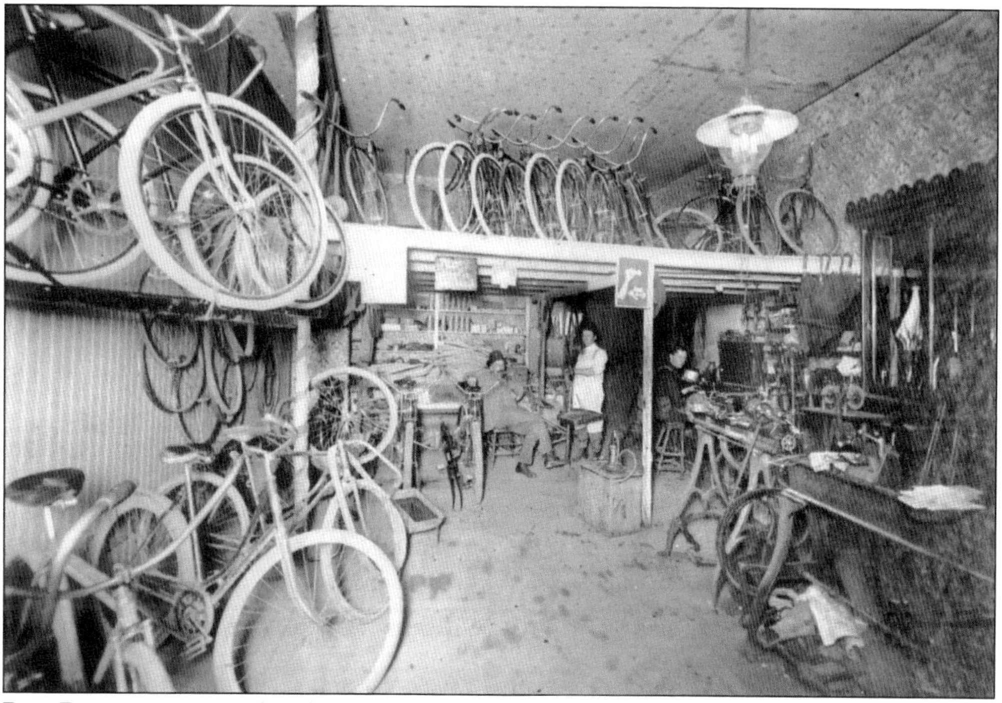

Pass Preparedness. Before freeways, when bicycles shared Cajon Pass roads with horses and wagons, bikers saw to it that their bikes were in top shape before they attempted the climb. Leffen's bicycle shop in San Bernardino did a good business in those days. Since bicycles are not allowed on the freeway, bikers have to find alternative routes, none of which are easy. Leffen was Fred Perris's son-in-law. (SBHPS.)

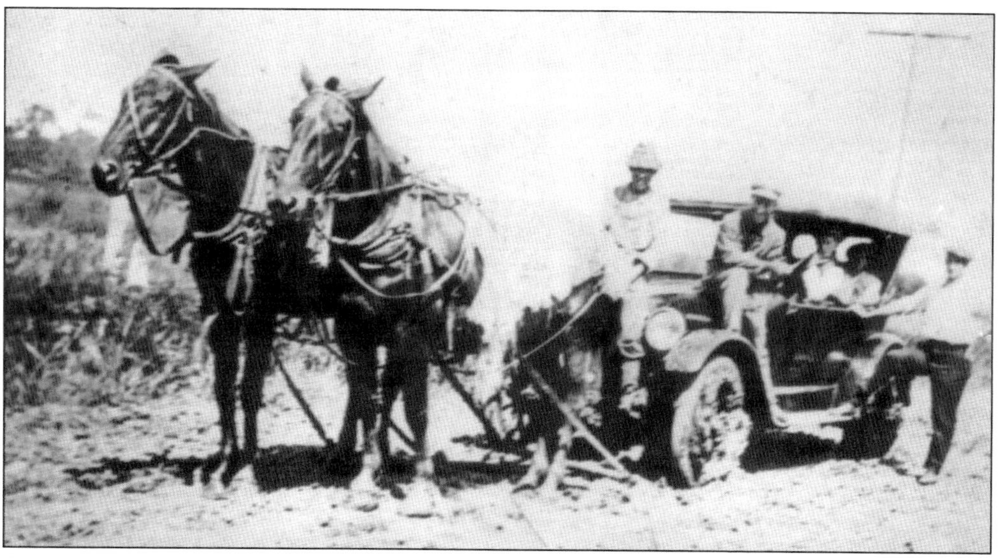

Team Pulls Car from Mud. Automobiles also must be prepared for the pass. With traffic pushing the 70-mile-per-hour speed limit, a lot can happen in a short time. In early Route 66 days, when speed was not yet king, a team of horses kept handy at nearby way stations or ranches could often give a vehicle a tow to the nearest mechanic or filling station. (MHS/VVM.)

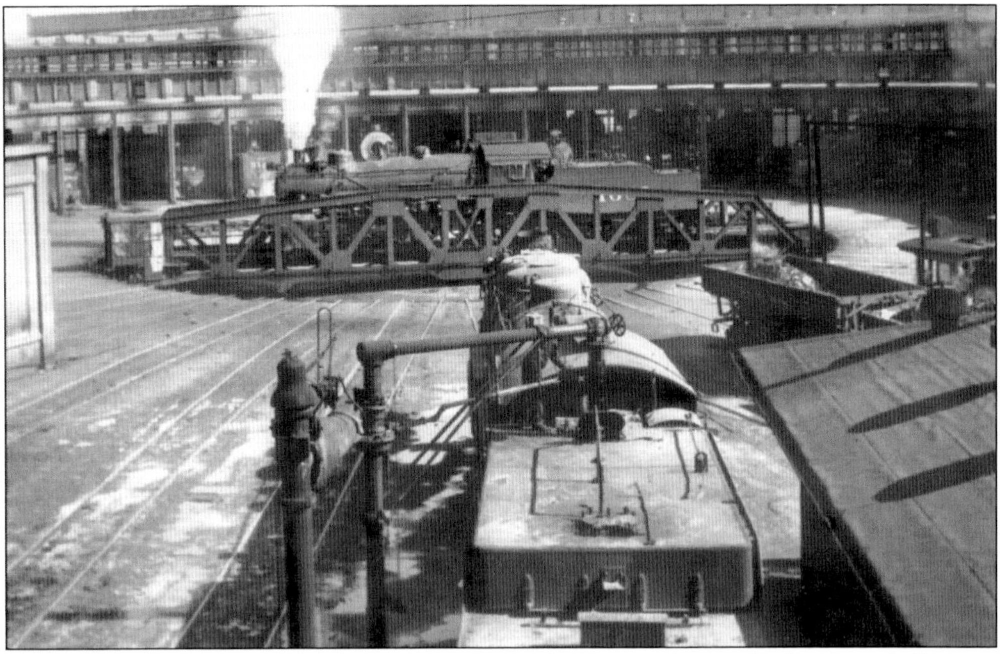

HORSEPOWER IS KING. The roundhouse in San Bernardino prepared trains for the steep, challenging grades of Cajon Pass. These photographs from 1925 show one locomotive taking on water in preparation for the pass. Below, a locomotive hangs from an overhead crane to be transported to another workstation for further repairs and adjustments. (Both, AHCRFL.)

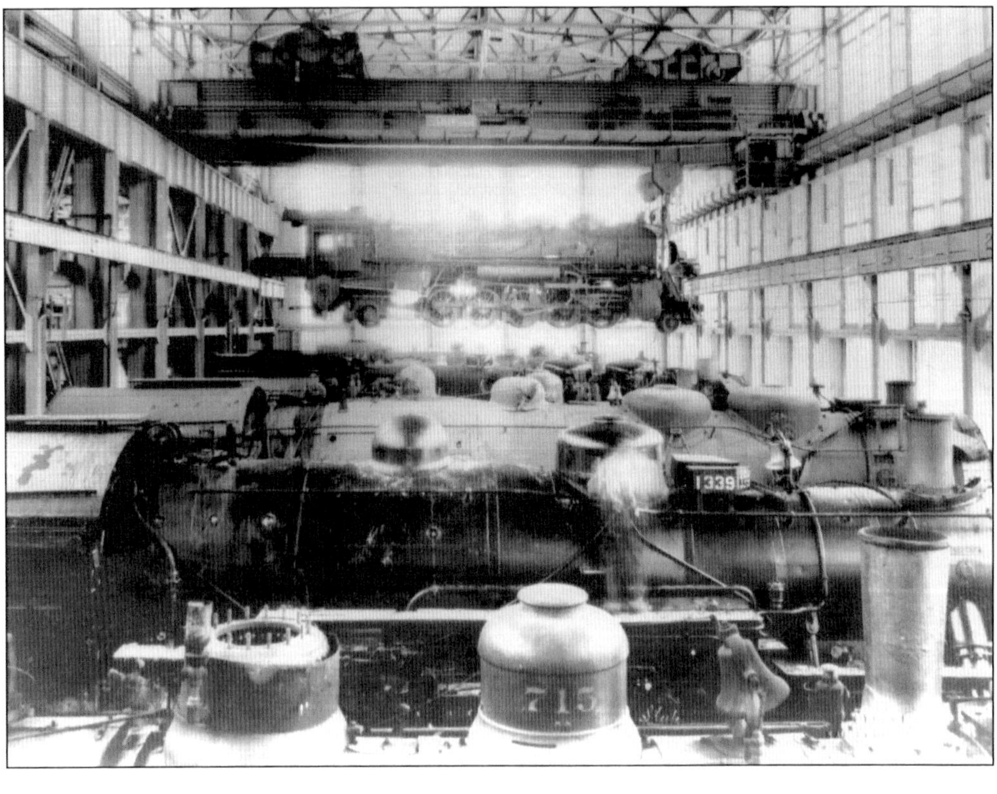

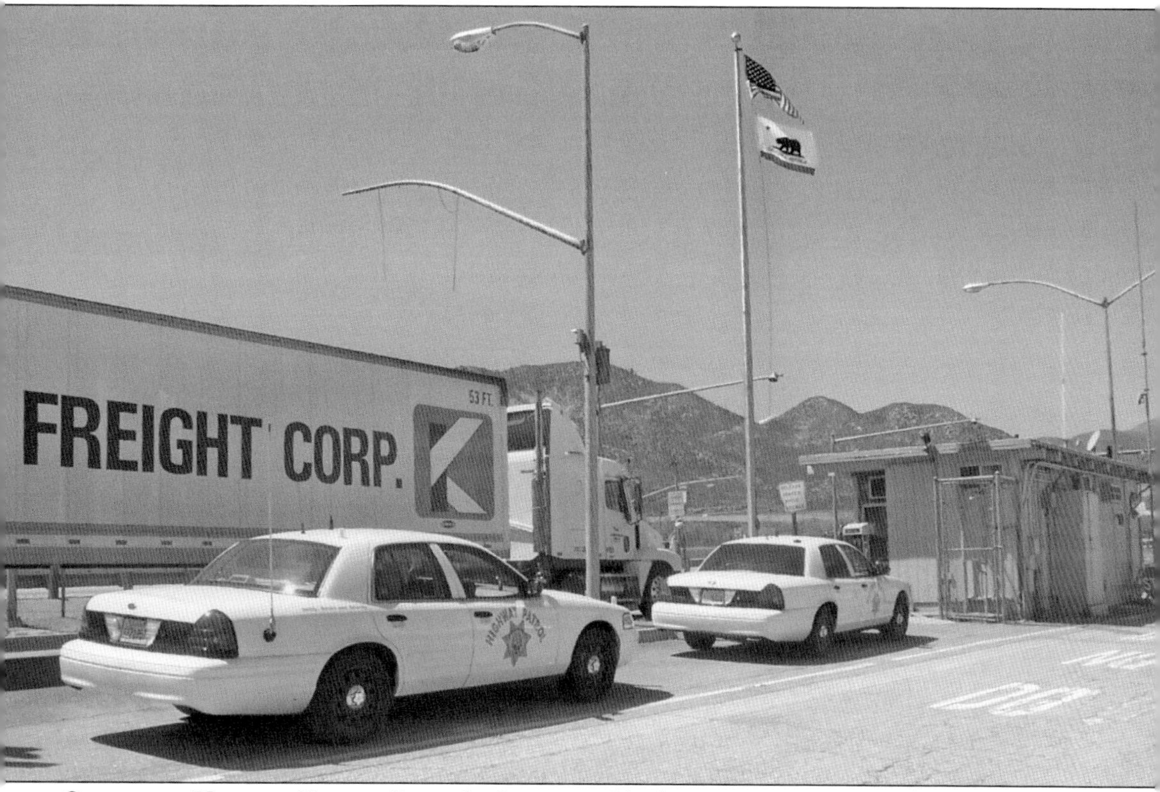

California Highway Patrol. Since the freeway and highways are so important through Cajon Pass, it is essential that a way is provided to protect travelers and enforce rules. California Highway Patrol was formed just a few years after Route 66 was named to do just that. In the first 10 years of the patrol, it increased to 730 uniformed personnel. CHP moved from the DMV to its own state department in 1947, and in 1995, it merged with the State Police. Now, in addition to its other duties, CHP is responsible for truck and bus inspections, air operations, vehicle theft prevention and investigation, and even a little wildlife care as Department of Fish and Game cuts back the number of wardens. CHP even uses its own helicopters and fixed-wing aircraft for patrolling highways. The truck scales on I-15 at Highway 138 are computerized—quite a difference from the old scales on Route 66 at Blue Cut. (AH.)

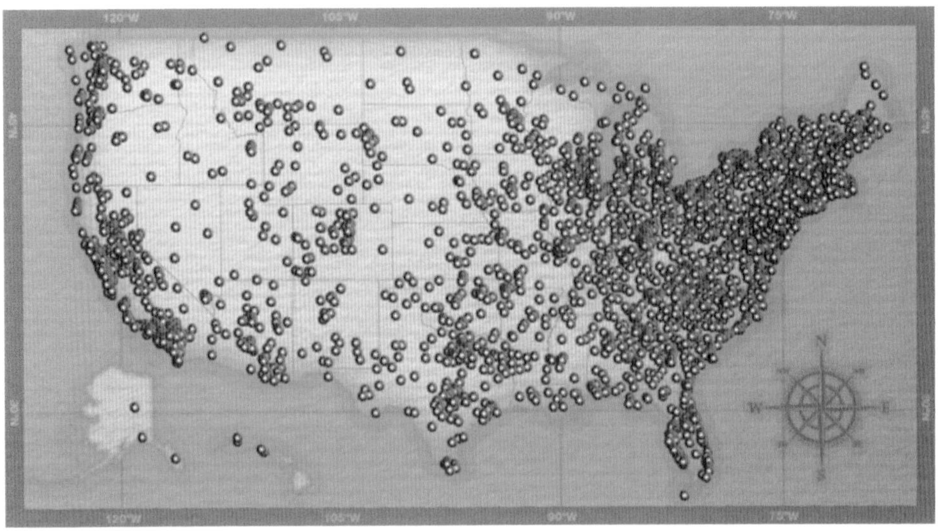